MW01518662

The Isle *of* Monte Cristo

The Isle *of* Monte Cristo

Finding the Inner Treasure

S. T. Georgiou

NOVALIS

© 2010 Novalis Publishing Inc.

Cover design and layout: Audrey Wells
Cover photograph: Christopher John Rozales

Published by Novalis

Publishing Office
10 Lower Spadina Avenue, Suite 400
Toronto, Ontario, Canada
M5V 2Z2

Head Office
4475 Frontenac Street
Montréal, Québec, Canada
H2H 2S2

www.novalis.ca

Distributed in the United States by Twenty-Third Publications
www.twentythirdpublications.com
1-877-944-5844

Library and Archives Canada Cataloguing in Publication

Georgiou, S. T. (Steve Theodore)
    The Isle of Monte Cristo : finding the inner treasure / S.T. Georgiou.

Includes bibliographical references.
ISBN 978-2-89646-229-2

    1. Spiritual life. 2. Meditations. I. Title.

BL624.G45 2010   204'.32   C2010-903968-8

Printed in Canada.

All rights reserved. No part of this publication may be reproduced, stored in
a retrieval system, or transmitted in any form, or by any means, electronic,
mechanical, photocopying, recording, or otherwise, without the written permission
of the publisher.

The Scripture quotations contained herein are from the Revised Standard Version of
the Bible, copyrighted 1952 by the Division of Christian Education of the National
Council of the Churches of Christ in the United States of America, and are used by
permission. All rights reserved.

We acknowledge the financial support of the Government of Canada through the
Book Publishing Industry Development Program (BPIDP) for our publishing
activities.

5   4   3   2   1   1 4   1 3   1 2   1 1   1 0

For my sister, Maria

Meh Agape En Christo

With Love In Christ

The Isle of Monte Cristo is really inside us.
Monte Cristo means "Mountain of Christ."
It's our sanctuary. It's where we're
heading, day by day, and when the
time is right, we'll all meet at the summit.

—*Robert Lax*

For where your heart is, there also will be your treasure.

—*Luke 12.34*

The heart is a small vessel, but all things are contained in it.
God is there, the angels are there, and there also is life and
the kingdom, the heavenly cities, and the treasury of grace.

—*St. Makarios of Egypt*

The beauty that dwells within us is a hundred times brighter
than the sun.

—*St. Isaac of Nineveh*

The kingdom of God is within you.

—*Luke 17.21*

Contents

"God will always have something new to teach us en route to the Kingdom" (Robert Lax)

Christopher John Rozales, 2010

Acknowledgements

Warm thanks are extended to the following individuals who helped make this book a reality:

Br. Patrick Hart, O.C.S.O.; Joseph Sinasac; Anne Louise Mahoney; Kevin Burns; Michael Morris, O.P.; Donald Main; Christopher John Rozales; Fr. Aris P. Metrakos; Anastasia Georgiou; Jane Dillenberger; David Miller; Jonathan Montaldo; Jacqueline Chew; Anne Escrader; Kathleen Kook; Gary Palmer; Winifred Ireland; Serah Kahahu; Maria Kerosky; Mary West; Anne Melson; Pantelis Kleudis; Gianvito Lo Greco; Gary Bauer; Gabi Papanikolaou; John Skinas; Stan Themoleas; Barbara Ulmer; Br. Andreas (PAO); Sr. Florence Vales, O.S.C.

Infinite gratitude is also extended to the late Robert Lax, without whom this book (and this trilogy*) would not have been possible. Thanks for being there, Bob, when I knocked on your door that windy night on Patmos in May of 1993. I still remember you standing behind a thin white screen that rippled in the breeze. In the darkness, your eerie visage, pressed up against the diaphanous cloth, resembled the face of the Turin Shroud. Only when you led me into your home and turned fully around did I see you clearly for the first time, your

---

* The first two books in the trilogy are *The Way of the Dreamcatcher: Spirit Lessons with Robert Lax – Poet, Peacemaker, Sage* (Ottawa: Novalis, 2002 & Templegate Publishers, 2010) and *Mystic Street: Meditations on a Spiritual Path* (Ottawa: Novalis, 2007). *The Isle of Monte Cristo* is the final book in the series.

deep-set, ancient eyes illuminated by a small antique desk lamp. The warm amber light spread across your fissured features like sunrays passing through a forest. If you had said that you were King Arthur or the wizard Gandalf from *Lord of the Rings*, I might have believed you. But I'm happy you were Bob Lax the Lightgiver.

Thanks for the spirit lessons. Thanks for the walks and talks, the joy and laughter, the seaside reveries, the blessed peace, the poetry of the heart, and the holy silences that took on the radiance of candleflame. Most of all, thanks for being a friend.

Once you told me that the ultimate purpose of life is to generate enough love so that every living soul might unite with God. But rather than meditate on that weighty thought, I recall asking you, perhaps with a bit of youthful impertinence, "And what happens after that?"

Your eyes lit up like stars. A smile bright as the sun beamed across your calm, unperturbed face.

"We go on to something greater," you answered, without missing a beat. "You'll see. But the most important thing to learn now is love. Just keep on loving, and there'll be more lessons to come. God will always have something new to teach us en route to the kingdom. The journey is forever."

Thanks, Bob. Love always as we sail toward *Monte Cristo*. Each day a little more of the Mystery reveals itself; each day brings us closer to the joy of the living Christ.

S.T. Georgiou

May 2010
San Francisco

Pantelis Kleudis, 1993

Robert Lax and Steve Georgiou at the waterfront in Patmos, 1993.

In *The Seven Storey Mountain*, Thomas Merton said of Lax, "The secret of his constant solidity has always been an inborn direction to the living God ... Lax was much wiser than I, and had clearer vision, and was, in fact, corresponding much more truly to the grace of God than I ..."

To the Reader

What first drew me to *The Isle of Monte Cristo* is its provocative title, derived, of course, from the famous novel by Alexandre Dumas, *The Count of Monte Cristo*. Exactly why S.T. Georgiou draws from this nineteenth-century classic is explained in his prologue, but suffice it to say that his latest book, like Dumas' epic, has much to do with finding a liberating and life-changing treasure.

Yet the treasure to be found in Georgiou's book is not material (as in *The Count of Monte Cristo*), but is wholly spiritual, incorruptible, "not of this world," meant to glorify Creator and creation rather than serve one's self-centred purposes and inexorable ego. As Edmund Dantes (the Count of Monte Cristo) himself discovered, such treasure is ultimately found within the sanctuary of the heart, that inner kingdom of love wherein the penitent wait on God.

This is Georgiou's third book of spiritual reflections. Concise and substantive, these meditations continue to relate his interior trek that began in 1993 on Patmos, the isle of the Revelation. On this Biblical site—itself a kind of "Monte Cristo"—Georgiou fortuitously met the poet Robert Lax (1915–2000), an American writer and sage who was one of Thomas Merton's closest friends. Merton had said of Lax, "He had a kind of inborn direction to the living God."[1]

Georgiou's first book, *The Way of the Dreamcatcher,* records his wisdom lessons with Lax; his second publication, *Mystic Street,* describes his spiritual experiences en route to his doctorate in theology. *The Isle of Monte Cristo* goes on to explore his understanding of the divine Presence in everyday life, particularly how God communicates with us through people, places, and ideas.

Georgiou, who teaches world religions in the San Francisco Bay Area, thinks this communication to be primarily instructive. He reveals how the manifold beauty of creation is meant to steer us toward the presence of the Creator in our hearts. Robert Lax said of this sacred and intimate domain,

> God the Holy Spirit dwells within us,
> as life within the seed. He is outside
> and beyond us too, encouraging,
> sustaining the growth of the seed.

> Still, though, let us think of Him as being
> within—He is within—and let us honor
> Him too, in ourselves and in others.[2]

Drawing from a wide range of scholastic and creative experiences relating to his own faith journey, including colourful flashbacks of Lax and holy Patmos, Georgiou imparts how all of our living on this transitory planet points to the everlasting "kingdom within." There we shall one day ascend *Monte Cristo,* the Mountain of Christ, and, like Edmund Dantes, inherit a treasure that has been prepared for us ever since the foundation of the world.

In many ways, *The Isle of Monte Cristo* is the crystallization of the author's spiritual odyssey. Herein a circle of love completes itself, for Georgiou, like his mentor Lax, is now a teacher whose lesson plan centres on *agape*. The book concludes a unique "trilogy of grace" initiated on holy Patmos and inspired by her blessed poet.

A treasure map concealed in a breviary ultimately led Edmund Dantes to his providential fortune and destiny; in like manner, may this journeybook of love help guide searchers to the "Isle of Monte Cristo," and to the infinite riches of the heart.

Br. Patrick Hart

Br. Patrick Hart, O.C.S.O.
Last Secretary to Thomas Merton
General Editor of the Merton Journals
Abbey of Gethsemani, Kentucky
June 2010

Prologue

The title of this book should bring to mind one of the greatest adventure stories of all time—*The Count of Monte Cristo,* by Alexandre Dumas. But why should a classic tale of revenge set in the Napoleonic era serve as a springboard to the inner quest? Simply put, because Dumas' celebrated epic is also a story of spiritual transformation and renewal. Understood in its entirety, it may be interpreted as a romance of the heart leading to the supreme mystery of *agape* (pronounced *ah-gah-pay*), the highest and purest form of love, a love wholly selfless, and, according to Christian tradition, centred in God.[1]

In the opening chapters, the young hero, Edmund Dantes, loses everything—his fiancée, his family, his promising career as a sea captain, his very freedom. Betrayed by men he thought were his friends, he is falsely jailed for a crime he did not commit and is thrown into the terrible dungeon of the Chateau d'If, an "inescapable" island prison similar to San Francisco's Alcatraz. Condemned to solitary confinement for the rest of his life, he undergoes incredible suffering.

While Dantes' eventual escape and carefully wrought revenge dominate the novel, beneath this elaborate tale of mystery and intrigue runs a spiritual current that is distinctly Christian in nature. First of all, it is Abbé Faria, a priest and fellow prisoner, who helps to deliver

Dantes from his six years of utter isolation. Through sheer chance, the priest makes contact with him while digging an escape tunnel. Dantes hears the digging and through auditory means, communicates with the priest. The two men then dig toward each other and so form a passageway linking their rooms.

Highly learned and immensely compassionate, Abbé Faria mentors Dantes in a wide variety of academic disciplines: the humanities, the sciences, even economics, politics, and psychology. For eight years Faria perfects Dantes' mind and gives him hope that one day, both shall escape through digging a seaward tunnel together. Indeed, the two men bond as father and son.[2]

When the Abbé is suddenly struck with a fatal seizure, he reveals to Dantes the secret location of an immense treasure hidden since the days of the Renaissance. The fact that this treasure is buried on the remote and rocky island of Monte Cristo imparts a profound Christian symbolism, for Dantes, like Christ on the desolate heights of Golgotha, is soon to "come into his kingdom," and with his great riches, dispense "divine justice."

Moreover, Dantes, like Christ, undergoes a kind of death and resurrection. His ingenious escape from the Chateau d'If is accomplished through removing the body of Abbé Faria from the canvas burial shroud the jailers had enclosed it in and then stitching himself up inside it. In essence, he trades places with the dead priest, an exchange reminiscent of Jesus taking the place of the fallen Adam, that Christ might annihilate cosmic corruption and death, brought on by sin.[3]

Eventually, the prison guards come to the Abbé's cell. They take what they presume to be a "lifeless" body, tie a weight to it, and throw it over a cliff into the churning sea. As Dumas relates, "The sea is the cemetery in the Chateau d'If."[4]

Like the shrouded (and once betrayed and imprisoned) Christ, Dantes plunges into the hellish abyss of certain death, only to cut himself free of its bonds. Hurtling through the depths, he rips open the canvas sack with a knife. Reborn, he miraculously bursts forth from the seemingly invincible confines of the deep. At thirty-three, the same age Jesus was when he resurrected, Dantes "rises from the dead"—he escapes the inescapable.[5]

Liberated at last, he soon finds his fortune of gold coins, ingots, and precious stones on Monte Cristo, and consequently purchases the uninhabited isle, using it as a hideaway and base of operations. After rewarding the few who remained faithful to him during his long absence, he then proceeds to carry out his slow and deliberate plan of revenge upon those who instrumented his incarceration, sometimes taking on the guise of a priest. While doing so, he sees himself as an agent of divine providence, a Christ-like avenger. It is God, he believes, who brought him out of a living death to punish his betrayers; for Dantes, it is the sole reason for his existence as the "Count of Monte Cristo."

Yet while dispatching the last of his enemies, he experiences tinges of remorse. Dantes begins to realize the moral (if not mortal) limitations of his power. He understands that his actions, however just, can have dark and unanticipated repercussions, as when the suicidal wife of one of his betrayers also poisons her nine-year-old son, a peripheral result of the Count's mechanizations. He also comes to see how despite the utter wickedness and treachery of the men who almost destroyed him, their offspring have turned out noble and true, especially where matters of love are concerned. As a result, he jettisons his original belief that the "sins of the fathers" are to be visited upon the next generation and then prays to God that his unrelenting quest for revenge "has not done too much already."[6] In essence, *mercy*—perhaps even forgiveness—gradually begins to replace his insatiable demand for justice.

By the end of the book, the Count is a changed man. Many years before, when he escaped from prison, he dared to exclaim, "I want to be Providence, for the greatest, the most beautiful, and the most sublime thing is to reward and punish."[7] And yet in the final chapter, his parting words, written in the form of a letter addressed to Maximilien (his "spiritual son" and apparent heir to his fortune), reveal a deep inward transformation, a spiritual maturity based on repentance:

> Tell the angel who will watch over your life to pray now and then for a man who, like Satan, believed himself for an instant to be equal to God, but who realized that supreme power and wisdom are in the hands of God alone .... And never forget that, until the day God deigns to reveal the future of man, the sum of all human wisdom will be contained in these two words: *Wait and Hope.*[8]

Thus Edmund Dantes, the Count of Monte Cristo, experiences *metanoia,* contrition leading to inner change. No longer does the inexorable avenger declare, "My will be done" but "Thy will be done." He selflessly yields to the almighty God who declares, "Vengeance is mine, I will repay" (Rom 12.19). This submission is supremely Christian, because the Count of Monte Cristo's obsession with revenge ultimately gives way to the incomprehensible mystery of love, and to all its known (and especially unknown) promises and possibilities.

Like many Christian mystics, Dantes undergoes an inward transformation; he comes to wait on the God of the Heart, in whom he has found his greatest treasure. Thus he sails off with his beloved Haydee in love and toward Love. He has found the meaning of life. Once a prisoner, even of his own vengeance in the world, he is, at last, free.

* * *

How can this epic spiritual story be allegorically applied to ourselves? Like Dantes, many of us have, at some point in our lives, felt betrayed, falsely accused, perhaps even victimized. Somehow the Chateau d' If—that is, the cold, hard world—has transformed our innocence and idealism into a grim discontent that has left us numb, alienated from our own hearts. And then, perhaps in our most intolerable hour, someone or something enters our existence, gives us hope, and shows us a way out of the darkness and into the light.

This liberation may be initiated through the insight and compassion of a friend, teacher, perhaps a stranger; this freedom may be generated through a book, a song, even a spirited word or smile. By whatever means, whether familiar or unfamiliar, subliminal or overt, some kind of blessed catalyst helps to free us from the prison in which we find ourselves, and we are empowered, reborn, en route to a new beginning. We rediscover the pathway that leads us to the core of who we are, the miracle and treasure of love.

And yet this interior journey is not immediate, nor is it effortless. Like Dantes, we must escape not only our worldly prison, but the limited confines of our own self-centred thinking—the very hardness of our hearts—if we are to find the peace within where we may "wait and hope" for our King to come. This inner kingdom is the real *Monte Cristo,* the Mount of *Agape* that Dantes finally finds inside himself. It is the hallowed peak rising from this world to the next, the spiritual summit that every lover of God is called to ascend.

This book centres on that interior ascent. The following reflections impart that whatever we find (or finds us) in this life, whatever events and transformations we may undergo on this earth, ultimately, everything is preparing us for a far more lasting destination—the coming kingdom of God, already stirring in our hearts. Each day we are graced with intermittent signs and blessings, spirit-lessons meant to wake us to the riches of the inner life, and to the tangible Presence of Christ, the Lord of Love who holds everything together, even unto the end of the world.

Robert Lax, my own "Abbé Faria," once compared the spiritual quest to Edmund Dantes resolutely "digging his way out of the Chateau d'If with a fork."[9] Indeed, all lovers of God are gradually breaking free of this world's temporary confines, that they might embrace the Lord in the infinite paradise of the next. But this is not to say that the transient cosmos should be dismissed en route—quite the contrary. Creation, though perishing and racked with struggle, may still be likened to an exquisite tablet on which are written the holy commandments of God.[10] The entire universe is a kind of spiritual school, a cosmic classroom designed to ready us for our entry into paradise, our bright eternal home.

The ephemeral cosmos points, like a universal compass, toward the Kingdom of Love which will never die, and from which life once began. This incorruptible realm is our rightful inheritance, our inexhaustible treasure, our "lasting city" (Heb 13.14), as long as we, like the Count of Monte Cristo, at last open our hearts and let Christ work his will and grace in us. Whether we know it or not, earth is something of a crucible; here, bodies of carbon may transform into spirit-vessels of diamond, all through the fire of Love.

St. Paul said, "While our outer nature is wasting away, our inner nature is being renewed every day" (2 Cor 4.16). It is this "inner nature" that we are increasingly making sense of as we wait on and hope in Christ, the Bright Lord of Love who also waits and hopes for us at the summit of *Monte Cristo.*

> It shall come to pass in the latter days,
> that the mountain of the house of the Lord
> shall be established as the highest of the mountains.
> Many peoples shall flow to it,
> and many nations shall come, and say:
> "Come, let us go up to the mountain of the Lord,
> to the house of the God of Jacob,
> that He may teach us His ways,
> and we may walk in His paths."[11]
>
> Isaiah 2.2-3

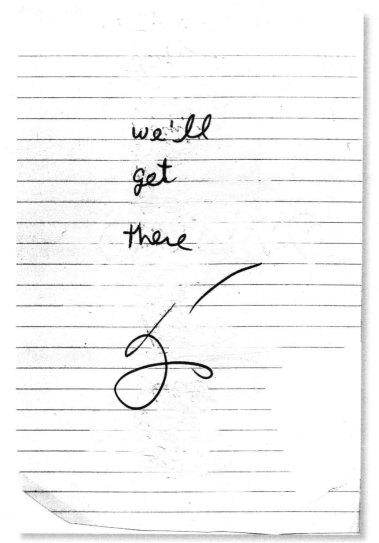

Robert Lax, notebook entry, July 1993.

I. Gates of Entry

Enter eagerly into the treasure-house within you,
and so you will glimpse the riches of heaven.

St. Isaac of Nineveh, *On the Inner Kingdom*

Cross at the summit of Mt. Davidson, San Francisco.

Christopher John Rozales, 2010

Inner Isle

Late January 2007. Thursday night. 10:15 PM. I had finished teaching a weekly world religions class at San Francisco City College and was gathering my things for the drive home.

Exiting the Humanities office, I noticed that my classroom door, just opposite the hallway, was wide open; this was unusual, since the custodian regularly shut it by 10 PM.

I peered into the dim room. Moonlight streamed in through the windows directly in front of me. But what caught my attention most was the dark mass outside, looming in the distance.

It was Mt. Davidson, the highest point of San Francisco, surrounded by the lights of many homes leading to its forested summit. Having seen the mountain countless times over the years, I had come to take its massive presence for granted, but now, in the silent and acute darkness, something about its wooded peak captivated me, as if I was seeing it for the first time.

I walked into the moonlit room and stood motionless by an unlatched, half-open window. A cold winter breeze was blowing, rocking the distant trees. As they swayed, the brightly lit houses, interspersed in the woods, flickered like will o' the wisps through the shifting branches.

All the while, though, the great hulk of mountain appeared to brood in the darkness. Immovable, remote, mysterious, it seemed to hang on the skyline, and eerily beckon. The intense scene reminded me of a stirring natural setting I had beheld long ago, yet could not immediately place.

The trees continued to sway in the breeze, and the scattered tiers of house lights twinkled against the black backdrop of rock. A sliver of moonlight now highlighted the very top of the mountain. Slowly I began to make out the immense concrete cross at the crest, densely ringed by eucalyptus blown to and fro. Over a hundred feet tall and constructed in the early twentieth century, the cross remains one of the largest in the world.[1]

Increasingly I sensed myself moving with the wind, rocking back and forth, much like the swaying, far-off trees. Each cold, invigorating breeze was like an uplifting wave buoying me, carrying me toward the mountain. In some fantastic way I felt as though a sea of darkness had spread itself out before me, and I was floating closer and closer to the rock. In my imagination I had boarded a kind of fanciful dream ship and was circumnavigating the mountain's expanse. The shimmering homes perched along the summit, pulsating like lighthouses in the distance, were guiding my vessel into port.

One fleecy cloud blew over the mountaintop, then another. In the distance, the faint bellow of a foghorn sounded out by the coast. Then, all at once, I realized why Mt. Davidson had so transfixed me: subliminally, the high, wide peak and its brightly tiered environs hearkened to the late-night approach to Patmos, the remote Greek island that I had visited repeatedly between 1993 and 1999.

It was on Patmos that I had serendipitously discovered the poet-hermit Robert Lax (1915–2000), a humble, soft-spoken sage.[2] His close friend, the famous monk Thomas Merton, thought of Lax as his spiritual superior, and said of him: "Lax had a mind full of tremendous and subtle intuitions ... he was born with a natural, instinctive spirituality ... he was much wiser than I, had clearer vision, and corresponded much more truly to the grace of God than I."[3] Br. Patrick Hart, last secretary to Thomas Merton, had termed the gentle sage "the isle's holy man."[4]

The son of Jewish emigrants from Austria, Lax converted to Roman Catholicism at twenty-eight, prompted largely by Franciscan influence and his developing interest in Christ as Peacemaker. The poet's favourite saints were Francis of Assisi and Seraphim of Sarov (a popular Russian Orthodox hermit who, like Francis, embraced charity and poverty, and expressed a great love of nature).

Even in his twenties, while living in his native New York, Lax had been considered "saintly," as testified in the writings of Catherine de Hueck Doherty, founder of the Madonna House Apostolate. Doherty said of the youthful poet, "Love spoke loudly in his every gesture."[5] Jack Kerouac called Lax, "A Laughing Buddha ... a Pilgrim in search of beautiful innocence."[6] Charles Harbutt, who served with Lax on the staff of *Jubilee,* a prominent Catholic magazine, remarked that many who had worked with Lax thought him to be "a saint—a kind of mysterious clown saint."[7]

The "clown saint" reference was indeed apt. Lax had worked as a clown in a travelling circus prior to becoming a hermit in the mid-1960s—one of many odd jobs that supported (and inspired) his writing. Lax had also found employment as a bartender, security guard, college English instructor, staff worker at the *New Yorker,* movie critic for *Time,* and screenwriter for Samuel Goldwyn Studios in Hollywood.[8] After finally settling into his hilltop hermitage on Patmos, Lax—one of the great unknowns of modern American literature—perfected his minimalist style of poetry, his art of saying deep things simply, reverently.

As grace would have it, Lax eventually became my mentor. This was an especially fortuitous event, since I had first arrived on Patmos stressed out and dejected, having suffered the end of a long-term relationship and employment difficulties. Through our meetings over the years, Lax encouraged me to pursue studies in spirituality and the arts. This advice led me to the Graduate Theological Union in Berkeley, California, where I completed my Ph.D. dissertation in 2005, the subject of which was Lax himself.[9] Things had come full circle, in essence.

While gazing at Mt. Davidson, watching the faraway lights twinkle and momentarily fade, dimmed by dream-like wisps of fog, I thought again of my first voyage to Patmos, in the summer of 1993. As the ferry drew near to the moonlit isle, I left the passenger lounge and hastily climbed to the top deck, eager to glimpse the hallowed rock. Only a handful of people were there, staring intensely across the luminous waters and into the black void ahead.

Early morning approach to Patmos, the "Isle of the Revelation."

The approach to Patmos, a biblical site most famous for its association with St. John's Revelation, stirs the soul. After a nine-hour passage from Piraeus, the isle's dark mass slowly and almost hauntingly takes shape on the horizon. The first thing one sees is a massive amorphous shadow poised in the distance, almost indistinguishable from the rolling black swells.

But then a rugged silhouette spreads out and intensifies. Hewn like a citadel, the isle juts up to the stars, taking on a "contemplative *gravitas*," a solemn and hierarchical solidity. The sensitive pilgrim feels the site to be very much alive, a sentient zone of prayer and holiness.

I recall moving to a more secluded spot on the ship and leaning over the railing; the wood was wet with spray flying from the bow. Far off on the dim horizon I could see lights faintly blinking, and then more pulsing lights that turned out to be houses coming in and out of view as the ship circled its way around the sprawling rock.

Higher above, at the crest of a colossal peak, loomed the imposing Monastery of St. John. Built in the eleventh century like a medieval fortress, its floodlit and turreted ramparts increasingly shone out of the surrounding darkness, lifting the traveller's gaze toward heaven. The old stone abbey seemed to be an ascetic microcosm of Patmos, the "Isle of the Saints."

We sailed closer. The steep volcanic cliffs drew very near as the ferry circumnavigated the rock's perimeter. A towering and tree-lined crag slipped by silently, almost eerily, and then, all at once, the sweeping radiance of the main port streamed into view.

Arranged like a brightly lit amphitheatre, the harbour town of Skala spread out enchantingly before me. The multicoloured lights rose in tiers up into the hills, toward the Cave of the Apocalypse, where St. John experienced the Revelation. Still higher spanned the darkness of the mountains, save for the illuminated Monastery of St. John, fashioned like a castle in the night sky.

Something powerful was here for me, something salvific. I had felt this sensation intensify as the ferry circled round the isle and entered into the bay. While most of the passengers moved on into town, I quietly made my way over to the nearby shoreline and sat in the sand, mystified by the pervasive presence of the Holy—a holiness that would come to manifest itself in the person of Robert Lax.

S.T. Georgiou, 1997

The eleventh-century monastery of St. John, surrounded by the old town of Hora, rises in the distance. In the centre stands the Monastery of the Apocalypse, which houses the cave where St. John—Disciple, Evangelist, Seer—witnessed the Revelation.

Yet now, as I continued to gaze on moonlit Mt. Davidson from San Francisco City College, it was apparent that even though my Patmos days were past, I had once more returned to the sacred isle, albeit in a more metaphysical fashion. In my psychic reverie I had again spiralled into the harbour, but why?

Lax had died years ago, and I was no longer a graduate student returning to Patmos repeatedly to meet with him. I had earned a Ph.D. and was teaching courses in the world religions. What had prompted me to return in my mind to the place where, in many ways, I had been "born again"? The answer came to me slowly, subtly, almost as mysteriously as the streams of fog now drifting toward the cross.

Over the years, and especially as of late, I had come to see that while my initial trek to Patmos had been oriented to the "outer isle," my repeated voyages to this sea-ringed sanctuary had, by almost imperceptible degrees, led me to the *inner isle.* In circling into Patmos summer after summer, I had actually been spiralling into the deeper reaches of my own self, where dwelled not I, but the mystery of "Christ in me" (Gal 2.20). Thomas Merton aptly said of this inward transit, "The real journey in life is interior. It is a matter of growth, deepening, and of an ever greater surrender to the creative love and grace in our hearts."[10]

Much of life, then, is about awakening to the interior experience. In our day-to-day living, we come to see how all of our physical journeying is not simply a temporal exercise, a transitory, earthly trek, but increasingly points to a shared and liberating inner passage that has metaphysical implications and outcomes. As Christianity (and all the great religious traditions of the world) testifies, our surface-level living is the symbolic acting out of a deep inward pilgrimage leading to—and beyond—the gates of the heart.

These gates of entry (represented by the portals of holy Patmos), once more stood before me. Psychically I had brought myself to this interior threshold not to relive the physical journey there, but to better appreciate (and reflect on) its spiritual and inward dimension. Embarking on this theocentric quest is, in fact, our prime and communal directive, for in the hearts of each of us Christ dwells, waiting for us to find him, both in ourselves and in others. All we need do is knock and the gateway to the interior castle will surely be opened, as will eternity. "We just need to be attentive," as Robert Lax once told me, "and patient."

The sudden chiming of my wristwatch indicated that it was already 11 PM. Billowing waves of fog now drifted over the cross and descended from the heights of Mt. Davidson, curling through the cold night air. Closing the classroom door, I walked out of the building, into the dream-swirls of mist, sensing a *kairos* at hand.

A Sign to Steer By

The day after my "inner passage" to Patmos, I delivered a lecture on Lax at St. Joseph's Basilica, on the island of Alameda, near Oakland. My presentation had closed with slides of Lax walking along the Patmos waterfront. The images were accompanied by an audio recording of him reading one of his early poems, "A Song For Our Lady," written when he had visited the port of Marseilles in the 1950s.[11]

Interestingly, I had recorded Lax reciting his poem in 1999, less than a year before his passing. The aged poet, close to death, thus read a poem he had composed in mid-life, a hymn of peace that not only praised Marseilles, a city consecrated to the Madonna, but also hinted of the heavenly kingdom that Lax would soon be entering.

The poet's gentle, reverberating voice echoed through the church. Slow, deeply rolling, it rippled out like a mystic wave:

> Mother of God, do you love this city?
> Do you hear its singing as a prayer
> of light and water, earth and air? ...
> *Oh, Lord, let me find peace in this city;*
> *Let us bring peace to this city.*
> *Let thy Peace be upon this city!*[12]

As the echoes of Lax's voice receded into an intensely moving quiet, the poet laureate of Alameda, Mary Rudge, rose to give the final words. She had brought with her a poem with which she had intended to conclude the evening, but instead announced that the verse had just been recited, and by none other than Lax himself. Seemingly by chance, Rudge had chosen to read "A Song For Our Lady," the very poem that Lax had read via audiocassette!

Marvelling at the coincidence, Rudge handed me the March 1957 issue of *Jubilee,* the acclaimed Catholic magazine in which the poem had first been published. "It's yours," she said. "It's definitely a sign— Lax would want you to have it."

Gratefully thanking her, I opened the fifty-year-old magazine, its cover and pages tinged and faded with age, and then turned to the poem. While the text was there, illustrated and still eminently readable, what immediately caught my eye was the riveting black-and-white photo opposite the title page.

It had been taken by Lax himself! Pictured was the magnificent view from his old hotel room in Marseilles, situated at the far side of the bay. Through a window opened wide, the port was spread out exquisitely; its long stone quay, fishing boats, and tall-masted ships hearkened back to an enchanted, almost bygone world, a kind of mythic isle.

Robert Lax, 1957

View of Marseilles from the Hotel Calais.

Sunlight rippled on the water. On the opposite shore, behind the docked vessels, rose a promenade of waterfront businesses and apartments. Above them, tiers of homes ascended along a steep and distant hill, *La Garde,* the highest point of Marseilles. At the crest stood the Basilica of Notre Dame, famous for its huge statue of Mary holding the Christ-Child, its dim form barely visible atop the belfry.

Set against a great backdrop of sky, the large, ornate church looked like something out of a fairytale. All of Marseilles seemed to aspire toward it. I, too, was drawn to the distant sanctuary, just as I had been drawn to the towering Monastery of St. John on Patmos, and to Mt. Davidson. Once more, something far away was beckoning, this time through an old photo taken by my friend and teacher.

I carefully scanned the snapshot and especially examined Lax's room, as if in it I could find a hidden clue that might tell me more about why the image had so moved me. The poet had always been meticulous with his camera work, just as his minimalist verse had demonstrated a laser-like precision. Perhaps he had arranged his quarters a certain way to enhance the meditative quality of the photo.

Lax's room was in the Hotel Calais, an inexpensive place along the wharf. The old building was always in need of repair. He would check into this lowly inn when visiting Marseilles as a roving reporter for *Jubilee.* His little room with cracked windowpanes sometimes doubled as a temporary refuge for the poor—those practising "the art of living in the ruins," as Lax put it.[13] The poet's simple, peaceful presence uplifted them and drew them out of their poverty, as did his charity.[14]

An incredible tranquillity, a relaxed sense of being still radiated in the photo; it was readily discernible, imparting a holiness that transcended time.

On the desk, immediately below the open window, lay binders, notebooks, papers. A mysterious antique beauty graced the room, a poised and shining presence. In the same manner that Lax had helped people to discover the hidden blessings of their lives, so in this photo he had caught a "hallowed something" that was intensely evocative, mesmerizing, iconic.

In the middle of the table, directly in front of the desk-chair, was an open book, most likely a journal. A pen lay beside it, ready to be taken up by the poet at a moment's notice, when inspiration would infuse him.

A shoreline breeze coming in through the window ever so slightly fluttered the buoyant pages. The whole setting seemed to be an open invitation to come, see, and write of the blessed vision radiating on (and beyond) the bay waters; to sing of the spirit-journey winding through the ruins and riches of Marseilles; to climb up to the faraway church-castle set high on a hill, a sanctuary in the sky leading to Mary, Protectoress of the Faithful, and, ultimately, to Christ and his eternal Kingdom.

Literally and allegorically, this heavenward "spirit trek" mirrored Lax's lifelong theocentric travels. Heeding a contemplative call, he had journeyed far and looked deeply into people, places, the very dregs of common everyday living and discovered that in all of his wanderings he could glimpse the perennial presence of God. Though seemingly distant, Christ was, in actuality, wholly intimate. His kingdom was the "treasure within," the castle of the heart (dramatically symbolized by the Basilica of Notre Dame) that transcended all worldly needs and concerns.[15]

Lax had photographed this "kingdom" from his small and simple hotel room where his impoverished friends sometimes gathered. This, too, was deeply symbolic, in that the snapshot was not taken from a lavish and prestigious lookout point, but from a less-than-ordinary dwelling, a place in disrepair where "less" was obviously "more."

As I continued to examine the photo, Lax's indifference to materialism increasingly made sense. Throughout the poet's life journey—travelling lightly with a circus in Canada, working with the poor in Harlem and Marseilles, living ascetically on Patmos, crafting poems that stressed economy of form—Lax had come to see that God is best perceived not in conditions of fullness, but emptiness. The free-flowing blessings of the Spirit seemed harder to discern in those who busied themselves with storing up temporal wealth. Cloyed with material possessions, they could not function efficiently as channels of invisible, unbounded grace. Small wonder that many of the poet's close friends were fishermen, rustic folk whose frugal living could border on asceticism.

Lax's spiritual compass had therefore always been set for the Rock of Ages, the "Isle of Monte Cristo," that outwardly barren (yet inwardly abundant) domain of the heart from which all things came and to which all things are going. As he wrote in his lengthy poem "Port City: The Marseilles Diaries,"

> I have been coming
> forever
> to this city ...
> I have
> been coming

toward this
city
since
the beginning
of time,
singing
this city's
song ...[16]

Staring into the old photograph of Marseilles, I increasingly felt the presence of Lax, as if he were now singing this song directly to me. Once more he seemed to be gently pointing the way to the lasting peace and promise of the inner kingdom.

It was a passage I had unconsciously begun fifteen years before, when I first sailed into Patmos broken in spirit, and, through grace, met the isle's beloved sage. My journey continued through the twists and turns of graduate school, as documented in *Mystic Street*, a book of meditations I had written while a student of theology. Now, as a college educator, a new door had opened that I sensed could lead to a greater understanding of the Teacher within, the Christ of Love, the everlasting King whom Holy Scripture reveals as our greatest Treasure.[17] But before I could reflect more deeply on these things, another sign soon manifested itself, pointing to the pre-eminence of the inner quest and to life in the Spirit.

Plotting a Course

A week after my Alameda talk, I received an unexpected letter from my artist friend Gianvito (Vito) Lo Greco, living in Rome.[18] Vito had written about his recent visit to Patmos, having travelled there the previous autumn to paint. I was very interested in what he had to say because I had not gone back to the island since 1999, shortly before Lax's passing, and was now thinking of returning. Yet in reading Vito's letter, he seemed to suggest what the latest series of events had been telling me all along: that the real "Patmos," the true "Jerusalem," the imperishable "Mountain of Christ" is ultimately discovered within oneself.

January 2007

Dear Stavros:

Hope you are well. I'm just back from Patmos. The island's still beautiful, but things aren't the same. Every year Patmos has been changing, and now this change is really evident.

There's more tourism and noise here. More buildings are going up. Space is less. Young people seem to be living only for the present. They don't care much about the old ways, only surface-level living. Many have left to make money in Athens, and the foreigners who come here looking for work know little or nothing about the sacred traditions.

Do you remember how houses here were never locked and keys were left in motorbikes? Now it's different. There's more crime. Everyone is more guarded. Patmos is becoming like a big city with all its problems. The special energy we felt here when Robert [Lax] was alive is harder to sense. Things aren't what they used to be … but is it not the same everywhere?

All of us hope to find that place where there'll always be peace and beauty, but here on earth nothing is forever, nothing lasts. That is why we must do our best to live the *real life*—the life of the Heart! *Agape* is the only way. There's only time enough to love …[19]

Certainly I was saddened to learn of the changes taking place on St. John's "Isle of Love," the biblical site that I had associated with my own spiritual reawakening. And yet even in my regular visits there, I, too, had caught glimpses of the very slow (but steady) modernization, the spread of apartments, studios, and tourist shops, the profusion of private getaways in what had once been open fields and farmland. Even the headlands of the isle were shrinking; its mysterious wilds were eroding, replaced with concrete and metal.

Unfortunately, changes such as these would appear inevitable, considering our increasingly fast-paced and homogenous world. Despite Patmos' inherent holiness (it has remained a destination of Christian pilgrimage since the third century), the popular island was now steadily becoming part of a restless age addicted to noise, speed, violence, materialism, and insatiable greed. The corrupt intrusions of modernism threatened to make even this widely revered sacred site worldly and profane.

If Patmos (and, for that matter, all of earth's sacrosanct places) then faced the possibility of imminent spiritual and environmental dissolution, where best to consistently experience the holy? Where to find that pure, blessed, secure, and everlasting locale "where grace can flow," as Lax had advised, and as Vito had echoed?

As so many spiritual traditions emphasize, the "zone of grace," that most perfect meeting point between human consciousness and God (or a greater "Field of Awareness"), dwells within the core of our being. While everything in the cosmos is infinitely precious in itself, the transient universe points to an immaterial spiritual reality, an invisible "first principle of existence" from which all appearances arise. It is precisely for this reason that all the major world religions view life as an *interior passage,* a compassionate journey leading toward a blessed illumination within, and/or a transcendent realization of absolute consciousness.[20]

As evidenced in the Gospels, Jesus emphasizes the liberating and empowering value of the inner trek: *"The kingdom of heaven is within you"* (Lk 17.21); *"Seek first this kingdom, and all other things will be added unto you"* (Mt 6.33). And Judaic scripture declares how *"as a man thinks through his heart, so he is"* (Deut 4.29, Prov 23.7).

Christianity and Sufism express how the mysteries of the "inner kingdom" abide in us. This sacred domain may, in part, be associated with the animating inner energies found in Taoism (*Chi*) and Hinduism (*Prana*).

Buddhism teaches that since we exist in a transient cosmos, the "true treasures of life" are to be discovered inside the searcher. Therefore *Buddha Nature*—the clear spark of perception extant in all living beings—alone is real. Similar ideas apply to the *Atman,* the Hindu principle of soul.

The spiritual journey, then, is about awakening to the interior experience and cultivating the salvific blessings found therein. Purged of worldly concerns, the student of religion gradually becomes aware of a greater consciousness in which everything is participating, a realization leading to a heightened understanding of ultimate reality, how all things are deeply interconnected—in essence, One.

Robert Lax, like so many Christian mystics before him, believed this "Oneness" to be based on *agape*—divine, universal, interceding love. He understood this transcendent love to be unconditional, meant to unite all faiths and peoples. In our conversations he emphasized how the creative holiness of compassion was the central tenet of all world faiths. Indeed, everything Lax had taught me was explicitly about *journeying to the centre,* that is, discovering the sustaining core of being—the pre-eminence of love.

As a practising Eastern Orthodox Christian, I believed this journey to be centred in Jesus, the God of Love. Scripture relates that his vivifying energy abounds throughout creation (Rom 1.20). Through the Christ all things were made, (Jn 1.3), and to the Christ all things are returning (Jn 12.32). Humanity had been crafted in Christ's very image—the indwelling image of Love (Gen 1.26). Thus Christians are called to enter their hearts, so that, even now, they might live in the joy and peace of the inner kingdom.

In his poem "Jerusalem," Lax writes poignantly of this intimate entry into the heart, a holy passage leading to the fount of bliss within:

> Reading of lovely Jerusalem,
> lovely, ruined Jerusalem …
> For we must seek
> by going down,
> down into the city

for our song,
deep into the city
for our peace ...[21]

How to enter into the inner self and find these life-giving waters? Certainly prayer, meditation, asceticism, and participation in ritual are standard methods, as the world religions testify. These practices help to purge the obstructive ego and purify the seeker, initiating an inward transformation. Deeper states of consciousness are experienced, as are feelings of divine intimacy.

At the same time, the questing soul may live each day more keenly, attentively awake to the holy revelations discernible in everyday living. Once hidden "spirit treasures" become increasingly manifest. Ultimately, all things come to be seen as gateways to divine illumination, points of entry into a transfigured world. As Irenaeus of Lyons wrote in the second century, "Everything is a sign of God; the Christian discerns and encounters Christ everywhere."[22]

All of life is, in essence, a spiritual school. Throughout creation, the Creator has left "traces" of his infinite and imperishable holiness. The supercharged energies of the Spirit reverberate through matter; things natural hint of their supernatural foundation and origin. Our Christ-born souls sense the presence of something greater than the mere organic shell of things.

Like Adam and Eve, we, too, can hear the footfalls of God (however mysterious and faint) in the garden of life. And we innately know that for the garden to exist, there must somehow, somewhere live a Gardener. So we go on searching until, at last, we find Him, seeded in our hearts.

You are within me urging me to find you.
It is you who tells me of the longed-for being.
Your voice calls me to the far-off land.
If I wake, it is you who wakes me.
If I sleep, sleep falls from your hand.
You are the Spirit urging me to find you.

Robert Lax,
from *Psalm*[23]

Toward the Far-Off Land

Christopher John Rozales, 2010

Ocean Beach, near Fort Funston, San Francisco.

After reading Vito's letter describing the radical changes taking place on Patmos, I drove out to Fort Funston, a nearby coastal recreation area, for a run on the beach. Though it was a cold day in late January, the sun was out and the skies were incredibly clear, revealing a spectacular shoreline. From the cliffside lookout deck, I could glimpse the Farallon Islands on the horizon, situated about twenty-five miles beyond San Francisco.

An inner, mysterious longing swept through me while I gazed at the distant Farallones. The hazy silhouette of rocks hinted of a far-off mythic land, a quiet, imaginary place set apart from the world. While I may have been thinking of the Patmos of old, the faraway isles evoked something infinitely greater; their faint silhouettes, almost hovering in the marine haze, conjured a romantic vision of the "kingdom to come," the celestial city toward which the faithful in Christ are journeying. C.S. Lewis said of this blessed abode,

> There have been times when I think we do not desire heaven; but more often I find myself wondering whether, in our heart of hearts, we have ever desired anything else .... It is the "secret signature" of each soul, the incommunicable and unappeasable want, the thing we desired before we met our wives or made our friends or chose our work, and which we shall desire on our deathbeds .... *All of our life an unattainable ecstasy has hovered just beyond the grasp of our consciousness ....*[24]

The idyllic sight of the Farallones poised on the rim of the horizon increasingly suggested to me that heaven is indeed our innermost desire and aim, because everything created bears God's "secret signature"—we are sealed with His love from birth. Thus our real identity, the very fount of our being, is in the Lord. Quoting St. Augustine, "You made us for yourself, and our hearts will find no peace until they rest in you."[25] Daily, the God of Love calls out to us, and, if our hearts remain open, we respond in love. It is the way of journeying toward Monte Cristo, to the inner treasure that is Christ.

I walked down a long flight of steps set into the massive cliff and made my way to the pristine shore. The brisk wind and salt air felt exhilarating, and I broke into a run. Save for the birds and sea life, the long, wide beach was completely deserted—for the hour or so that I was out there, the shoreline had become my private paradise. But as I jogged back to the cliff, I received a sombre, if not unsettling, wake-up call.

At the crag's base I saw a man lying on his side, clad only in running shorts. He was nearly pressed into the rock. At first I thought he was sunning himself or even asleep, though this seemed highly unlikely on a cold winter day. I drew closer and still he seemed oblivious to my presence. But then I saw his swollen face, half hidden by black matted hair, and blue-green discolorations on his arms and torso. From his inner thigh down to his ankle, his leg was opened, revealing congealed nerves, tissue, and bone. A few crows were poised on boulders, their beaks blood red.

It was not the first time I had found a corpse on the beach; a few years before, I came upon the remains of a man who, as I would later learn, had jumped from the Golden Gate Bridge.[26] But finding the body of someone in his mid-forties (close to my age) and who may have also been running along the coast (he was still wearing his waterlogged Nikes) definitively hit home—death may come at anytime, in any manner, though we may think ourselves invincible. As expressed in the eighth-century Christian epic *Beowulf*,

> For a little while you will be at the peak of your strength,
> but it will not be long before sickness or the sword, or the
> hand of fire, or the raging sea, a thrust of the knife, a
> whizzing arrow, or hideous dotage, or failure and darkening
> of the eyes, will plunder you of your might; and in the end,
> brave soldier, death will defeat you.[27]

I prayed for the deceased, then climbed to the top of the cliff and notified the park patrol. After relating the details of the grisly find,

I returned to the lookout deck and sat there for a long while, collecting myself.

How strange that I should chance upon the dead man so soon after receiving Vito's letter, a missive in which he fervently expressed that nothing lasts, that the real life to pursue is that of the heart! And why was it that in such a short time I had experienced a consecutive series of signs pointing to the transience of this world and the pre-eminence of the inner life?

I think it was because over the past few years I had gradually (and sadly) forgotten my spiritual awakening on Patmos, my spirit-lessons with Robert Lax—the day-to-day living in love, the patient way of the heart, the joy of giving oneself wholly to God. While I was lecturing about Lax (and other topics related to my courses in religion), I was not really living the teachings he had imparted to me—I was not "walking the talk." Instead, I had been caught up in the more worldly aspects of academia, especially struggling to find a permanent place of employment and seeking a tenure-track position.

Seventeen years had passed since I began teaching, yet I remained a part-time instructor, commuting to a handful of Bay Area schools. Even my recent Ph.D. in Religion and Art, which followed my Master's degrees in the Humanities and in Theology, had not significantly changed the situation, nor had my diverse classroom experience, fieldwork, and publishing record. I was now in mid-life and my status as a college educator seemed to differ little from that of a new hire fresh out of graduate school.

Why, at this advanced stage in my career, was I still financially insecure, living semester to semester, unsure of my academic future? Why did I remain an expendable lecturer, despite superior evaluations by students and faculty? Numerous times I had come close to landing a permanent position at various colleges, yet nothing had come through. The subterranean tension felt among instructors vying for full-time posts (and navigating their way through campus politics) could be overwhelming at times. Years were going by, and my life seemed locked in a perpetual holding pattern.

As a result, I had become increasingly cynical and frustrated, even bitter, for there seemed to be no means of professional advancement. What was the point of all the education when I could not exercise my experience to its fullest as a vested professor? The increasing budget cuts and poor economy did not help matters, nor did the nationwide disappearance of tenure-track positions that had been transformed into "part-time employment opportunities." Where to go when the doors of academia were essentially closed, save for temporary appointments that relied on available funding and adequate enrollment?

Looking out toward the Farallones, a one-word answer sufficed: *within.* For the spiritually minded instructor, "Higher Education" ultimately transcends position, institution, prestige, and pay— everything the world values. The life of the dedicated teacher at every academic level is, in essence, a non-profit, transformative ministry. The profession demands that one channel all one's training, experiences, and enlightenment into the "now moment," both inside and outside the classroom, so that human consciousness might perfect itself.

Teaching centres on "inner ripening," on "bringing fruit to bear" (Rom 7.4). Real education instills wonder, inspiration, and hope. Authentic learning is grounded in "greeting every person, student or not, with power, wisdom, and love," as Lax had advised.[28] When paths cross in this way, "a jungle might (eventually) transform into a garden."[29]

All of this was something I already knew, but, as of late, had failed to consciously and consistently live because I was too often outside the God of my own heart. The frustration of perennial job searches that led nowhere and my inability to secure even a local tenured post had come to obscure the holiness of the task at hand: *imparting (and receiving) knowledge through wisdom and compassion, and, in the process, helping minds and hearts to grow.*

The only way to accomplish this sacred and scholastic task—despite the stress of part-timing at multiple institutions—was to take good care of the immediate present. My mentorship with Lax had demonstrated this very point. Whether I was talking with him about life in the Spirit, walking along the shore, visiting islanders, or sharing a meal, the sage always had a way of revealing the divine Presence in every act and moment. Time and again he would tell me, "If you take care of each moment, you take care of all time."[30]

Everything thus had become a lesson in his company; everything I had experienced with Lax had generated a nurturing, transformative, near palpable wisdom, simply because everything we shared was free in the love of God—we were tuned into the *Agape of the Now.* Nothing else really mattered, because we understood that in love, everything good and profitable would eventually come to pass, just as it was meant to be. In love, every experience had the potential to be baptismally renewing, wholly transcendent, capable of elevating the soul toward an enhanced understanding of the divine.

Into the heart of that love I was journeying once more; all things contained within them the treasure of the Christ, patiently waiting to be discovered. But the inner way was not to be undertaken too fast, too hard. As Lax had written,

> I'll try to say it the way it is, the way I see it.
> But I won't try too hard.
> Trying too hard gets me off the track.
> I know where I am now.
> I know I can get some part of it said.
> I can, if I don't try too hard.[31]

Inflow, Outflow

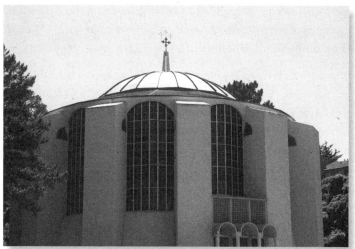

Christopher John Rozales, 2010

Holy Trinity Greek Orthodox Church, San Francisco.

The Sunday following my sobering find at the beach, I attended services at Holy Trinity Greek Orthodox Church in San Francisco. While kneeling in prayer, I began to take note of my posture, which, in humility and reverence, had turned inward and was bowed; my bent frame had assumed an interior direction and emphasis.

Closing my eyes, I had withdrawn from the noisy, turbulent "outer world" to enter a domain of infinite tranquillity, and this by degrees. Holy Trinity was situated on the outskirts of the busy city, near the restful sea; the church itself was an inner refuge, a place to find peace in a tumultuous society. The serenity within the spacious edifice led the worshipper to the mystic doors of the heart, the innermost sanctuary.[32]

Like a shell winding toward its centre, I was quietly contracting, spiralling into my deepest self in order to make contact with a life-giving, nurturing Power, a foundational and restorative Presence. Here dwelled not I, but the mystery of "Christ in me" (Gal 2.20).

This salvific zone, accessible to every believer, can be thought of as an "inner isle," a place apart, a "secret inward room" (Mt 6.6), where stillness in the Godhead radiates without end, imparting to believers a timeless peace, so necessary in a fallen, transient world. Though the universe remains unstable, the sanctum of the heart is changeless. Its inmost essence is Almighty Love, the "Holy Irreducible," sustaining life forever. The Christian is called to discover this unchanging *Agape*, this immutable God through whom humanity (and the cosmos) will one day be transfigured.[33]

Many religions profess that an infinite and changeless reality exists beneath a fleeting world of change and dwells within everything that lives. Creation is commonly seen as a "realm of awakening" in which the searcher experientially discovers this ultimate reality. On finding the divine, the seeker receives the supernatural means by which to escape the dissolution of the cosmos and the finality of death.

For the Christian, this lifelong journey begins with *baptism*. The sacrament is a conscious, definitive response to the Love that not only birthed creation, but had gone on to sacrifice itself for the life of the world; baptism is then a kind of "answering love."[34] The rite is a formal acknowledgement (and confirmation) of the inborn agapaic bond existing between Creator and created. The holy ceremony supernaturally opens the inner doors of the soul (made obscure since the Fall of Adam), that the believer might more directly and intimately commune with Jesus, the risen "God-Man" in whom the initiate "dies, and is born again" (Rom 6.1-11).[35]

A new light thus shines out of the believer—the same light that shone out of the tomb when Christ rose. Indeed, the first light of the resurrection radiates in the heart of the baptized. Baptism, in Greek, denotes *Photismos,* illumination, to be endowed with light. The inner eye opens, and the illumined is blessed with the capacity to recognize the Christ, not only in oneself, but in all things. Gifted with this greater vision, the baptized exercises a powerful intercessory role in stewarding the cosmos toward its ultimate apotheosis; the Christian serves as a caretaker of the earth, a "Priest of the laity" (1 Pet 2.4-10), nurturing creation, as best as possible, until the return of the King.

While kneeling in prayer, I reflected on the treasure to be found within the bright and boundless spirit-mansion of the heart. I thought of how the riches of the Christ are vast, measureless, exceeding anything the mind can conceive. Jesus—the infinite embodiment of beauty, wisdom, and love—can never be completely fathomed by intellectual knowing (which is ultimately limited and has no lasting unity); he can be perceived only by faith, via the intuitive, illimitable heart. In Christ, *love transcends knowledge*; thus it is through the gateway of the heart that God touches souls. Stirred by his agapaic essence, they are granted the blessed means to "partake of his divine nature" (2 Pet 1.4).

Only love—the almighty love of God—can rescue a transient, fragmented planet, and can deliver creation from death. Divine love is stronger than death, promising salvation and resurrection, and so is surely the highest wisdom. Hence St. Paul writes, "We impart a wisdom, but not a wisdom of this age or of the rulers of this age who are doomed to pass away; we impart a secret and hidden wisdom of God, decreed before the ages for our glorification (2 Cor 6-8). We preach the wisdom of the Christ, in whom the whole treasury of knowledge is stored up" (Col 2.3).

Thus when Christ rose and appeared to his disciples, it was not their minds that experienced a wave of recognition and joy—it was rather the *hearts* of the apostles that burned and quickened in the presence of their loving Master (Lk 24.32). Jesus fired a much more sensitive, intrinsic, emotive aspect of his creation which, in essence, *spiritualized the entire body.* God did not ask for elite savants with finely trained, self-sufficient minds, but humble individuals who had purified and opened their hearts.

This "way of the heart" reveals that it is not necessary to be a philosopher to know God; one has only to love intensely, to think and act "through the heart." The mind is somehow outside itself until it humbly obeys the promptings of the intuitive heart, and in love turns to Christ, the compassionate, bright Lord who endows the intellect with a kind of "agapaic reason."

The energy of love is the prime power, the searching, sensitive, and saving principle that moves believers to approach God in what may be termed "inward and ascending" stages. Especially among the saints, this inner and upward psychic movement is so intense that the elect are caught up in divine ecstasy; in essence, they go out of themselves in rapture, faintly mirroring the bliss of God's love, which is so wholly concentrated that it explodes in creativity ("Let there be light!" [Gen 1.3]).[36]

Similarly, a prayerful contemplative may also descend into himself and bring forth interior treasure, fertile spiritual riches to be shared with all, be they assurances of Christ's love, kind words, peaceful blessings, acts of mercy, inspirational art, visions of the new Eden, anything to uplift a jaded, desensitized world. This inward-outward movement—so much like inhaling and exhaling, like blood coursing to and from the heart—is actually part of a divine cycle, a rhythmic pulse and flow. The seeker goes into his holy core to find Christ, and, having found him, emerges to share his discovery, only to return again, that heaven might infuse him with yet more spiritual power so that love's blessings might once more be disseminated (and this *ad infinitum,* that all things may draw nearer to their transfiguration).[37]

Praying myself into the mystery of the Christ, into his indwelling divinity, I began to see how throughout creation and at all times, beings are either going deep into their hearts for inner sustenance, or are emanating from them, infused with life and light. Everything alive is travelling into or out of the kingdom, coming in or going out of a deeper dimension of love uniting us all, a love yearning to be recognized and revealed, that the glory of God may be manifest everywhere.

Later that morning, as I walked out of Holy Trinity, a jet roared overhead. Indeed, like planes arriving or departing, or as angels descending or ascending, we are all moving through the same sky, sharing the joys and struggles of our journey toward paradise.

Intimations

My progressive efforts to live a theocentric life, free of energy-draining concerns having to do with employment difficulties and the pursuit of tenure, began to take on greater significance. Day by day, I sought to put into practice what Robert Lax had told me years ago: that is, to live (and especially *to love*) in the moment, no matter what the situation. *Agape* elevates the soul beyond worldly desires; it lifts the heart toward the divine and makes one more receptive to God.

The more I exercised this transcendent love, the more I discovered hidden blessings both inside and outside the classroom. Rejuvenating signs and symbols began to surface in my daily activities, many of which brought back memories of Lax and my spirit-lessons with him on Patmos. Once more, life took on a highly substantive and synchronous feel. My conscious desire to love (and to pray myself in the love of God) made me better able to sense the Christ in all things.

As I progressed along this spiritual path, I increasingly reflected on the indwelling presence of Jesus. At what point do we feel him alive in us, gifting us with consciousness, sustaining our very being? When does the God-journey begin?

While an early awareness of Christ directly depends on religious upbringing, social traditions, and family influences, he calls each of us in a special way because everything that exists has a unique relationship with the Creator. Oftentimes our personal *theognosia* (knowledge of God) begins without our even knowing it, especially when we are very young, open, empty of preconceptions and prejudice, living innocently, spontaneously.[38] At this time, a certain "inner sensibility" may be catalyzed through images, sounds, sensations, encounters, and dreams. We quicken to a deeper rhythm permeating life—a "conscious communion" with God mysteriously begins. Robert Lax writes of this intimacy:

> Times of feeling you were there,
> that you were close. A hall, a corridor,
> walking down a corridor, the damp stone walls,
> a smell of dampness, cold, but a feeling of what?
> That I wasn't alone? That someone was near,
> not visible, but near me, that someone was there?
> Who, though …? Do I know you? Do I, at all?
> Have I had some signs or flashes? Any clues?[39]

Every believer has their account of how they first came to feel the nearness of the divine presence. We all have probably sensed, however fleetingly, the presence of a world within, and a world beyond. But as most can testify, these intimations quickly fade once the noisy distractions of modern-day living take over. In a media-driven age, we tend to throw ourselves into a spectacle-driven, want-based lifestyle that proves to be ultimately draining and hollow. Thomas Merton writes:

> The modern child may, in the beginning of his conscious life, show natural and spontaneous signs of spirituality. He may have imagination, originality, a simple and individual freshness of response to reality, and even a tendency to moments of thoughtful silence and absorption. But all these qualities are

> quickly destroyed by the fears, anxieties, and compulsions to
> conform which come at him from all directions .... The con-
> scious life of today's individual is completely lost in intellectual
> abstractions, sensual fantasies, political, social, and economic
> clichés, and in the animal cunning of the detective or salesman.
> All that is potentially valuable and vital in him is relegated to
> the subconscious mind ....[40]

Thus we come to forget our first awareness of the divine, supplanting
it with anthropocentric excesses. We gradually lose sight of how we
hearkened initially to God, not to the avaricious demands of popular
culture, so inordinately bent on satisfying immediate desires. We
were living in the world then, but we had not yet become worldly.
Our contact with Christ was pristine because we were simply awake
to life, not ego-oriented and self-centred.

Eden was then close to our hearts because very little separated us
from our origin; an intimacy with our holy beginnings prevailed. We
still had a faint ability to tap into *Genesis consciousness* (the pre-Fall
psychic state of Adam and Eve born of original innocence). Christ
himself makes clear that to receive the Kingdom of God, we must be
as gentle and trusting as children (Mk 10.15).

I recall a brief time during my own childhood when certain "inner
experiences," both positive and negative, seemed to suggest that
there was a kind of deeper, more mysterious dimension in life. I
remember standing in the middle of a school playground during
recess and slowly biting into an apple. Its kaleidoscopic taste was
overwhelming—in that first mouthful, all my senses felt as though
they had been fed. The absolute whiteness of the fruit's interior remains a powerful memory.

I also recall seeing, late at night, above my bed, a brooding shadow-form that exuded a disconsolate, negative energy. For perhaps a week after this unsettling experience, I repeatedly dreamed of a bright city besieged by dark forces.

With time, I understood that these childhood episodes had something to do with the transformative, multi-dimensional struggle between good and evil, a conflict into which every mature Christian is called to enter, that through prayer and good works, the cosmos might one day be reborn entirely in light.

Indeed, as we grow in Christ, we come to see how the whole world is bright, and yet the whole world is burning. In this fallen realm, nothing is assured; all things are vulnerable, susceptible to instability and decay. Here we go through happiness and despair, much like Jesus did while on earth, illustrating how this transient cosmos remains a temporary place of struggle (and purification) where lasting peace is found only in the love of God.[41]

Like Jesus, every Christian is both crucified and resurrected in this life. The believer undertakes a journey that, in many ways, is similar to Christ's (as the sacraments exemplify, beginning with baptism). Yet sometimes we experience such ecstatic moments in this world that they can make us feel as if we have already entered heaven, however briefly. Our first glimpses of the coming Kingdom begin here, on this side of paradise, even as we wait for the life of the world to come.

I recall one spring morning, as a college freshman, when I approached the campus library. All at once, and for only a few seconds, everything went into a "slow-motion rhapsodic roll": the people around me, the trees I passed, the building, my body and thoughts, everything had slowed down and melded into an exquisite, resonant harmony. I had entered a deeper zone, a hidden, inner reality—the universe made perfect sense, and was wholly radiant and beautiful.

Just a few months after this "otherworld entry," I experienced yet another numinous moment. I had come home from school and sat at the kitchen table where I opened the Bible and turned to the Gospel of John. Slowly, almost imperceptibly (though it lasted for a mere few seconds), I felt the Word and creation becoming as one. A fertile and aromatic smell of land rose from the well-worn pages, as happens after a rainfall. Scripture had taken on an earthy, tactile feeling, even a taste—the words and passages had seemingly transfigured; they became like wheat and grapes, greens, olives; somehow everything was in harvest and tangible to all my senses. The New Testament, open before me like plowed land, was laden with a teeming, instantaneous richness fired by a late afternoon sun, its orange-gold light spreading across abundant fields.

This highly transcendent experience stayed with me for days, and, as Providence would have it, returned to me many years later, while visiting Robert Lax in his hermitage on Patmos. He was stirring a kettle of vegetable soup for our dinner, and asked me to taste its consistency. Since a stack of dishes was in my hands, I bent down slightly, that he might spoonfeed me.

"So you want to taste it that way?" he asked, faintly smiling. "All right, that's possible, too." And as soon as he placed the broth in my mouth, I seemed to taste all the fields of the holy isle, all their organic richness. It was a kind of reverberating, multi-sensual communion experience, similar to what had transpired so long ago when I had opened the Bible and turned to the "Good News."[42]

Intimations of God and theophanies of the inner kingdom are always possible and have no end if we remain open, loving, and perceptive. While each experience is unique in itself, oftentimes they integrate and echo, meld and play off each other like ripples of sunlight on water. Perhaps at first they make little or no sense, but as the years pass, deeper insights and patterns form, and their meanings continue to blossom, bearing much fruit.

S.T. Georgiou, 1995

The holy isle of Patmos with the town of Hora rising in the distance. In the centre looms the Monastery of St. John.

Field of Vision

Close to mid-semester one morning, I picked up some papers in the hallway outside my office. Printed on one of them was a striking photo of deep space taken by NASA's Hubble Telescope. The brief caption beneath the star-strewn picture read:

> This Hubble Field Image, assembled from 342 separate exposures, is the deepest view of the universe ever seen. In this tiny speck of sky—equivalent to a dime held 75 feet away from the naked eye—1,600 galaxies are shown. *A single galaxy is believed to contain 100 billion stars.*

I was awestruck—the sheer magnitude of these figures was staggering. If in such an incredibly tiny area of space 1,600 galaxies existed (each with 100 billion stars), then what of all the other spaces in the universe? The illimitable size of the cosmos became, quite suddenly, overwhelming. How to make sense of it all? And how to find one's place in this starry vastness?

Precisely because the Hubble photo prompted such deep metaphysical questions (which directly relate to the study of religion), I decided to show the powerful image as a class opener. Not only did the photo generate thoughts about the immensity of the universe and its relationship to the individual, the image helped to create a heightened sense of mystery and wonder in the classroom, complementary when studying theology. Like space, the subject of God was vast; many early faith systems probably began, in part, by people looking into the night sky and trying to fathom the great expanse.

In showing the Hubble image (via large-screen projector), I noticed how an initial hush swept over the students—their nervous, scattered energy had stilled. For a few quiet moments everybody was on the same spaceship, mystified by the grandeur of the infinite. In an academic climate where specialization, compartmentalization, and deconstruction reigned, a kind of "unity in awe" briefly (and refreshingly) prevailed. Moreover, for the spiritually minded, a discernable holiness seemed to radiate through that celestial vastness; only a God could have put such an infinitely complex and exquisite cosmos together, where, if the gravitational constant were off by one part in a hundred million, then the origin and expansion of the universe could not have transpired in a fashion capable of supporting life.[43]

As Socrates points out in Plato's *Theatetus,* amazement helps to awaken human consciousness and prepares it to receive higher knowledge. Wonder opens the door to an "inner space" wherein enlightenment is wholly possible. Thus the Hubble photo prompted my students to ask deep spiritual questions that the world faiths have addressed since earliest times, each in their own way: *How did all these points of light come to be? How do they interrelate both with themselves and with us? Where did everything come from? Where is everything going? What is eternity? What is God?*

Most of these questions, pared down, echoed my own immediate reaction to the Hubble image: how do we make sense of the limitless universe (the *macrocosm*), and how does the individual self (the *microcosm*) orient itself in the midst of such immensity?

Mystical traditions of both the East and the West base their answers to these interrelated questions on a twofold fundamental premise: first, the immeasurable universe is representational of God's infinity, and second, while the human mind is always "catching up" to rationally comprehend this holy expanse, the awakened heart is already at peace within it, intuitively at one with its sacred Source.

In essence, the heart is the intrinsic sensory organ through which the cosmos (and one's place in it) can be best understood. Via the immensity (and intimacy) of the heart, God is most clearly perceived, even in the far-flung reaches of the universe. Over time, we learn how all of our ceaseless thinking and "busy doing" ultimately surrenders to the infinite calm of this inner sanctum, which, like the Deity, is eternal, and is the inborn locus of communication between Creator and creation. As the Hindu *Upanishads* proclaim,

> The little space within the heart is as great as this vast universe.
> The heavens and the earth are there, and the sun, and the
> moon, and stars; fire and lightning and wind are there, and
> all that now is, and all that is not. For the whole universe is in
> Him, and He dwells within our heart.[44]

The measureless universe therefore points not toward endless realms beyond our own, but to the immediate infinity within. Outer space mysteriously inspires inner awakening and realization, contact with the "All in all"—the divine and luminous Essence in whom we have our deepest being and fullest identity.

For the Christian, Jesus is this "almighty All." The Lord of the Heart is the irreducible and sacrosanct core of everything that exists, the God of Love "through whom creation was made" (Jn 1.3), and, as a consequence of the Fall, remade via the Incarnation and Resurrection: "Behold, I make all things new" (Rev 21.5). Christ is therefore entirely and perpetually present in the cosmos, both through *divine energy* (his indwelling glory permeates creation) and *presence* (he lives within the illimitable heart).

Infinity then takes on transcendent meaning. Jesus is the sustaining core of eternity, and is everywhere alive in it. That eternity we are in the midst of now, and is ours to partake of, if only we let go of our intellect-driven and ultra-analytic approach to life and deign to think "through the heart." When we place our minds in our hearts, we are guided by the love that birthed creation and gave its precious All for our salvation.

In his last years, Robert Lax used to say, "Put yourself in a place where grace can flow." That place is the heart, and the flow is love. Or, as Pascal put it, "It is the Heart which perceives God, and not the Reason, for all of our reasoning comes down to a surrendering to feeling. The Heart has its reasons, of which Reason knows nothing."[45]

In the loving Christ, distances annihilate. He is the eternal bridge uniting heaven and earth, spirit and body. When we draw near to him—especially when receiving the Eucharist—we partake of an exceedingly holy mystery, for we embody infinity in God.

In embracing Christ, we transform, take on a greater form—we are transfigured. The stars, at long last, are no longer distant points of light; they begin to shine out of us, out of our radiant hearts, the joyous, bright, ascendant suns of the new heaven and new earth.

Dream House

Ten miles south of San Francisco is the seaside town of Pacifica, spread along a stretch of coastal hills and valleys. The most popular beach is Linda Mar, widely known for its surfing. Next to it is Pedro Point, a rocky, semi-wooded bluff overlooking the Pacific and nestled with eclectic homes.

One afternoon after a lecture, a number of faculty friends and I drove down to Linda Mar for lunch. None of us had ever ventured to Pedro Point, so after eating, we drove to the scenic promontory.

After crossing a bridge, we rounded a grove of trees, passed an open field, and entered a quiet residential area. Climbing up a long grade, we turned a slight corner and stopped near a magnificent Mediterranean-style villa. The three-storey sienna house was decorated with beautiful multicoloured tiles and bordered by palms and lush vegetation.

The home was for sale. Though certainly none of us could afford the property, we were intrigued by it, particularly when a passerby told us that it was vacant.

Pulling over, we walked up the steep incline leading to the entryway. At the top we could see that the house was dramatically set near the edge of the cliff—the sunlit blue Pacific was visible beyond.

Nothing was preventing us from accessing the rear of the villa, so we continued on around the grounds and gasped at the stunning panoramic views that took in Linda Mar and the winding coastline. Even Pt. Reyes was clearly visible, fifty miles north of San Francisco.

We felt like we were at a resort. The back of the house boasted a spectacular outdoor terrace, rose-hued and complete with an exterior fireplace. Above this patio, stairs led to a luxurious master suite that looked out toward the Farallone Isles. Through the large-scale tinted windows we glimpsed high ceilings with wooden crossbeams, a chef's kitchen, and an intimate dining room facing the open sea.

All of us entertained the same question: *What would it be like to live here?* The thought of such luxury sent our heads spinning. One friend said she would host lavish parties. Another acquaintance said it would be the perfect place to paint, write, and generate art, to which I agreed. And a priest who had come with us thought that the building would make an excellent spiritual institute, as well as a great getaway from life in the city.

As we drove back to San Francisco, I could see how the house had, in a way, changed us, if only briefly. Though we had left Pedro Point, none of us had really let go of the villa—we were still entertaining the fantasy of living there, even conjuring up wild ways to purchase the property for our own particular interests. The dream of owning the exquisite mansion would not leave us. We kept on talking about it, until finally, on returning to the city, we went our separate ways.

What had happened to us? Why were we so completely taken by the home? Simply put, we had a "close encounter" with manifold beauty and desired that beauty for our very own. Though our interests were largely self-centred, we were nevertheless driven by an innate and holy desire for the beautiful.

This inborn passion for aesthetics is part of our very DNA, going back to Adam and the paradise of Eden. We are spiritually wired for "beauty without end," since ultimate beauty is in God. It can be said that the great value society puts on large homes, fast cars, bright gems, and svelte physiques is ultimately symbolic of the space, freedom, speed, radiance, and harmony of soul and body that the blessed will enjoy in heaven, through Christ.

When we crave and surround ourselves with temporal comforts, subliminally, what we really desire is the joy and peace of God—a secure, exquisite bliss that comes without cost (unlike perishing riches), because all things are free in God. Yet because we may be spiritually numb, we think that acquiring more possessions will satisfy our hungry souls. Instead, though, the reverse happens—we become even more ravenous because we sadly continue to feed on the husk of life rather than partake of its inner and sustaining essence, *the manna of love.*

Every generation is captivated by the illusory notion that money, power, prestige, and sensual pleasure will win lasting happiness. Especially today we live in a materialistic society set on satisfying self-centred (and artificial) needs, which, when seen from a global perspective, would seem especially superfluous, considering the state of suffering in the world.

Years ago, as a graduate student, I remember asking Lax what he thought about me getting my own residence, because for many years I had shared my living space with others, and it seemed time for a change.

"A little studio would be good," he said, "yes, a special place to write, but a house … well, I don't think you can ever plan to settle in. Who can? Our real home's in heaven—everything else is a temporary stop. So keep your bags packed—we all have to be ready for the next move."

"But what about creating my own space?" I insisted. "I mean, I've acquired things, and I'd like to get some more stuff to make my life happier and more comfortable … what's wrong with that?"

He smiled. "Just be careful you don't block the flow. Too much 'stuff' can block the flow. I mean, first you put everything on hold to get what you want, then after you get it, you fuss over it, worry about how you're going to take care of it, and by then, you may be off to get something else. Best thing to do is base everything on the *one thing necessary*—your ability to maintain a clear communion with God, and to do his work in the world."[46]

Lax was so right. Too many possessions restrict one's ability to live in the moment, to feel the moment in Christ, to disseminate divine love, and freely move with it. Amassing property (and constantly striving to increase one's capital) can dim the perception and glut the soul. Excessive "ownership" of goods ultimately becomes obsessive, territorial, ugly. Instead of "sharing the wealth," riches are hoarded, guarded, and, in this way, become utterly useless. Indeed, as many saints have discovered, the only true and lasting riches are those that are given away—the "flow" continues unobstructed.

Certainly if the love of God moves through the cosmos without restriction (that is, unconditionally), then we, too, are meant to love similarly, extending ourselves to others, without reserve, through "faith and works" (Jas 2.14-17). We were not created to "store up treasure on earth, where moth and rust consume, and thieves break in and steal," but rather to "lay up for ourselves treasures in heaven" (Mt 6.19-20).

Too often we forget that we are already in possession of our most precious treasure. Christ explicitly tells us that the kingdom is within us (Lk 17.21). In Buddhism as well, there is a popular saying: "In the house of the poor, tired, and lonely man, lies the treasure, forgotten."

To find this immensity of riches, it helps if we dispossess ourselves of everything unnecessary, as all the world religions repeatedly emphasize. Entropy itself teaches us that we shall inevitably become empty. In such a dissolutive and perishing universe, we are called to be "inward pilgrims"—silent, prayerful, attentive—that we might hear the Lord's "still small voice" bidding us enter the temple of our heart. There he waits in love for those who love, that everything may be renewed in his saving glory.

> For we are all wanderers on the earth, and pilgrims.
> We have no permanent habitat here ...
> We are wanderers on the earth, and only a few of us
> in each generation have discovered the life of charity,
> the living from day to day, receiving our gifts
> gratefully through grace, and rendering them,
> multiplied through grace, to the Giver.
>
> Robert Lax, from *Mogador's Book*

S.T. Georgiou, 1993

The rustic port town of Skala, Patmos, with Mt. Kastelli in the distance.

Walls

After class one day, I walked over to a nearby bookstore and took a seat in the fiction section. Glancing at the nearby titles, I was surprised to find *The Count of Monte Cristo* directly in front of me. (I had recently begun to write *The Isle of Monte Cristo*.)

Opening the book, I turned to the chapter having to do with Edmund Dantes' incarceration. The young hero is sentenced to prison for a crime he did not commit and suffers in solitary confinement. His initial hope for a reprieve gives way to prayers of deliverance, only to be followed by despondency, anger, despair, and, finally, a longing for death.

In his sixth year of imprisonment, however, Dantes hears a scraping sound coming from a wall in his dungeon. Joyfully realizing that it is a prisoner tunnelling to escape, he strikes the wall three times.

There is immediate silence. Later Dantes hears the vibrations continue, and excitedly proceeds to dig in their direction. Eventually, he meets his fellow prisoner, Abbé Faria, the remarkable priest and mentor who later bequeaths to Dantes the map that leads him to the treasure of Monte Cristo.

The important point, in this case, is that the two prisoners become aware of each other via the very confines meant to keep them apart.

While the thick wall of stone continues to serve as an unyielding partition, it also becomes a kind of "sounding board," a method of communication.

On thinking about this passage from Dumas' classic, I remembered a selection from Simone Weil's *Gravity and Grace,* in which this great religious thinker of the twentieth century writes,

> Two prisoners whose cells adjoin communicate with each other by knocking on the wall. The wall is the thing which separates them, but it is also their means of communication.[47]

Weil goes on to state:

> It is the same with us and God. Every separation is actually a link .... This world is the closed door. It is a barrier. And at the same time, it is the way through.[48]

Weil's reflection led me to consider how in this unstable, transitory life, made imperfect through the Fall, we are all, in a sense, temporary prisoners. And yet in Christ, the Fount of Creation in whom the universe is sustained, we are simultaneously free. Our earthly existence may therefore be seen as both a "barrier" and a link to God.

The same may be said for sin, whose ultimate consequence is death. Sin separates us from the Deity and demonstrates our fallen, mortal, and ultimately helpless state. But sins can also be seen as "links of contrition" if we resolve to atone for them in Christ. For this reason, the angelic powers do not dwell exceedingly on the "sin" of a sinner; rather, they focus on his potential to seek forgiveness, that the transgressor might make his way through to God. The modern Greek writer Melissanthi hints of this in her poem "Atonement":

> Every time I sinned it was as though a door had opened, and tears of sweet compassion dripped among the grasses ... Every

time I sinned a door half-opened, and though men thought me ugly, the angels thought me beautiful.[49]

To save us from sin and effect our union with the divine, God liberates us through the Incarnation—our means of "escape" from the confines of a perishing cosmos.[50] In taking on flesh, "God became man so that man, by infinitely successive degrees, could become like God."[51] Christ broke down the "dividing wall" preventing humanity's access to Eden and prepared a lasting lightway for us to enter heaven, climactically accomplished with his Crucifixion and Resurrection.

Consequently, nothing may separate us from God. In the love of Christ, walls ultimately cease to exist. As St. Paul makes emphatically clear in his letter to the Romans:

> For I am sure that neither death, nor life, nor angels, nor principalities, nor things present, nor things to come, nor powers, nor height, nor depth, nor anything else in all creation, will be able to separate us from the love of God in Christ Jesus our Lord. (Rom 8.38-39)

And yet, because we continue to dwell in a passing, disintegrating universe until the Second Coming, this world may oftentimes feel more like a prison than a paradise. We struggle not only within a fallen cosmos, but strive for salvation in a turbulent realm wherein malevolent powers still remain active, according to Scripture: "For we wrestle not against flesh and blood, but against the principalities, against powers, against the rulers of the darkness of this age, against spiritual hosts of wickedness in the heavenly places" (Eph 6.12).[52]

These disruptive, calcifying forces prey particularly on the human ego, stirring pride in a man, and arrogance. The unwary heart may harden. A soul may come to feel "walled off" from everyone and everything.

Once again, however, the walls of a prison (whether of heart or stone) may serve a higher purpose: though their confines are tormenting, they continue to allow the prisoner to communicate, even helping to effect his liberation, for, over time, and with divine intercession, a wall may actually be a "way out." The struggling soul—conditioned through fervent prayer and strengthened by God—may develop such irrepressible inner fortitude that no enclosure or barrier can contain its luminous energy. Wholly radiant, it may project its psychic essence where divine grace desires; the spirit anticipates the "age to come," when, like the risen Christ, the elect shall transcend matter and go anywhere at will.[53]

Yet in this present darkness, when too often all seems lost and faith gives way, when every effort of escape looks as if to lead nowhere, oftentimes all we can do—as Edmund Dantes discovered—is keep tapping on the wall and listen.

Every tap is like a prayer. There are fellow prisoners everywhere tapping, listening, waiting for a response that never seems to come. But even if, for years, our "dark nights" persist and our attempts to make contact have seemingly failed, one day a light unlike any other will break through our cells, through our very souls, and all captives shall be made free. For our bright liberator is Christ, whose infinite love makes all things new.

Doors

Corridors and doors abound in the antique town of Hora, built around the Monastery of St. John the Theologian, Patmos.

S.T. Georgiou, 1999

For the last time I stood by the door before turning out the lights. I did this at the end of every semester—that is, stand by the door and reflect on how the course had progressed, how for months we had entered and exited the same room, within which our mutual "inner cultivation" had transpired.

Class had started in the cold of January; it was now a balmy evening in mid-May. The night sky, visible through the open glass windows, was still on fire with the afterglow of sunset.

Flashbacks of our weekly evening sessions replayed in my mind. The students usually came in while I was writing lecture terms on the board. Small talk would be exchanged while they settled back and listened to meditative music I had selected earlier and piped in through the classroom's stereo system.

Usually I brought a bag of bagels for those who were hungry, leading a few generous students to regularly supply cream cheese and coffee. These the class consumed while reading news articles relating to religion, as well as inspirational quotes I had distributed.

All of these preparations helped our sessions to progress smoothly, comfortably. It was Lax who would tell me, "Sit back and relax, and you can journey anywhere." At the same time, the students naturally understood that a healthy interrelationship exists between "food for the body" and "food for the mind"; we require both to prosper.

It was good seeing the class evolve, over the months, into a warm and communal assembly, an "academic family." My students not only wanted to learn about religion, but were also focused on how to become better, kinder people through studying the world faiths. Our "homework" included improving human relations, and so saving the planet.

A lot had changed since the first day, when students hurriedly rushed through the hallways wondering where the classroom was, fearing they would be late (and even though they were on time, some seemed scarcely able to sit quietly, collectively). But soon they understood the truth of the Taoist proverb "Those who hurry never arrive." In other words, be gathered in the present moment, both with yourself and with everything around you, since that is the only place anyone can ever really be; to live in the past and future is illusory.

Many of my students came to share their spiritual experiences with the class, as did I—the range of religious and cultural backgrounds was extraordinary. Some pupils had embraced a monastic way of life in the countries of their origin, though later they abandoned these pursuits. Enrolled was a former Buddhist nun from Burma, a young ex-monk from Nepal, and two men who, for about a year, had been a part of the Taizé ecumenical community in France.

While many of my students were searching for a religion that they might feel comfortable with, a handful were already deeply immersed in spiritual practice. One was studying with a Tibetan lama to be a Vajrayana master; another, a Muslim from Kuwait, was determined to become an imam; yet another was thinking of going to Greece to investigate becoming a monk on Mt. Athos.

Though our interfaith class discussions were lively and animated, even passionate at times, they were always respectful. We understood that each of us has a special relationship with life and with the Mystery that catalyzed creation. Consequently, it was clear that for co-existence to thrive, "wisdom and compassion" were necessary—a belief championed by the Dalai Lama for decades. *Wisdom* implies that we are all interrelated; *compassion* is the only way this cosmic interaffinity (and interdependency) can happily continue, that life may flourish.

As I stood by the classroom door reflecting, watching the last light fade from the sky, I thought of the new doors that, even now, were opening for my students. Some were graduating and continuing their scholastic paths; a few were looking forward to getting married over the summer; most were set on finding employment.

Other doors had opened as well. Midway through the semester, a dearly loved professor in the department—who had taught humanities and religion for over forty years—had died, despite heroic efforts to halt the spread of his cancer. Early in life he had entered a Catholic seminary, but later found education to be his true calling.

An unusual series of events transpired at school shortly after he died which involved, of all things, doors. One evening I was teaching my world religions class when it seemed as though someone was faintly jiggling the room's outer door handle. Thinking it to be a student who sought entry, I went to the door and opened it, only to find the hallway empty.

A few minutes later, the same jiggling, only sharper, louder. This time a student bolted from his chair and quickly flung open the door, but nobody was there.

Yet again it happened, and to everyone's amazement, the door opened wide by itself, with no trace of anyone outside.

For about a month, other department faculty experienced similar strange incidents with their classroom doors. Then, at the professor's memorial service, his relatives revealed that throughout his life, he liked to randomly jiggle doorknobs in his home, and so catch family members off guard. Faculty who for decades had taught with this instructor confirmed that he was, indeed, something of a prankster. So the "haunting of the doors," as it came to be called, was attributed to this mischievous late educator.[54]

As someone devoted to the study of religion and spirituality, what I found interesting about these "hauntings" was that they focused on doors. Symbolically, a door represents physical and metaphysical passage, continuity, growth. Portals imply liberation, inner transformation, a change of worlds, new life. Since the beginning of time, they have been central to the human psyche.

The professor who had died was himself a "door" (and a "doormaker") for his students, helping them to create inner gateways of enlightenment that could lead to their graduation and eventual careers. He himself had gone through a cosmic door that opened to the world beyond. In focusing on doors, perhaps his spirit was indicating that it was making the transition from this life to the next, and that a way was possible for all of us.

That my classroom door had suddenly opened wide was especially intriguing, pointing to how the natural and supernatural realms are directly interrelated; there are no real barriers or lasting boundaries in the multidimensional levels of existence. The relationship between life and death, earth and heaven, the visible and the invisible is like an "open door."

The day after concluding my class, I drove out to the Graduate Theological Union Library in Berkeley to do research. Later, on the way out of the building, I noticed that the entryway double doors, when closed, looked like a solid cross, with sunlight passing through the four glass quadrants, two on either side. Then, when I saw a patron open the doors, it looked like the "cross" had dramatically parted, flung wide its "doors" to a brand new and brilliant world.

This "opening of the cross" effect was startling, because it suggested that the cross of Christ is indeed like a door to which all paths lead, a kind of physical and spiritual axis gate (and access portal) opening to heaven and eternity, and also to our very souls. Hence one of the great "I Am's" of Jesus: *"I am the Door. All who enter by me are saved"* (Jn 10.9).

We open this mystic inner door when we pray, help another, touch (and are touched by) anyone making their way home. This door opens to the infinite treasure of the Christ radiant in our hearts. When we swing it open reverently, confidently, with faith and love, we bring forth his light into all places and realms, that the universe may be wholly reborn, transfigured into his glory.[55]

Every day is therefore an opportunity to draw near the gates of the heart, and to open them. We are ever on the threshold of enlightenment.

II. Spirit Currents

Give heed to the inner workings of God …
Give yourself to inward things,
and you will see his kingdom in your heart.

Thomas à Kempis, *The Imitation of Christ*

S.T. Georgiou, 1993

Sunrise from the Monastery of St. John the Theologian, Patmos.

Address Book

At some point in the inner journey, there comes a defining moment when the searcher is serendipitously directed to a person and/or place that is meant to serve as a foundation for his or her spiritual growth. Heinrich Zimmer, the eminent scholar of Indian religion and culture, writes,

> It is only after a pious quest to a distant region, in a strange land, a new country, that the meaning of the inner voice guiding our search can be revealed to us. And added to that strange and constant fact is another: that the person who reveals the meaning of our mysterious inner voyage must himself be a stranger ...[1]

Zimmer's quote typifies my initial trek to the isle of Patmos and my chance meeting with Robert Lax. As described in *The Way of the Dreamcatcher,* I had fled to this Aegean sanctuary in 1993 in a quest for solace and renewal. The end of a relationship and job difficulties had left me distraught.

While Patmos has always been a popular refuge for Christians (owing to its close ties with St. John the Evangelist and Seer), I had been corresponding with a monk there who accentuated the isle's restorative powers. He said that Patmos was an idyllic paradise, a blessed sanctum, a place to escape the chaotic world and be born again.

Everything told me that this was the time to travel there. Within weeks, I was on a plane bound for Athens. Two days after arriving, my ferry sailed into the main harbour of the holy isle.

Expecting to meet the monk, I was dismayed to learn that he had gone to visit the Patriarch of the Eastern Orthodox Church in Istanbul, and would return in a few weeks. At this point, I decided to settle into a seaside guesthouse and explore the island and its spiritual treasures on my own.

One evening, I was sitting by the waterfront when a young stranger, a Greek waiting to board a ship, started a conversation with me. In the course of our exchange he learned that I was a teacher and writer and promptly suggested that I visit Lax. Interestingly, he referred to the poet-sage as *Pax* (meaning "peace" in Latin), which to me seemed most fortuitous, considering I had journeyed to Patmos to find inner tranquillity.

Since the young man insisted that I find "Pax" that night, I followed the directions leading to his home. After a long uphill trek, I finally found the poet's hermitage, at the base of Mt. Kastelli, and knocked on the door.

At first there was no response. The wind had picked up, so I repeatedly struck the door, shouting, "Pax! Pax! Are you there?"

About a minute later it opened, and a tall, lean, bearded old man, half-concealed behind a diaphanous curtain, stood at the threshold. After determining that I was not a reporter or a deranged tourist, he clarified that his name was "Lax," and led me into his small dwelling.

S.T. Georgiou, 1999

Robert Lax looking out of a window in his hermitage.

I did not clearly see his face until we had turned a corner and sat down at a table opposite one another. A desk lamp, the only light on in the house, illuminated his long and narrow visage. As I later wrote in my journal,

> Lax looked like a figure in a Rembrandt painting. Though robed in shadows, his ancient, white-bearded countenance shone out of the darkness. Somehow I felt the warmth of a sunset, the gentle heat of a candle steadily burning, its amber flame motionless, if not mesmerizing ... His deep blue-grey eyes seemed all-knowing, and, at the same time, *all-loving*. Everything—the dimly lit room, the surrounding darkness, the wind outside—everything melted away except for his near omniscient (and yet gentle) gaze ....[2]

Very quickly I discovered that something intensely real was happening. I had left San Francisco feeling as if nothing mattered, and now, quite suddenly, everything did. I acutely sensed how all things were charged with an interrelated holiness, a sanctity that humanity had been entrusted to sustain, both personally and communally. Whether I loved or hated, did good or evil, had faith or despaired, it affected the balance of the universe. Blessed by Lax's presence and example, I longed to exercise *agape*.

Why did I feel these things so deeply? I think it was because the calm and subtle presence of the sage demonstrated that anything is possible in God, providing one is compassionate and attentive. As I would soon discover, Lax's life in itself proved that a man could love so much that he became a living blessing, and, as such, could give birth to radiant possibilities. There was no "growing old" in Lax, only the joy of new beginnings. It was that kind of superabundant inspiration I had come to Patmos to find.

Lax seemed to be a microcosm of the holy beauty surrounding him. Through the years, the sacred rhythms of the isle had worked their way deeply into his heart and now flowed out of his luminous spirit like an irrepressible tide. Simply put, the self-effacing and peace-loving hermit was a springboard to a higher reality. He had learned how to transmute his earthly, everyday existence into the paradise of the kingdom of God.

I remember him reaching around and bringing forth what looked like an old patched-up notebook wrapped in twine. In the shadows, its jacket seemed to be made of fine leather, covered with cracks and abrasions; inside were many yellowed, time-worn pages.

Slowly his long, thin fingers undid the knot holding the contents together. Even while loosening the delicate, frayed cord, he remained totally focused on me, still searching the depths of my being, bringing to mind a truth common to all spiritual traditions: *For the saint, only the person counts, the stranger at hand, the neighbour given by God.*

"This is my address book," he said, smiling. "It's kind of beat-up, but still does the job. I'd like to write you into it."

He opened the weathered register. As I saw him write my name on a slightly wrinkled page, I felt it was the first day of class, and Lax was signing me into his course. Moreover, it seemed as though I were being written into some sort of "greater book" in which all my thoughts and actions would be mystically recorded. Being scripted into it was akin to crossing a threshold, a kind of inner initiation into a deeper dimension. In this sense, the old book's cover seemed like an illuminating door, a transcendent portal through which I had entered and at last dropped anchor in an increasingly radiant universe.

"Now for your address," he said. Lax laughed aloud when he learned I lived on Ocean Avenue. "Sounds like you live near the sea, too," he exclaimed. "Always good to feel her flow."

His articulated fingers slowly and precisely moved the pen like an artist wielding his brush, or a meticulous scribe dedicated to every letter. He looked like a Zen master engaged in calligraphy, who, in the process of composing his spirit-script, kept the cosmos on beam, in balance.

When he wrote "ocean," I think he felt himself become the sea, serenely flowing with it. He put his entire being into every movement of the pen, and I was steadily relaxed by it, made peaceful. In his quiet, poetic resonance, he reminded me of an Eastern sage, the "Man of Tao" who in motion is like water; at rest, like a mirror; in response, like an echo; who in his stillness, remains pure.

Later that night, when I left his house, I reflected on how a part of me still remained in his home, that is, my name, written into his "Book of Life." Perhaps from time to time he prayed over the many names inscribed within the register (as did I, when I periodically glanced through my own student roll book). In any event, after leaving Lax, a quote from the French Jesuit priest Jean Pierre de Caussade came to mind. It was something to think about as I made my way down to the waterfront, strengthened and renewed:

> When we open
> our hearts to God,
> the Holy Spirit
> begins to write in them.[3]

Rhythm of Work

One evening as I was setting up my classroom for a weekly lecture, I thought of the countless times I had gone through the same routine: picking up papers off the floor, emptying the wastebasket, opening the windows to freshen the air, putting the chairs and tables back into order, cleaning the bulletin board and chalkboard, positioning the podium.

Next I would run through my selected slide images, then program the "mood music" that I played for students ten minutes before class. Afterward, I photocopied and assembled the extensive lecture handouts. Finally, after checking my phone messages and email, I visited the mailroom, talked with my department coordinator about administrative matters, and then sat down to review the evening's lecture.

Extensive preparation is required to effectively teach a weekly three-hour class. It is the necessary and repetitious "background work" so commonly overlooked in all of human activity. We tend to see the finished results, the outcomes of things, and do not give much thought to the recurring preliminary labour that allows our lives to run as consistently and smoothly as possible.

Even when visiting Lax on idyllic Patmos, the wisdom that I learned from him tended to be based on a fixed routine. By 6 PM he and I would meet at the dock, go for a meditative stroll, perhaps visit an ailing friend, shop for groceries, then head for the hermitage.

Once there, I proceeded to cut fish for his outdoor cats and feed them. After sweeping the porch, we prepared dinner, then talked leisurely over our meal. Later I'd wash and dry the dishes. Sometime around 10 or 11 PM, I'd head down to the dock and think about our time together.

I remember asking him if he ever got tired of our routine. It was, after all, similar to how he shared his evenings with others who had visited him through the years.

"Routine is everything," he would say. "Priests, performers, crafts-men, labourers, everybody in the world tends to do the same basic thing over and over again."

"But what's the point?" I'd ask with a smile.

"Might as well ask the earth why she spins every day, or why the sun rises and sets. All things stick to that creative beat set up before we were born. Everything's got a fundamental rhythm and flow. Lots of clarity comes from moving with that tempo, also a sense of calm and play. Sooner or later you open up to something bigger than yourself—you want to sing and dance, love more, pray."[4]

It would seem, then, that repetition is one of the defining elements of spirituality. It is the sure and steady means by which one can experience a *deepening of the present.* It sets up the framework for living in the moment, both in a practical and a metaphysical manner. Everyday tasks, attentively performed, have the potential to transform into transcendent realities. From such concentrated, rhythmic labour, creative blessings may flow. As Lax expresses,

> each day
> the same
> walk up
> the hill
>
> same turns
> same shadow
> of the tree
>
> each station
> of the way
>
> takes on
> its own
> set of
> meanings.[5]

Depth of practice ultimately demonstrates how ordinary activity, mindfully conducted over time, can lead to inner wisdom, even holiness. Thus monks from all spiritual traditions claim that illumination is possible simply by watching a blessed elder sweep a floor.

Certainly the little things we do daily are, in their own constant way, helping to sustain the world. Any conscientious, attentive work, quietly and diligently performed over and over again, nurtures and purifies the cosmos, transforming it for the better. The rhythms of labour, often conducted in solitude and perceived by only a few, are like steady and silent prayers, honouring God.

This very real, honest work, ongoing everywhere, is perhaps the most important in creation. Repetitive acts—much like the cyclic seasons and our inhalations and exhalations—contribute to a greater awareness of the divine perpetually operating in the universe. Surely all work points to the presence of the Worker, in whom we "move, live, and have our being" (Acts 17.28). Every occupation therefore has the power to illumine and transfigure, be it preaching, painting, or shoemaking.

As a poet whose craft centred on minimalism, Lax regularly pointed to God through his repetitive, mantra-like verse. Using an ascetic, meditative style focusing on the "purity of essentials," he cut through worldly excess and accentuated the foundational level of reality, as illustrated in the following selection:

> forms
> forms
> forms
>
> basic
> basic
> forms
>
> basic
> basic
> basic
> basic
> basic
> basic
> forms.[6]

The poem's taut linear body and "heartbeat rhythm," hinting of the Jesus Prayer, emphasizes the wisdom of living a consistently simple life wherein less is more. In kenotic fashion, Lax empties himself of everything save for what is necessary. Like a true spiritual master, he does not draw attention to himself but to the holy building blocks of creation. Solid and foundational, they serve as "cosmic cornerstones" and glorify the divine architect.

Since Adam, every generation is given the chance to see how everything we do here points not to ourselves, but to the Power empowering us, working alongside us, that our labours might not be in vain, that is, a transient mortal enterprise.

The repetitious nature of existence (and all its infinite variations) allows us to keep on honing the craft of our lives until we at last see how only one thing matters—the Life that brought us out of nothing and blessed us into being.

We have only a brief time to make good the light within us, to discover and access its warmth, to cultivate its holy radiance, and to let it shine out meaningfully, as a blessing unto others.

Until then, our work continues; the routine goes on. Every day may be said to be a "repeat performance," until we get it right.

Heart of Gold

Ever since journeying to Patmos, I realized what a blessing it was to live near the shore. As often as possible, I would drive to Ocean Beach and run its lengthy expanse. It was a tactile way of connecting with Christ and rebirthing myself in a cosmos fashioned to honour God and evoke manifold love and praise.

It was good to escape the confines of a busy schedule and offer thanks by the water. The beach was a place to rejoice and be glad.

All my senses came to life there, triggered by an unlimited expanse of sea and sky, the pulse of the tides, exploding surf, and the smell of brine. In this aqueous paradise I became human again, that is, like Adam, no longer wired to my cellphone and laptop. Stripped of the electric coils binding me to an increasingly artificial, microchipped existence, what remained was the wild shoreline and the rhythms of the sea.

The beauty along the Pacific was breathtaking. To see the morning sun rise over a peak; the pelicans dive for fish; the cliffside willows dance in the breeze; the mist swirl through the clefts of mountains— all this delighted me, sent shudders through my soul, because in everything I felt the presence of God.

I was like a poppy opening in the light, unbound, ecstatic, like a man delivered from the darkness of prison. The truth was that I was changing, quickening, returning to an original state of consciousness, as it was in the beginning, when all things enjoyed a deep and abiding communion with their Maker.

Proof of this re-creation was evident not only in how I felt, but also in how sea life related with me. Gulls didn't scatter when I ran past them, nor did the sea lions rush back into the water. Sometimes porpoises close to shore followed me down the coast, even corkscrewing directly toward me until veering away at the last moment, lest they be beached.

In this joyous and open state of being, in which I was more conscious of God and nature than of myself, I periodically found things on the shore that I probably wouldn't have discovered otherwise. Somehow the universe was directing me toward "spiritual bounty" that had significant personal meaning.

Most of these unusual items had washed up from the deep, a dark and apophatic realm representing the unknowable mystery of the Divine. What I found strengthened my inner growth. The unique meanings of these wave-born gifts inspired me to continue living in a theocentric manner. Altogether they served as "signs" of the inner passage, elemental indicators pointing toward "Monte Cristo," the treasure of the Christ within.

I found many of these items while pursuing my doctorate in theology: among them a cross, a Christian hymnal, and a piece of driftwood with the word "icon" written on it.[7] These finds continued after graduation and through my teaching.

For example, one afternoon I found a compass that had washed ashore. In its resemblance to a cross, the compass hearkens to the missionary nature of Christianity, a faith meant to be disseminated in all four cardinal directions. Lax had once told me that love is like a compass, giving us bearings when we might feel lost.

On another visit to the beach I found a shattered ship's clock pressed into a cliff, with sand running down its metallic face. The useless clock indicated how time stops in paradise; in the eternal God, there is no time.

A little farther down the shoreline, I found what appeared to validate this interpretation. Bobbing on the incoming waves was a blue-tinged glass ball the size of an apple, within which twirled a plastic green fish. Perhaps a child's toy, but certainly a sign of a Christ-filled, timeless universe.

A few weeks later, I was traversing a steep cliff and happened to spot a small slip of paper jutting out of an iceplant. The paper had been torn out of the Bible. The single quote on it, from Isaiah 11.13, was highly apropos because my car had recently been burglarized, and I remained upset over the incident. The words hinted of forgiveness and consummate peace:

The wolf shall lie down with the lamb.

While these discoveries were deeply moving, the find that had the greatest impact on me was a heart of gold. The piece of jewellery was about the size of a bottle cap and bore two engravings: on one side, a small radiating cross, and on the other, the letter "A" rendered in ornate calligraphy.

The discovery had come at a highly significant time. At once I thought of Alexandria, my first cousin. She had died months before, having suffered a fatal blood clot shortly after the birth of her third child. She was only in her mid-thirties.

Her father had been visiting her in the hospital. He had briefly stepped out of the room. When he returned, he found her unconscious. She died soon after.

An immediate crisis of faith hit family members and friends. How could a good and loving God have allowed this tragedy to happen? How could he take Alexandria and leave her three young daughters, including a newborn, motherless? How could this have been God's plan for her, and for her children and husband? She was happily married, outgoing, a beloved schoolteacher with so much to live for. And then, quite suddenly, she was dead.

In a world where people are used to quick and easy explanations, here there were none. Shock and disbelief, pain and grief, anger, despair, numbness, and feelings of bitter emptiness all ran their lengthy, excruciating course.

Over the months that followed, clerics and friends who sought to console the family often referred to Scripture. They would counsel how in a world broken since Adam, anything can happen from second to second. Life remains an arduous test of faith, and this in the face of peril, suffering, and death.

In this temporal realm of struggle, nothing is assured. Here "we can only see in a mirror dimly" (1 Cor 13.12). Our single hope is in Christ, the Resurrection and the Life, "who sacrificed himself for the salvation of the world" (Jn 3.16) that "all things may be made new"

(Rev 21.5). *Everything is therefore meant to be understood in the light of the age to come.*

While there were numerous attempts to examine Alexandria's passing from a spiritual perspective, the magnitude of her sudden death prevented me from absorbing any possible analysis of the tragedy. There were too many words, concepts, quotations, references. People were looking for succinct phrases and formulas that could help ease or explain the situation, and though they meant well, it was hard for me to focus on anything in particular, let alone meditate on page after page of Bible passages.

"Only one thing is needful," Jesus once told Martha (Lk 10.42). In such a critical time of loss, this "one thing" seemed to best equate with a simple (perhaps even childlike) trust in love, in an energy stronger than death, supremely transformative, infinitely creative, deeply nurturing, universally active, interrelational, working in ways and on levels beyond our grasp and knowing. Faith in love was about all that my wounded heart could handle at this devastating time.

I think it was because of love that I found the gold heart shortly after Alexandria's passing. The pendant poignantly revealed how love lives beyond the grave and seeks to bridge the divide between this life and the next. The inscribed "A" certainly stood for Alexandria. But in this case the letter was also emblematic of *Agape*, and, with regard to the kinetic power of that energy, *Anastasis* (resurrection) as well.

Out of the unknown depths a bright and precious heart had washed ashore. On it, a triumphal cross and the initial of my late cousin's first name were distinctly engraved. Taken altogether, the message—more appropriately, *her* message—seemed to say,

"Love, In Christ, Alexandria."

The choice to love and to trust in love, even in the darkest hour, is always ours. In times of great tragedy, some hearts close forever and remain sealed in their own suffering. Hardened, embittered, they are unable to let go of their pain and be infused with a Mystery transcending the violent shudderings of a passing world soon to be transfigured. Stubbornly, they insist on their own way.

Other hearts, after enduring terrible misfortune, come to open, and grow in ways previously unimaginable. A kind of inner enlightenment is attained through suffering. The long dark night of "waiting on God" and "praying for the answer in him" leads to the realization that trials endured in faith, hope, and, most especially, love can be both redemptive and transformative. Certainly the mission of Christ is a sign of this truth. Though he took on the sins of humanity and in horrific pain perished on the cross, out of his heart flowed rivers of living water; out of his tomb, new life entered the world.

In our current age of anxiety where nothing seems certain and many continue to search for ultimate meaning, hearts are sure to break. But there is a difference between a heart that is broken and a heart that *breaks open*. Though both are wounded, the former shuts down, withdraws; the latter keeps the faith, beats on, prays itself out of darkness and transcends its former condition.

Like a germinating seed, such a heart quickens to new possibilities. The life within its husk bursts free and shoots up through the depths toward an infinity of light.

Hearts are very much like seeds. Both start small. Both require nourishment. Both are cores of life, containing great power. And both are blessed with the ability to open and bear fruit for the living God.

Not on the Program

The church dinner-dance had been long anticipated. I had to book a seat months in advance for the event, to be held in late December at a landmark hotel in San Francisco. Over 500 guests filled the dining hall that evening, many arrayed in gowns and tuxedos. Numerous priests and deacons were in attendance, and more than one bishop. Everything was set for a night of great celebration and pomp.

Three days before, one of the deadliest natural disasters in recorded history shook the planet. An undersea earthquake registering 9.2, the second-largest quake ever recorded on a seismograph, struck the west coast of Sumatra, Indonesia. The mega-trembler triggered a series of enormous tidal waves that swept over the coastal land masses bordering the Indian Ocean.

Initial reports had it that possibly 10,000 people had perished. Within hours, this number swelled to 15,000, then 20,000. The toll quickly escalated to 30,000. Obviously, the scope of the catastrophe was only beginning to reveal itself. No one could know that the relentless waves had decimated the shores of eleven Indo-Asian countries and wiped out nearly a quarter of a million people in mere minutes. One third of the dead were children. Two million people were left homeless.

In the days following the disaster, I regularly kept up with news reports. Even while attending the church gala, I caught snatches of broadcasts in the hotel bar. I couldn't help thinking about the suffering and devastation going on across the world, and on such a horrific scale. Strangely, however, hardly anyone at the dinner-dance spoke of the tragedy.

As the last of the champagne and appetizers made their rounds and people headed for their tables, it suddenly dawned on me that I was at a church event—around me were clerics galore. A communal prayer for the disaster victims would no doubt be offered at the invocation or during the post-dinner speeches. But I wanted to make sure.

I walked quickly over to the raised stage area and spoke to a priest near the lectern.

"Father," I said. "That tidal wave in Indonesia was catastrophic. Tens of thousands were killed, maybe more. It would really be great if we could all say a brief prayer."

He looked at me with a slight frown, as though I had disturbed his focus. In a slow, metered tone, he replied, "I'm sorry, but the scope of our program is too narrow to allow for that."

"But can't we fit in a communal *'Kyrie Eleison'* at some point?" I pleaded.

He shook his head.

"Not even a minute of silence?"

"I'm sorry, we just can't do it."

I went to my table dumbfounded and took a seat. The rest of my dinner party was already there.

"Why the sad look?" asked a friend. "Something bothering you?"

I related what had happened. Nobody could believe it. However, we all had hope that during the program, someone scheduled to speak, priest or layperson, would say something about the disaster out of sheer compassion and lead us in prayer.

Two hours later, the speeches had concluded. The benediction was given by a bishop: not a word about the catastrophe. Nothing.

Big-band music began to play and people started to dance. Making my way through the thickening crowd, I went outside to get some air and clear my mind.

The scene didn't make sense—it seemed surreal. I felt as if I was locked in some kind of fantasy world that remained oblivious to a tragedy of epic proportions. Though I understood that we had gathered to celebrate, this was still a church-related event, a Christian assembly. The numerous priests in attendance could have at least encouraged everyone to keep the tsunami victims in their prayers, and to send aid.

So many faithful were gathered in one room, all sharing one supernatural baptism. What holy energy our united prayers could have generated in helping out the victims of this cataclysm, both living and dead! The Book of James states, "The prayer of a righteous man has great power in its effects" (Jas 5.16). And St. John Chrysostom said, "Prayer can change even the substance of things."[8] Had the clergy forgotten about the strength of spontaneous love, of luminous "arrow prayers"[9] reaching their mark? Were supplications for "deliverance from all affliction, wrath, danger, and distress"[10] reserved only for Sunday?

Souls had perished and were perishing, mass devastation prevailed, and still, no time could be afforded for a communal prayer born of immediate and unconditional love—not even a minute, because such an intercessory act did not "fit into the scope" of the night's program. And yet, didn't Jesus remark that if an ox falls into a well on the Sabbath, then even on the Sabbath its owner will straightaway pull the ox out? (Lk 14.5). If this concern be true for an animal, then how much more for people!

Nearly a month after the tragedy in Indonesia, I was attending the Divine Liturgy at a local church. The same priest with whom I had spoken at the dinner was presiding. At the end of the service, he called for donations to help victims of the tsunami. Then, a short time later, when the congregation filed to the front of the altar to receive holy bread and a blessing, he stopped me for a moment and said with a broad smile, "See, we came through, we're helping them."

"Thanks, Father," I said. "The money is vital and necessary. But what I was asking for back in December was something beyond cash. The victims needed our intercessions more than anything at that time, especially those who suddenly lost their lives—only prayer had the power to reach them then, or even now."

Prayers travel faster than light. They help to stabilize any situation, permeate every dimension, sustain the life of things seen and unseen, give succor to souls in this world and the next.

It's never too late to pray. As Robert Lax said:

> Prayer is a way of doing instantaneous good for
> all things in all places. It's a way of sending out
> love everywhere at once. It's a power everyone
> has access to, and it can transfigure the universe.[11]

One Project

When I lecture on Lax, students sometimes ask me what I learned most in his company. It is hard to compress the essence of a seven year student-mentor relationship into a succinct answer, but I often speak about his trust in supreme and unconditional love. The hermit believed that every sentient being is called to let in the light of love and become a conduit of compassion. *Agape* is the place to start from.

Interestingly, Lax felt that a primary way to open up and love more was to *relax*. His lifelong interest in meditation and yoga gave him many insights in this regard. He encouraged people to "slow down" and live thankfully, attentively, mindful of grace and each day's blessings.

Lax also wrote about the importance of forgiveness and fellowship, of living simply, peacefully, free of non-essentials. He maintained that when the mind and heart become clear, then wisdom's incessant call becomes distinctly audible. The awakened individual proceeds to study more of the world's great books, particularly classics pertaining to philosophy, religion, and the arts.

For Lax, inner clarity naturally led to creativity. This creativity manifested itself in writing, painting, dance, even prayer—all ways of communicating with (and sharing) the superabundant love that had set creation into effect. Ultimately, all of human wisdom and expression pointed to the "one project" everybody was meant to work on, ever since the time of Adam. In Lax's words,

> There aren't a bunch of projects, there's only *one project:* survival on the planet and the salvation of the soul. They are parts of one project. Pick it up at any point, start working, and you get into it.[12] This seems to be the advice of those who study. Order the earth then, man, for its own good, and for your own good. Fulfill, in love, your duty and your life.[13] Take care of God's creatures, as many as you can handle, increasing the number as you learn how to do it.[14] Turn jungle into garden without destroying a single flower.[15]

In continuing to share these insights with my students, almost inevitably some will raise their hands and ask, "How come more of this isn't taught in schools? This kind of thinking makes clear why we're here, why education is important. Stuff like this gets us motivated to learn!"

Such forthright comments indicate that a collective sense of purpose, transcending "G.E. requirements" and "units needed to graduate," is lacking in much of academia. There is no confident, compassionate vision to be pursued and realized. Without a holistic and vibrant plan of learning—an overarching and unified directive integrating mind and heart—the college experience morphs into a dry, fragmented, and labyrinthian enterprise. Any chance to inculcate in the young a deep and abiding respect for human solidarity and achievement in all disciplines is lost.

This is not an unknown dilemma. For nearly a quarter of a century, a good deal has been written about the negatives assailing higher education.[16] Colleges and universities have partially ceased to be centres where self-discovery and the cultivation of the human spirit can take place. Instead, they have largely become training institutes for quick career growth, "commuter campuses" where technological skills are more valued than the ability to read, write, and express one's thoughts with clarity and ease. Sadly, this same emphasis on "technology proficiency" also applies to faculty hiring—online instruction experience can bear more resume weight than years of regular classroom teaching.

In such a sterile and depersonalized intellectual environment, students might indeed feel academically shortchanged and/or remain disenchanted with their college experience. According to an AP-mtvU poll surveying students at forty American colleges, a vast majority of college students feel depressed and apathetic.[17] Likewise, faculty—already stressed with endless committee meetings, the "publish or perish" principle, colleague rivalry, and budget cuts—may fail to inspire and enlighten their students. They cease to be illuminating role models.

Colleges once used to be communal and interdisciplinary centres of learning, exemplary institutes of scholastic harmony and integrative goodness. But over the years, their many departments have become compartmentalized, overly specialized, highly territorial. Little wonder that much of liberal education has steadily been reduced to a vapid and spiritless exercise in deconstructive analysis. To compound the problem, the fast-rising tide of academic fundamentalism, where professors refuse to acknowledge ideas that do not fit their social and political agenda, has transformed elements of education into something akin to indoctrination.

Given this critical state of affairs, the "lesson plan" of Lax, steeped in common sense and compassion, was like a breath of fresh air to my students. His love of life and learning, grounded in the "wisdom of simplicity," cut through the cold and clinical cynicism of academia (and all its mind-numbing excesses) like a laser.

Much like the ancient Taoists, Lax understood that "right doing" begins with *right being*. His "philosophy of the open heart" set up the proper conditions and environment for good learning. Love was the key means to transcend the ego and draw out the agapaic power radiant within oneself and all beings.

Love remains the compassionate inner energy upon which everything depends, the very foundation for self and universal understanding. As St. Paul expressed, "If I comprehend all mysteries and all knowledge, but have not love, I am nothing" (1 Cor 13.2).

Certainly, all world religions would agree with the notion that the "highest education" centres on discovering and cultivating the supernal love in both oneself and in others, that the entire cosmos might be perfected, transfigured. The major faiths of East and West have always believed in the transformational and liberating powers of love.

In the *Bhagavad-Gita,* Krishna advocates keeping "the mind in the heart," and emphasizes the pre-eminence of *bhakti,* the yoga of love. In Buddhism, exercising *ahimsa* (loving kindness for all beings/non-injury to sentient creatures) is paramount. In Taoism, the greatest of the "three treasures" is compassion.

Judaism maintains that God, neighbour, and creation are to be loved with "all the mind, heart, and soul" (Lev 19.18, Deut 6.4-5). The

Christian is called to exercise *agape* daily, and the Muslim is taught to trust in Allah, the "Merciful and the Compassionate."

This manifold emphasis on love, so deeply ingrained in the world religions (and, in turn, in the cultures and peoples practising them) has much to teach a fragmented educational system, if not a divided planet. Though certainly a college is not meant to function as a seminary or ashram, the peaceful, meditative intent of these traditions, as designed in their inception, can help to strengthen an academic climate wherein both faculty and students are stressed and jaded. The heartfelt insights of these faith systems can help repair the fragmentation and brokenness shared by both parties, and restore the lost vision of an interconnected universe created in love and meant to flourish through love's integral and renewing power.

My mentor made clear to me the pre-eminence of *agape* the night that I knocked on his door:

> Everything is here because of love.
> That's why we were created—to love.
> Love keeps things going now, and for forever.
> Love sets us out on our journey and ensures
> our safe return. We're all moving toward a more
> unified, loving universe as we journey to the stars.
> So just keep on loving—that's the bottom line.[18]

S.T. Georgiou, 1995

Robert Lax conversing with friends on a beach in Skala, Patmos. Seated, left to right, are the artists Marko Roetzer, Ulf T. Knaus, Gianvito Lo Greco, Helge Jorgensen (Sun Wheel Hawk), and the singer Galatea Psonis (seated with her mother, also named Galatea).

Ashtray

The honey-gold evening light bathed everything in a holy glow. For about an hour we sat beneath the awning of the Arion café, sipping our milkshakes, watching the boats sailing in and out of the harbour. It was the end of May 1993. Lax and I had just completed our first walk together down the long concrete pier bordering the waterfront. Our calm, good-natured stroll had been punctuated by deep silence and occasional laughter.

In subsequent meetings he and I would trek up to his house and eat dinner, but on this first get-together, he treated me to a milkshake, then went into the hills alone. Though our talk in the café was minimal (mostly about how the evening was making "a poem of itself"), with each passing minute I felt I was experiencing a catharsis that had actually begun a few nights before, when by chance I met the sage. Even then I sensed that Lax had been a definite Godsend, giving me hope and inspiration at a time of inner unrest.

All too quickly, our time together drew to a close. I suddenly desired something to commemorate my first meeting with him. On our table was an ashtray. Lax had pointed to it as we idly chatted, commenting on the simple beauty of a yellow-blue flower painted in its interior, partly obscured by cigarette butts.

After he left, I asked a waiter if I could pay him for the "souvenir." He advised that I go to a nearby shop and purchase a new, identical model, free of any chips or stains. But after insisting that I wanted the used ashtray, he said that this would be possible only if I gave him a new one in place of it. I agreed, and the "original" was in my possession by nightfall. A month afterward, it was on my desk at home, where it has remained, serving as a penholder.

Long after Lax had passed away, I was reaching for a pen to make a note, and my gaze fell upon the flower in the centre of the ashtray.

Instantaneously, I experienced a kind of "enlightenment." In Zen-like fashion, the inner meaning of the memento had suddenly revealed itself—fifteen years after I had acquired it! Before, I had never thought deeply of the ashtray, other than it reminded me of my first get-together with Lax. But now, the spiritual symbolism of the keepsake was immediately apparent.

An ashtray represents what is old, discarded, if not dead. The fire has gone out. Echoing Scripture, "Ashes to ashes, dust to dust" (based on Gen 3.19).

When I first arrived on Patmos, I felt like ashes. Stressed out and disillusioned, I had nearly lost faith in love, in the possibility of finding lasting joy in life, and put myself at the mercy of God.

And then, on the holy isle of St. John, I met Lax. Through his presence and counsel, my darkness was transformed into light. Hence the decorative flower at the bottom of the ashtray—the very flower that Lax had quietly drawn to my attention so many years ago, alluding to my eventual restoration.

The spiritual searcher may be likened to a flower, slowly breaking from its seed. A flower inches through the mysterious dark soil, is drawn toward the light of creation, and, at long last, blooms, its petals turned to the sky like hands outstretched in prayer.

Rising from earth to heaven, a flower points to life's spiritual direction and ultimate transfiguration. Though temporary, its remnants fuel the growth of yet more flowers, an infinite array, demonstrating that life is inexhaustible, stronger than death.

Taken altogether, the symbolism of the ashtray was prophetic. My near "end" was, in actuality, a beginning; dissolution would lead to deliverance. Out of the ashes new life would quicken, bringing to mind the ancient myth of the phoenix, and, most significantly, the reality of the Christ. In rising from the dead, Jesus had fulfilled every resurrection story, hero myth, and hope, creating an imperishable lightway from this world to the next.[19]

Yet what is the energy that transforms ash into flower, cinder into blossom? The lives and teachings of the saints reveal it is love, the benevolent power coursing through the universe, bringing life out of original nothingness, sustaining every level of creation, and, through sheer compassion, calling all things that have lived back into existence again.

It was this almighty love, imparted to me by Lax, that restored my spirit; by gradual degrees, love had healed my heart. Likewise, this same transcendent love is the divine alchemical fire that entered into human history in the person of the Christ, the Tree and Flower of Jesse who reduced himself to ash, only to rise again in glory. In the process, Jesus heroically transformed the collective pain of humanity into something noble, endurable, refining, faith-enhancing. His sacrifice of love inspires and redeems us; steadily we draw nearer to the riches of the inner kingdom, and a transfiguration most precious and holy.

Through a supreme and selfless love, God gave himself up for the life of the world. By means of an "answering love," we consent to live compassionately and temperately on this fragile, perishing planet, enduring anything that may come our way with deep peace and confidence, that together we may rise again when all things are restored in Christ. For love "bears all things, believes all things, hopes all things, endures all things" (1 Cor 13.7). Ultimately, the God of Love makes all things new, for he is the consummate creative power in whom we shall be changed (1 Cor 15.51).

In the midst of great trials and suffering, it is often hard to love—there is too much "ash" to think of anything else, let alone flowers. Yet as figuratively demonstrated by my keepsake from Patmos, if we dig deep into the ashes of our suffering, we will find a bright energy that no ash can obscure, that brought us into being, and that calls us out of the embers of this passing realm, that we may be born anew.

Sometimes ashes exist in order that we may discover the original Fire.

Room to Grow

As with every profession, in teaching there are good workdays, bad ones, some highly memorable, and others best forgotten. And then, every so often, perhaps once every few years, there comes a day on the job that seems like a gift from above.

It was a day in mid-September, the beginning of the school year. Since I had only one class to teach and was not "freeway flying" to other campuses, I bicycled to work, a relatively rare event for a lecturer usually driving from school to school.

From the time I began cycling until my return home, everything I experienced that day had an enhanced feeling about it—my senses had somehow amplified, and happily so.

A light wind cooled me as I cycled; the morning sun vivified me in its glow. The ride was refreshingly clean and organic—pure, simple, self-generated, it made "sacred sense." The rhythmic whirring of the wheels sounded like a wordless hymn.

It was good to see the spokes glisten, to wrap my fingers around the chrome handlebars, to hear the click of the shifting gears. Unenclosed by metal and glass, unconfined to a tight lane on a congested highway, my own pedal power propelled me forward. Revolution after revolution, I was free.

Autumn was fast coming, and without any barriers I could feel the turning of the seasons. Falling leaves, tinged red and gold, rained quickly past; in every leaf ached the end of summer. The fire of harvest-time already coursed through their crisp, brittle veins—at the fractal level, fall was exploding.

Riding into campus, I saw waves of students moving to their classes. The crowd seemed endless. Year after year came more students, a successive flow of incredible raw energy coursing into classrooms, power gathering to be illuminated, channelled, refined, perfected.

Students on the campus of San Francisco State University.

Younger people sometimes had little idea of the brilliance locked within the heart of their being; if only they could find and access it, amazing things could happen. As Lax had once told me, to have inner fire is a manifold blessing, but first it must be discovered, then carefully tamed, cultivated, brought to a fine, keen intensity, like a laser meant to keep oneself (and the entire cosmos) on beam, awake in love and wisdom.

Wheeling my bike to the mailroom, I found a letter from Nepal in my box. A Buddhist institute was seeking to enroll students interested in overseas study. Inside the envelope was a string of tiny prayer flags, along with a pamphlet depicting the mountainside academy. Monks were shown conversing with students; a sweeping valley spread out below the building.

Though I had received letters such as this from other religious schools and institutes, the colourful mailing, marked with a "Katmandu" stamp, drove home how all over the world, even in the farthest reaches, people were gathering to study ways of faith and enlightenment. Just as I was on the verge of entering my classroom to begin a discussion on religion, so other teachers (and their students) were doing the same, whether it be in Rome, Nicosia, Tel Aviv, or Nairobi. All over the planet, instructors and students were assembling in their respective rooms. Education suddenly took on a universal quality.

Parking my bike in the office, I picked up my bookbag and headed down the hallway to lecture. The letter from Katmandu had put me in a happy mood, prompting me to direct a smile to a few students chatting in the corridor. Their reciprocal smiles buoyed my spirit in a heartfelt, palpable way. Wordlessly we understood that we were here to learn, grow, and share, not only for our immediate good, but for *all good.*

On entering the classroom, I found most of the students taking their seats around a ring of tables that formed an octagon. This eight-sided desk arrangement had always been pleasing to me. Aesthetically, it invited face-to-face discussion; symbolically, an octagon pattern suggested key spiritual truths of the East and West.

For example, in Taoism, eight foundational "trigrams" exist, each representing a force of nature through which the Yin and Yang ceaselessly change. In Buddhism, the Fourth Noble Truth is the "Eight-Fold Path." In early Christianity, baptisteries were almost always eight-sided, representing the "Eighth Day of Creation"—the "New Genesis" that had been set into effect through Christ's resurrection.

When I voiced these observations to my class, most were genuinely interested, although one fellow, about eighteen or twenty years old, kept staring at me expressionlessly, with an attitude of defiance. His eyes seemed to say, "I don't want to be here. What you are telling me doesn't really matter. I'm only here to get this requirement completed."

Certainly, every student has had similar feelings about a required class. For some reason, the pupil has little interest in the material or instructor or both, and shuts down. Oftentimes in these instances, words cannot remedy the situation. They cannot readily ease the student's lack of interest in the subject matter.

But the presence of the teacher can. People can be influenced not so much by what is said, but how one lives or moves, by the slightest of gestures. We innately know that if an instructor puts his words into practice, they are reflected in his bearing. Wisdom is thus taught by example. Merely by sitting next to an enlightened teacher, one may receive the inspiration to learn, which is the beginning of wisdom. Hence St. Francis of Assisi said to his disciples, "When preaching the Gospel, use words only when necessary." And Lao Tsu advised,

"Teach without words, perform without actions; this is the Master's way."

Robert Lax demonstrated this ability many times. I recall one evening on Patmos, when I was sitting at the dock looking into the water and he happened to come by.

It had not been a good day for me. For most of the afternoon I had been in something of an inner funk, half-wondering if my regular visits to Patmos had exceeded their worth. A kind of doubt and apathy had descended on me, an "inner dryness." My spirit felt that it had reached a saturation point.

With a gentle wave of the hand he quietly sat next to me on the white stone bench. Saying nothing, he opened a worn canvas cloth bag slung over his shoulder and brought out a little copy of the New Testament that I had left in his house a few days before.

Delicately cradling the book in his hands, Lax opened it. On the blank page opposite the frontispiece, he carefully wrote in his slow, meditative style: *Steve, Many Blessings.* Then with a twinkle in his eye and a loving smile, he gently handed me the book, tipped his cap, rose, and went on his way.

The poet's impromptu (though well-timed) visit had turned me around; my confidence was quickly restored. The old sage had an inscrutable way of turning darkness into light. He channelled grace at the most appropriate time.

Remembering this encounter with Lax, I took a seat next to the malcontent student and began class not with a customary opening monologue, but instead by wordlessly reaching into my bag and drawing out a well-worn copy of *The Way of the Pilgrim,* a classic of Orthodox spirituality focusing on the Jesus Prayer.[20]

This text was the first of our readings. The profound work, urging its audience to "pray without ceasing," had moved countless seekers over the years. I sought to give it the attention it deserved. But for the time being, this respect was rendered in silence.

With movements that hinted of ritual, I placed the book on the table. As I carefully turned the thin, creased pages, saying nothing, waves of peace (were they shudderings of grace?) ran through me.

All at once my mind flashed back to my bike ride to campus. My heightened senses had delighted in the turning of the wheels, the rhythm of their revolutions, the shining of the spokes. Now, a similar pleasure flowed through my spirit with every page I touched. In their brown-tinged, leafy texture I could feel trees, roots, pulp, earth, an organic unity of being. Once more, my senses had somehow augmented.

Cradling the book and feeling its inner, contemplative power, I understood, in a deeply pedagogical sense, that learning is not only something that is measurable and attained through intellectual study; it is also an art. Education is a tactile mystery that is stimulated through the senses, perceived (and disseminated) via the heart.

In retrospect, the entire morning had essentially been an exercise illustrating this truth. My invigorating bike ride, the colourful letter from Nepal, my happy encounter with the pupils in the hallway, and now, the beginning of class—all these situations confirmed that learning is not only an intellectual exercise, but an empathetic and spiritual one as well. The bright resonance of inspiration catalyzes thought and perfects it, harmonizing its essence.

But what of the disinterested student? Just as I had silently drawn *The Way of the Pilgrim* out of my bag, so he seemed to have mellowed a bit, relaxed, opened up, not because of anything I had said, but because of my quiet, deep regard for the subject matter and its metaphysical reverberations.

Silence had provided a space in which both of us could meet. Like the empty "blessing space" in the octagonal centre of the room, the stillness had served as a channel through which something higher could be educed, and at last born.

Nick of the Dunes

Christopher John Rozales, 2010

The coastline at Fort Funston, a part of the Golden Gate National Recreation Area, San Francisco.

He looked like Ezra Pound with his white tousled hair, short scraggly beard, narrow weather-lined face, and piercing blue eyes.

He was somewhere in his sixties. He spent most of his time along the shore eating out of garbage cans, traversing cliffs, or sitting by the water, staring out to sea. He never begged.

A lean man, he was built like a marathon runner. Despite his poor diet and lack of a home, he had a wiry strength that was unmistakable.

I think he began frequenting the beach, particularly the Fort Funston area, around 2004. Though other homeless people came to the shore, they did not stay long because of the drastic climate changes—within a day the temperature could dip twenty degrees.

There was also stiff wind and flying sand. Icy fog and mist tended to hug the shoreline for weeks, leading into months. The nights were cold. Drifters didn't spend much time at Ocean Beach. But he did.

He probably had about two changes of clothes. I usually saw him wearing a rust-coloured hoodless sweatshirt or a blue T-shirt. He wore tan jeans and tennis shoes that had holes. Sometimes he had on a pair of scuffed-up work boots. His only possessions were four plastic shopping bags that he always carried, two dangling from each hand. They looked to be stuffed with old newspapers.

How he was able to endure the elements year-round remains a mystery. He reminded me of Milarepa, the Tibetan yogi who was able to survive the snows of the Himalayas dressed only in a loincloth. Even through the rains of winter he would still be out there, scavenging and making his way across the dunes.

People kept their distance. They usually appeared not to notice him, but after he went by they would exchange comments like, "Where did *he* come from?" or "Another homeless nut." Others gave him hostile looks. Hardly anybody seemed to smile at him or offer a simple, spontaneous "hello."

On certain days he could look quite dishevelled. During the summer months his face was deeply burned, his lips severely chapped. Frequently he talked to himself, muttering nonsense. Once in a while he screamed out whatever came to mind, like an angry prophet.

I usually saw him out at the beach two times a month. I'd wonder about his past, what had broken him, led him to live this way. But then the beauty of the shore (and my desire to immerse myself in it) would take over. After saying an intercessory prayer, I'd soon forget about him.

Eventually, he and I had a direct, momentary encounter. It was on a cold, blue-sky Sunday morning, around 7 AM. I had driven to the coast for an early morning jog.

The parking lot was nearly empty. Save for the chirping birds and crashing breakers, a marvellous stillness hung in the air. Excitedly I ran down the winding steps cut into the cliffside, eager to "hit the beach."

And then, out of the morning shadows, he came silently up, ascending slowly, two bags in each hand. His breath-clouds drifted through the air.

His clothes were wet with dew and dirt. Obviously, he had spent the night on the beach. His red-rimmed, bloodshot eyes and chilled, wind-beaten face clearly spoke of his ordeal.

"Good morning," I said, as compassionately as I could, feeling the great distance that lay between his way of life and mine. The old adage "There, but for the grace of God, go I" echoed in my mind.

He looked at me for about a second, then shrugged his shoulders and let out a long, loud, tired sigh, like one who has climbed one peak, but knows that there are many more ahead. Lowering his gaze, he trudged on up the steps until he disappeared over the ridge.

As I headed toward the breakers, it suddenly struck me that my brief meeting with the homeless man had been my "church" for that morning. I was certainly planning to go to liturgy on my return, but it was that close encounter with the stranger that had me praying for him, deeply thinking about him at length.

At the same time, I was angry at myself for not having given him anything. He asked for nothing, but I could have gone back to my car and given him money for breakfast, had I made the effort. As written in James 2.17, "Faith, without works, is dead."

I thought of Lax, who periodically gave drachmas to gypsies. Many shunned these nomads, fearing more would congregate, but Lax always had some coins ready. He also made sure to check up on Patmians who were ill or had fallen on hard times. As he had told me, "Any place where you love and care and pray for another becomes something like a church."[21]

That it had taken me an entire year to apply this philanthropic wisdom to the homeless man embarrassed me, particularly since I considered myself a "disciple" of Lax, as well as a practising Christian, a follower of the God who professed love in the face of the unknown stranger. "As you did it unto others, so you did it unto me" (Mt 25.40).

A few days later, I returned to the beach and saw the homeless man walking across the parking lot, his four bags at his sides. Parking my car, I walked up to him with a few dollars. He did not give any indication that he recognized me. Without making eye contact, he gladly accepted the money.

"Sure, that'll come in handy," he said.

"Great," I replied. "What's your name?"

He paused, as if thinking what it might be. "Sydney. But sometimes I'm called Seymour." (Only in a later conversation did I learn that his "real" name was Nick).

There was a minute of silence. "Looks like your bags are pretty full," I said.

He nodded. "Yes, someday we'll have to ask Dr. Einstein what's in these bags." Then he sort of looked through me and said, very slowly, "Thank you," and began to walk away.

"God bless you!" I called out to him.

He turned around and haltingly echoed, "God … bless … you."

From that point on, I gave Nick money, sometimes food and clothing. It was good to speak with him from time to time. We usually exchanged a few words that made sense, but all too quickly he would become incoherent, and then walk away talking to himself. Even so, he had a way of saying his initial words slowly and precisely, which made me think deeply about what he and I were saying. This was especially true when he would repeat greetings or congenial phrases, as if making sure they were being said with sincerity. In this sense, he was something of a witness, perhaps even a "holy fool."[22]

One late afternoon, as I was driving back home from San Francisco State University and coming around Lake Merced (which borders Ocean Beach), I was shocked to see Nick surrounded by police officers, their arms folded across their chests. Three squad cars were parked nearby. Nick was standing alone in the centre of the circle like a befuddled child, still clutching his bags.

If somebody had called the police because he was yelling and "disturbing the peace," then this response was overkill. He looked pitiful standing there, ringed by a formidable force. He appeared like a man unable to comprehend the world into which he had been born.

Since I was on the opposite side of the road, I had to drive down a mile before I had a chance to reverse my direction and see what was going on. But by the time I got back, Nick and the police were gone.

Had he been taken in for questioning? Was he to be incarcerated? Weeks went by, then months, without any sign of him at the beach.[23]

And then, one June morning, about four months later, I was overjoyed to see Nick walking through the seaside parking lot, holding his bags. He looked pretty much the same.

"Nick!" I cried, walking up to him. "Where've you been? Last time I saw you, you were surrounded by police!"

"Why, yes, that's true," he replied, looking up at the sky as if nothing unusual had happened. "Sometimes the cops do that. Can't help themselves, I guess."

While I laughed aloud, he began to momentarily drift, then quietly made his way toward the cliffs and descended the steps leading to the sea. From a nearby lookout deck, I saw him walk out to the waterline and make his way down the long, barren coast until he disappeared into the streams of mist rising from the warming dunes.

A week or so after, I was jogging on the beach and found a thin, hand-sized piece of driftwood, the shape of an icon. Someone had painted a halo on it using bright yellow acrylic, and had highlighted the rays with green-gold glitter. The face had been purposely left out.

To me this unusual find indicated that everyone has the potential to be a saint. Surely there are "hidden saints" (or holy fools) walking among us even now, testing us to see if we really do love and help those in need unconditionally, without judgment. Nick, of course, came to mind, as did this famous quote from the letters of St. Paul: "Do not neglect to show hospitality to strangers, for thereby some have entertained angels unawares" (Heb 13.2).

Whether we know it or not, we relive the Bible stories in our daily existence. Lazarus the poor man; the wayfarer beaten by thieves and left on the side of the road (and at last attended to by the Good Samaritan); the Prodigal Son, who, for a long time, suffered a "life on the streets" after leaving his father's house—all these episodes are happening here and now. God remains present in these hapless situations, oftentimes hiding in lowly places where we rarely expect him to be. And yet he is there, everywhere, inspiring us to find "the Christ in all things," that we may intercede with *agape*.

Innately we know this "exercise of love" to be our foremost duty, the prime directive given us by God. But too often we get distracted by worldly pursuits and egoistic ways of living. Society conditions us to live self-centredly, rather than base all our lives on love.

Love is what the world is starving, waiting, hoping for—everything wants to be acknowledged, honoured, embraced. Lack of love fragments the heart and consciousness, and the broken often go to faraway and lonely places, trying to comprehend the reason for their incomplete existence, to fathom the meaning of it all.

What a blessing it would be for them to meet bearers of love in these remote haunts, that even by a word, a mere glance, they might know they are not alone, that there is another way, a new life. Like Christ, whose example we are called to follow, are we not also called to save? Perhaps the twentieth-century Russian Orthodox nun and martyr Mother Maria Skobtsova said it best:

> At the Last Judgment I shall not be asked whether I was successful in my ascetic exercises, nor how many bows and prostrations I made. Instead I shall be asked: "Did I feed the hungry?" "Did I clothe the naked?" "Did I visit the prisoners?" That is all I shall be asked.[24]

Arrow of *Agape*

On a rainy Saturday I was strolling through the art galleries at the Legion of Honor Museum in San Francisco. In one display case I noticed a sixteenth-century gilt pendant depicting Mary and the infant Jesus, with St. Sebastian poised above them. Linked to the bottom of the medallion was a small crucifix, a little over an inch in size. But on closer inspection, I saw that Christ was not affixed onto a cross—rather he was set like an arrow into a crossbow.[25]

This intrigued me; I had never seen anything like it before. Was there a biblical reference to Christ portrayed as an arrow? Later that night, I found this passage from Isaiah 49.2-3:

> He made me a polished arrow, in his quiver
> he hid me away, and he said to me, 'You are
> my servant, Israel, in whom I will be glorified.'

St. Gregory of Nyssa (fourth century) elaborates on this "Jesus arrow" image:

> Love is the archer, and love is God .... *God shoots his chosen arrow, his only-begotten Son,* first moistening the three tips of its point with the life-giving Spirit. Now the point is faith, and faith makes not only the arrow but the archer also to penetrate its target, in accordance with the word of the Lord: "My Father and I are one and we shall come to him and make our dwelling in him."[26]

More than once I returned to the museum to meditate on "Christ the Arrow" (or "Crossbow Jesus," as a friend termed the image).[27] The Redeemer's upper body perfectly mirrors the half-moon shape of the bow. His sinewy arms are extended wide, his hands curl around the bowstring and forcefully draw his tapered form down the narrow stock of the weapon, locking his soma into place, that he might spring free on release and soar to the sky, toward the eternal Father.

Immense effort is required of Jesus to push his body down the length of the bow. His face grimaces as he exerts pressure on the coiled whipcord and loads himself into position, the incarnate "Arrow Prayer of humanity."

Both death and life, crucifixion and resurrection can be read in Crossbow Jesus. Christ strains and trembles as he forces his "arrowed self" downward. This subterranean thrust alludes to a passage from the first letter of Peter: "He went and preached to the spirits in prison" (that is, Hades) "who formerly did not obey" (3.19). If Christ the Arrow is to reach heaven, he first must die, draw himself unto the depths, fire his Spirit from the illuminated pit of hell. In essence, no place can remain untouched by his saving glory and illimitable grace.

In dying and delivering the Good News to the underworld, Christ becomes infinitely stronger, almighty. His mysterious descent, in which he pierces death and sin, lets fly a dynamic new energy into the universe.

> Hades was pierced and destroyed by divine fire when it received in its heart Him who was nailed to the Cross and lanced for our salvation ... O Christ our God, though you descended into the grave as one dead, you overthrew death, by death trampling

upon death, and have bestowed life to those in the tombs. Christ is Risen, the Light of the World is manifest![28]

Like an incendiary arrow, Christ penetrates hell and explodes in love. In divine fire he rises from the dead and hurtles through the outer limits of creation and beyond, toward the "right hand of the Father" and the beginning of a new world born of the Holy Spirit. As St. Paul declares,

> In saying, "He ascended," what does it mean but that he had also descended into the lower parts of the earth? He who descended is he who also ascended far above all the heavens, that he might fill all things. (Eph 4.9-10)

Already the King is victorious, even while drawing back the crossbow's coiled string. The chosen Arrow of God has found his mark, both under the earth and in heaven. The Bolt of *Agape* has slain death, the dark power that could not comprehend love, and sought its ruin; simultaneously, Christ the Arrow rises, speeds on into the heart of the Father, that together with the Father and the Spirit, the Son of God might pierce the hearts of all beings and renew everything in love.

There is an ancient Hebrew saying: *"Without the tension of the bow, the arrow cannot fly."* While this tension is dramatically seen in the figure of "Crossbow Jesus" as he struggles to draw back the bowstring and fulfill his destiny, the Saviour's struggle inwardly points to the arduous (and yet creative) tension that periodically surfaces between his "celestial" and "terrestrial" natures.

In completely identifying with the human condition, Christ was both God and Man. His inner wrestling is evident in the Garden of Gethsemani, ("Take this cup away from me" [Mt 26.39]), and especially on the cross ("My God, my God, why have you forsaken me?" [Mt 27.46]). Thus, when Jesus draws back the whipcord to complete his self-sacrificing and salvific mission, he wrestles with what he feels he *cannot do* (stemming from his mortal nature), and with what he *must do* (reflective of his divine nature).

How does the God-Man resolve the struggle? Through deep and abiding love, the assenting, unifying, liberating, and selfless power in which all dualities dissolve ("My soul is very sorrowful, even unto death .... Nevertheless, not as I wilt, but as thou wilt" [Mt 26.38-39]).

Like Christ, we, too, are caught up in a similar inward struggle. Though we be pierced by many desires and stretched to the limits of our human endurance in trying to do the "right thing" (often in what seems a very "wrong world"), we persevere. With faith and with love, we continue to live through the heart, for it is in our moments of trial and extreme desperation that we draw nearest to God. Through trust in his grace and mercy, we break through to a higher dimension; a new universe ultimately opens.

Like Christ the Incarnate Arrow, we, too, are spirit-arrows meant to fly from this world to the next. So we draw back our bowstrings, that with our Lord we might pierce death and rise again. And though we be as arrows, we do not hit the mark with hate but with love, imitating the Risen Christ. *Agape* is the clearest flight path, a lightway straight and true that stops at nothing because in love is everything.

Since ancient times, the arrow has been considered a powerful spiritual symbol in all world faiths. It represents a kind of penetrative awareness, a piercing of illusion, anxiety, and doubt to get to the heart of the matter. For Christians, the heart of the matter is love, as exemplified in the life of God's "Chosen Arrow."

Demetrios

Gheros Demetrios (Old Man Demetrios) had been a farmer most of his life. I first met him and his wife Angeliki at their home in Hora, the highest village of Patmos, situated near the monastery of St. John.[29] Both were young at heart and displayed a deep affection for each other. They radiated that special love that comes from living happily together for over sixty years.

Occasionally, I would visit the couple when I was up in Hora. After welcoming me with a cool glass of lemonade and exchanging a few pleasantries, Angeliki usually puttered about the kitchen or took up her knitting. Her husband tended to work in the yard. Though he used two canes to get around, he continued to amble about and tended a small vegetable garden. Often he would sit on the porch and gaze out over the countryside.

I liked talking to Demetrios. Straightforward and unpretentious, even abrupt, he displayed a deep, rustic wisdom, mostly gained through a lifetime of working with the rhythms of the land. God and creation were his favourite topics, as they were with many of the islanders. Refreshingly, his insights were peppered with a kind of wild, zany enthusiasm that bordered on eccentricity.

After visiting the Monastery of St. John one morning, I walked through the sunny fields to Demetrios' house and found him sitting on the porch, taking in the view of the hills and sea. Two kittens were playing at his feet.

"Yassoo, palikari!" (Health to you, young man!), he called out loudly, waving his cane. *"Ellah doh! Nah milisomeh!"* (Come here! Let's talk for a while!).

I went up the steps and sat on the concrete floor, next to his chair. Gingerly I picked up one of the kittens and began to pet it while the other one looked on longingly. Then Demetrios reached down and picked up the other cat, stroking its head.

"It's good to pet them," he said. "It's peace for them and us."

16. Demetrios and the author in Hora, Patmos.

For a few minutes we sat there petting the kittens, saying nothing. But every so often I glanced at Demetrios. His big, thick, wrinkled hands cradled the animal lovingly as he stroked its fur in repetitive waves, from the neck on down. Then he looked up and sighed.

"Touch everything this way."

"What do you mean?" I asked.

"Try to love everything. Everything wants love, just like these *ghatakia* (kittens). Let your love flow—let it be constant, like the seasons."

"You sound like Petros," I said, referring to Lax by his island nickname. "He also thinks we should love more."

"He's right," affirmed Demetrios, waving toward the fields with one arm, the other holding the kitten close to his chest. "We are called to love people, birds, beasts, trees, seas, stars … all the universe wants to be cherished!"

His sudden exclamation reminded me of Father Zosima, a famous character in Dostoevsky's *The Brothers Karamazov*, who exuded an intense passion for life.

Putting the cat down, Demetrios grasped both his canes and rose to his feet. For a moment he looked like a priest about to begin the Divine Liturgy.

"When we love with all we are … we help to bring every bit of nature nearer to God," he said slowly, and with a hush, as if contemplating the sanctity of his own words.

"Kalah toh eiphes!" (You said it right!), I replied. "*Agape* brings everything back to Christ."

Demetrios nodded vigorously and motioned upward. "Every year I offer my harvest back to him. In love he gave it to me, and in love I give it back."

Some minutes passed in suspended silence. The wind stirred the branches of a few nearby trees. Lazily they creaked; a few leaves fell. The crow of a rooster broke the quiet.

Demetrios leaned toward me, then struck the cement with one of his canes like an official ready with a pronouncement.

"Always give God the glory," he declared sternly, and with a sense of urgency. "Honour him. Through his love we were born, and in his love we live now. Christ is our life for eternity."

A few weeks later, I happened to drop in on Demetrios and found him reinforcing a stone wall in his garden. An old doormat, curled up on every corner, lay in front of him. He was kneeling on it.

"Let me show you something," he said, getting up. "If I stand on this corner of the mat, what happens to the rest of the corners?"

"They spring up off the ground," I replied.

"And if I stand on both end corners?"

"The opposite ends go up," I said. "But what's all this supposed to mean?"

"It's really simple," he assured. "If I wish to have all corners of the mat balance equally with each other, at the same level, where must I stand?"

"In the middle of the mat," I said, still unsure of where this was going.

Demetrios drew close and looked me in the eye. "That mat is the universe. Its centre represents God. That is where you should always stand if you want to live in balance with everything around you."

"This is all well and good," I replied. "But there's a difference between a mat and the real world. Here and now, how do I know if I'm standing in life's holy centre?"

Demetrios pointed to a palm branch quivering in the wind. Its green leaves rippled in the sunlight.

"Look how it's shaking!" he exclaimed. "Look at it! Isn't that little dance a miracle? Doesn't it do something inside you?"

"Of course it does," I said, almost matter-of-factly. "Nature has always moved me."

"Kali archi" (a good start), he affirmed. "Now when you feel that 'movement' building in you, so that there's a kind of burning in your chest, and tears of joy come to your eyes, and through your lips come the words '*Praise God*,' then you will know that you are nearing the holy centre of the cosmos."

I smiled and nodded. *"Ahmeh, gerondah!"* (I'm with you, wise elder!). "There have certainly been times when I've felt this way."

"And that 'feeling' is everything!" he exclaimed. "*God wants your heart on fire!* That's why he made the cosmos beautiful. How could Adam have been moved to pray if his spirit wasn't filled with passion for all of creation? It's the same with us."

Enthused by his fervour, I raised my hands to the sky and shouted out a line from the "Hymn of Thanksgiving," a popular Orthodox praise-song: *"Glory to God for all created things!"*

The devout old farmer smiled, and made the sign of the cross. "Glory to him in the highest," he echoed, once more voicing a phrase he often repeated: "Christ is our life for eternity."

The last time I saw Demetrios he was just beginning to wake from an afternoon siesta on his porch. He had fallen asleep in his chair.

"Ksipnah, papoulaki" (Wake up, grandfather), I said to him affectionately.

"Ach," he groaned, stretching himself with great labour. "In the winter of life, sometimes to go on dreaming is far better than to wake."

"What were you dreaming of?" I asked.

He chuckled. "Pretty much the same things that have been around me since I was a boy. Birds were flying across the sky. There were fields and stars. The hills stretched out to the sea, and the sunlight was bright on the water."

"Beautiful" I said. "That sounds so restful. In a way, you've always been living in paradise, and your dreams have become part of reality."

"Or the reality has become part of the dream," he said, with a resigned and happy smile.

"Stavros, my friend, soon you'll be going back to America, and I'll still be here, or perhaps will have gone home to heaven. But we'll always be in touch."

"Do you mean by telephone?" I asked, playing along with his sunset scenario.

Demetrios rolled his eyes. "We don't need the wires of the world to connect!" he exclaimed. "Here, let me show you how we'll speak."

Rising to his feet, he said, "Whenever I want to talk to you, I'll cup my hands around my mouth like this, and then I'll tilt my head back to the sky and yell, '*AAAAAAA-OOOOOO.*' Wherever you may be, you'll hear me loud and clear, and respond in the same way."

"Should we practise now?" I asked with a wide grin.

"Absolutely!" he replied, as if there were nothing more important to do.

So for a few minutes we stood on his porch facing one another, our hands to our mouths and our heads tilted back, yelling, "*AAAAAAA-OOOOOOO*" to each other, over and over again.

Within a minute Angeliki came out, and a few passersby in the distance craned their necks toward us, wondering what the commotion was all about. But we continued on with the wild and crazy din like two wolves braying at a midnight moon.

As our echoes drifted across the fields and down through the valley below, some memorable lines from *Black Elk Speaks,* on the life and times of a Lakota visionary, wherein the Great Spirit calls out to the whole of creation, resounded in my mind:

> His voice went all over the universe and filled it. There was nothing that did not hear, and it was more beautiful than anything can be. It was so beautiful that nothing anywhere could keep from dancing.[30]

III. Riding the Waves

Keep sailing for the inner star.

Robert Lax, *The Way of the Dreamcatcher*

S.T. Georgiou, 1997

Pavement stone leading into the Cave of St. John (shown with the key to the Monastery of the Apocalypse, Patmos).

Communion of Love

On my last trip to Patmos, in 1999, I visited a small monastery nestled in a remote seaside cove. I had been resting in the cool shade of its entrance when a motorcycle with bulging saddlebags roared up to the main gates. Driving the vintage black BMW was a young Greek with shoulder-length hair and a tattered Levi's jacket who looked like he had rumbled out of the road movie *Easy Rider.*

As it turned out, the biker was a gifted iconographer living on the nearby isle of Samos. Every few months, he took the ferry to various islands where he sold his sacred art to churches and monasteries.

After talking with him for a while, I learned that he was married and had three children. They lived a simple, grassroots existence. Though he was barely able to provide for them, the iconographer radiated a happy confidence that issued from a deep faith in God.

He told me that his family dwelled in an isolated cottage in the hills; half of it made up his studio. By choice they had no television or computer. Music was their primary form of entertainment (he played the guitar). They liked telling late-night stories, especially when relatives or friends happened to drop in.

Most of their food came from the surrounding land. The children, who participated in morning and evening prayers with their parents, were home-schooled. Church was the rhythmic and social centre of their existence. For recreation, there was always the sea.

Just before the iconographer left to speak with the *egoumenos* (abbot), I ventured to ask what icon, of all that he had painted, meant the most to him. I thought this might tell me more about his radiant spiritual solidity, rare for someone under thirty.

Without hesitation, he smiled and said, "In my house is a small copy of Rublev's *Holy Trinity.* I completed it years ago, and have kept it in the kitchen, by our table, ever since. For me, it is the icon of love."

Then he pointed to his watch, indicating he was late. Quickly opening his saddlebag, he gathered a few icons and disappeared into the abbot's office.

At the time, I was just beginning my doctoral studies at the Graduate Theological Union in Berkeley. Though I had heard of the fourteenth-century Russian iconographer Andrei Rublev and had seen copies of *The Holy Trinity,* I had never examined the masterpiece in depth. The young man's answer prompted me to study the icon in detail on my return to the States.

Even to this day, I continue to find manifold meanings of love in the icon. Meditating on its compassionate mystery has helped steer me toward the inner treasure of the Christ.

Image compliments of St. Isaac of Syria Skete

The Holy Trinity (the Old Testament Trinity), by Andrei Rublev, 1411. Tretyakov Gallery, Moscow.

The Holy Trinity is an image of *agape* because its theme is centred in the interrelational love of the triune God, a supreme communion meant to include the whole of creation. Every moment is an opportunity to participate in this divine love. Daily the Lord offers himself to us. We have the choice of welcoming him into our lives or turning him away. How does the icon exemplify this?

To begin, the holy image is itself a representation of open-hearted hospitality. The three resplendent angels are the heavenly beings who visited Sarah and Abraham at the Oak of Mamre (Gen 18). The elderly couple offered the trio, who appeared in mortal disguise, a meal, which they ate. The early Church has treated these "undercover angels" as an Old Testament prefiguration of the Holy Trinity: in essence, a manifestation of the living God who continues to visit us, oftentimes in the form of a stranger, in order to test our love and generosity.

From left to right, the angels represent the Father, Son, and Holy Spirit. All three beings display hand gestures meant to indicate the sacral moment when the heart is opened and the stranger is welcomed (that is, when a higher love is born).

The pre-eminent middle angel, symbolizing Christ, extends two fingers, signifying the famous words of Jesus, "Wherever two or three are gathered in my name, I am there, in the midst of them" (Mt 18.20).[1]

The fingers of the angel on the right, who represents the Holy Spirit, come together to form what seems to be a single finger. This "digital gathering" stands for the "Unity of the Spirit in the bond of peace" (Eph 4.3). The unifying gesture signifies the divine "oneness" that transpires when real love happens.

The angel on the left, symbolizing the Father, extends three fingers in blessing the two angels. He acknowledges their agapaic intent, and also participates in it, as exemplified by his Trinitarian benediction. In turn, both the Son and Spirit look toward the Father to receive the blessing, and to acknowledge his presence in every act of love.

Interestingly, the slim, articulate fingers of the Son and Spirit are extended in a "tapping" gesture, as if knocking on a door. They seem to tap a table surface, but on closer inspection the table is actually an altar. On it rests a chalice containing a calf's head, signifying the Eucharist, the sacrament par excellence. Thus the gesture of tapping is symbolic: the altar around which the three angels gather is figuratively Christ himself, the head of the Church, the veritable "Door" through which all things must enter en route to the Father (Jn 10.7). In him we seek access, for in him is everlasting life.

The tapping interpretation also fits because Christ explicitly states, "Behold, I stand at the door and knock. If anyone hears my voice and opens the door, I will come in to him and eat with him, and he with me" (Rev 3.20)—a declaration much in keeping with the icon's message of love-centred hospitality.

To enforce this door symbolism, Rublev placed a portal-like rectangle at the base of the altar. Its narrow dimensions closely align with the doorway of the mansion above the Father's halo (which represents the heavenly kingdom).[2] This approximate match indicates that when we partake of the Eucharist, we enter, even now, into the house of our Lord. Moreover, every house, in heaven and on earth, is meant to function as a place of love and welcome wherein a type of "holy communion" may happen, a blessed partaking of all things in God.

Indeed, this fruitful theme of communal, integral love is appropriately emphasized through the repeated image of a chalice. Not only is there a Eucharist cup resting on the altar, but the full-length profiles of the Father and Holy Spirit (who face the Son) form the outline to a second communion cup which Christ somatically fills: hence the symbolism of the "True Vine" emerging from behind him.

If two chalices exist, Orthodox iconography begs that there be a third. Where is it? In the foreground of the icon, below the altar table and flanked by the angels' feet, barely noticeable. The cup is roughly rendered, almost incomplete, because it becomes complete only when the viewer (worshipper) participates in the communion of the Father, Son, and Spirit: that is, in the interrelational "life of the Trinity."

Rublev's icon is essentially an invitation to enter into the transcendent, all-pervasive flow of divine *agape*, to intimately experience the interactive round of love. Thus the circle of Trinitarian communion is not closed, but remains open to the reverent beholder. In electing to become a part of its brilliant life-stream, the Christian is utterly transfigured, made beautiful, as evident in the exquisite angels who represent the Holy Trinity. Their radiant peace, quietly pulsing with an otherworldly light, hints of the mysterious ethereal joy that awaits the blessed in paradise.

Yet how to love? How precisely to enter into communion with God? Again, the icon gives us an answer. The calf's head in the central chalice represents the sacrifice of Jesus, who gave himself up for the life of the world. In a sense, believers must undergo a similar sacrifice. We are required to empty ourselves of ego, vice, and worldly passions if we are to draw near the table of the Lord. As St. Paul says, "Present yourselves as a living sacrifice, holy, acceptable to God, which is your reasonable service" (Rom 12.1).

This kenotic emptying is purifying and liberating. It allows us to transcend our limited self-centredness in order to better focus on the "other," the needy stranger who is nothing less than Christ himself. In letting go, we *let in God* and become open channels through which his blessings may flow. This is the great message all three angels impart: that if we dare to love others more than ourselves, we indeed become as angels, that is, vessels of God through which his life-giving (and life-saving) communion flows. Beyond this, nothing else matters; from this, everything begins.

In contemplating Rublev's masterpiece, our hearts increasingly open. What begins to shine out of us is precisely what the icon displays—*the communion of the Holy Trinity,* a liturgy of love that is going on continuously in everything that lives, moves, and has being.[3] Whenever we help another, and whenever we descend into our hearts in prayer, we enter into this holy service and help to dispense the communion of *agape* throughout the cosmos. We ride the waves of love.

A Holy Intensity

My students had been working on an in-class essay exam on how Christian *agape* compares and contrasts with *ahimsa* (the Buddhist doctrine of compassion). Their initial restlessness, punctuated by fidgeting and nervous laughter, steadily gave way to occasional coughs, forceful exhalations, and sighs. Eventually, a meditative quiet filled the room; for a long while, pen on paper and the turning of pages were the only sounds.

At this point a colleague knocked on my door. He had misplaced his keys and asked if I could let him into the department office at the end of the hallway.

Though I was gone scarcely five minutes, I was struck by the focused intensity of my students when I re-entered the classroom. Their concentration was steady, vibrant, reverberating like a mantra. From what I could sense, their collective energy exceeded that of any class I had passed in the hallway. I felt like I had walked into a teeming "mind-field."

Most of the students, intent on their work, had hardly noticed my return. While some were rapidly jotting down their thoughts lest any be forgotten, others carefully weighed their deliberations with eyes closed or fixed on some distant point. The students were in that delicate, refined zone where in the human consciousness intuitively senses one of its prime directives: to explore the inner reaches of the self, and to bring back accurate reports of the life within.

A calm, keen radiance shone out of the pupils; they were inwardly ripening. A rich and teeming innocence had sprung from their living depths because they had forgotten about themselves and had completely immersed their energies in a transcendent enterprise—the life of the mind.

Perhaps it was the honey-gold radiance of the sunset beaming through the windows, but a warm glow the colour of amber had filled the room, now humming with what seemed to be an almost holy intensity. Indeed, my deep-thinking students appeared as if they were praying; like those rapt in prayer, they had let go their egos and self-concerns and were in a state of undivided attentiveness. Pure and still as candle flame, they had given themselves to the inward mysteries of contemplation, especially because they were focusing on the nature of selfless love in both the East and West.

Suddenly it came to me that my students were engaged in *reflection*. This abstract term, steeped in metaphysics, intrigued me, for in Latin it implies a "bending back," as in the reflective action of light. But the students were engaged in a reflection (or mirrored likeness) of what?

To me it seemed that in their deepening ruminations, the class was accessing a higher power, the intelligent Source of life itself, the true Light that "enlightens everyone born into the world" (Jn 1.9). In their open, free, and earnest contemplation, they were making intimate contact with the All in All, thus reflecting, however minutely, the brilliant Being that long ago had set into effect transcendent levels of consciousness, the bright God who began life with the almighty command, *"Let there be light!"*

The twentieth-century German-Jewish philosopher Hannah Arendt once asked the question, "Where are we when we think?" Especially when we meditate on the nature of love, we may increasingly perceive that our thoughts (and our entire beings) are always in the presence of God. Contemplation itself happens because an exceedingly profound "Idea"—implanted in us like a seed, since birth—is intent on germinating: the realization that as divinely created, thinking beings, we are ever participating with the "Mind of Christ" (1 Cor 2.16), in whose thoughts we are.

In coming to this "right mind" (Rom 12.2), we consciously draw nearer to Jesus, the focal point of existence. We begin to mirror the peace of heaven, as demonstrated in the tranquillity of those who are immersed in thought (or prayer). Our deep-running "streams of consciousness," once clouded, now increasingly clear; in their sheer lucidity, the life-giving waters of paradise are reflected. We flow with an Intelligence infinitely greater than ourselves, and yet whose brilliance calls us to be generators and transmitters of light, like the divine Light itself. We interface with the Mind moving over the face of the deep.

Thinking is therefore holy. Somehow flesh and blood—temporary (and disintegrating) aggregates—are momentarily fused in such a precise and God-like configuration that they can process thought, an invisible energy that cannot be seen, and yet serves as the luminous foundation for every human construct. Moreover, the highest tier of thought (metaphysical deliberation, according to the world faiths) is not so much concerned with the utilitarian advantages of this fleeting universe, but steers us toward life's immaterial and spiritual origins, this being the "Light of the world." Thought, therefore, comes to reflect its holy Source; the intellectual ray we have been given at last "bends back" to its Origin.

As we refine our meditations, we come to see that we can process thought not only because we are natural-born thinkers, but because we are actively engaged with an Intellect that is ever guiding us back to its firstborn and eternal Idea, namely *life born of love.* Everything good we do in this existence is an affirmation of this original, transcendent blessing. Once we recognize this inward Light, we go on to the next level, whatever that may be. We are born again, newly conceived in Christ. In essence, our true Reflection liberates us; realizing ourselves in God, we are at last made bright, infinitely free.

Great Humility

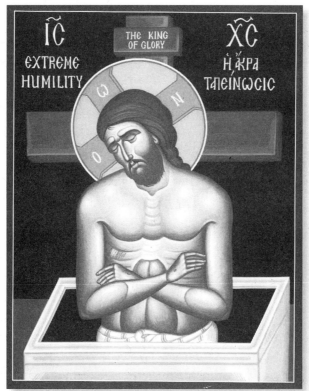

The Icon of Extreme Humility.

© Holy Transfiguration Monastery, Brookline, Massachusetts. Used with permission.

While visiting Patmos one summer, I remember speaking with a ninety-year-old monk at the Monastery of St. John and asking him what he considered to be the most direct path to Christ.

First he pointed to a wooden brace leaning on his cell wall, a crutch used to help him keep upright during services, indicating the importance of discipline and perseverance in prayer. He then motioned to an icon by his bed, *The Christ of Great (or Extreme) Humility,* in the West referred to as the "Man of Sorrows," a powerful image revealing the ultimate sacrifice of the Saviour.

Jesus, already crucified, is shown standing in his tomb, in front of his cross. At his sides are the lance and the sponge, the instruments of the Passion. His hands appear bound, but no rope ties them together, demonstrating that he willingly chose to be fettered and suffer unto death for the salvation of all. The wounds on his hands and side bleed openly, indicating that his agony was real, endured through his infinite love for every human being, and for creation itself. With eyes closed, he is empty, wasted, utterly dead to the world as he silently descends into Hades. Yet even so, he is inwardly alive with the Good News of the resurrection.

Though I understood the need for prayer and discipline in the spiritual journey, the icon of Great Humility, however poignant, did not instill in me an immediate sense of *metanoia* (repentance, leading to a greater love of Christ). The image did not deeply move me, at least not at that time.

To be truthful, I was quite a bit younger when I first came to Patmos, disillusioned, and unsure of my life's direction. Moreover, I had a greater (and perhaps more comfortable) liking for icons of the Madonna, Christ Enthroned, and particular saints. These images seemed more peaceful, gentle, aesthetically favourable. They were less obtrusive, softer, absent of the sheer, harsh, and naked reality of the crucifixion.

And yet, the sacrifice of the Son is the key to cosmic salvation. Only God could have repaired the break between Creator and creation, a schism traced to the Fall. The reconnective link is Jesus Christ, the incarnate God-Man, who set into effect a restoration of heaven and earth, to be consummated at the Second Coming.

It would not be until 2008, fifteen years after I spoke with the aged monk on Patmos that the icon of Great Humility re-entered my life; its deep inner meaning indeed revealed a clear path to the Saviour, just as the elderly Patmian father had said.

Sometime close to Thanksgiving, I had stopped by the Archangel Bookstore in San Francisco, near Golden Gate Park, to pick up some gift cards. Just as I was leaving, I glimpsed the icon propped atop a bookcase, by the door. I think what initially moved me was reading *The King of Glory* written on the cross, above Jesus' bowed head. The infinite God of creation had made himself finite, vulnerable, broken, dead, even for those who had been the instrument of his ruin: "Forgive them, Father, for they know not what they do" (Lk 23.34).

Purchasing the icon, I gave it to my parish priest to bless. Then, after leaving it in the altar of the church for forty days (an early Christian tradition), I brought the image into my home and set it on an icon stand.

Since then I gaze at it often, and with reverence. Especially after prayer, its "inner doors" open and allow me, a seeker in Christ, to journey deeper into the God of my baptism.

The icon of Great Humility holds no stops—beaten, scourged, crucified, entombed, and through it all obedient and silent, Christ the King, the Fount of Life and Master Architect, faithfully endures the will of the Father, trusting in his mercy and righteousness. And yet even though broken and embittered, a very faint tenderness may still be discerned in the face of Jesus, a mysterious sweetness, a gladdening sorrow, for he knows that his emptiness is our fullness. With absolute compassion he continues to love all. With his head inclined to his heart, he descends into the darkness of the tomb, whose door will be sealed.

This is extreme humility. The God who could have stopped his sacrifice "with legions of angels" halts nothing. Having taken on mortal flesh, Christ shudders, dies, and accomplishes everything. Emptying himself of all, the Chalice of the Uncontainable pours his lifeblood throughout time and space and makes the universe new, readying it for its ultimate transfiguration. In the most intimate manner possible, Christ has entered into this wounded life, that life may be healed, remade in his Light. Hatred and violence are paradoxically overcome by Incarnate Love.

As can be read in the icon, the three letters in his halo stand for the Lord's holy declaration, "I Am Who I Am" (Ex 3.14), clearly indicating that Christ is not a prophet or an emissary sent from heaven, but is the Deity Incarnate, *the living God.* As Jesus told the Pharisees, "Before Abraham was, *I Am*" (Jn 8.58).

A deep understanding of this pierces the heart. The soul humbles itself in awe and reverence, adoration and worship. This is the Most Holy Son, the Second Person of the Trinity. The God whom this icon depicts is no mere symbol conceived through a "spiritualized psychology," nor is he a humanly designed deity, cosmopolitan and worldly, fashioned according to the ideals of modernism. This time-less God is the *Good News* come down from heaven to earth. His promise of life eternal is sealed in everlasting love, as revealed in the Mystery of the Cross and the Empty Tomb.

In a cynical, analytic age that preaches how God is not to be taken "too literally" (and may even be reduced to an evolving myth or a genetic-molecular-neural phenomenon), a Creator addressed as *"Abba"* and *"Agape Incarnate"* would appear radically intimate, if not intuitively real. A divine Love that ultimately makes itself human so that humanity might be reborn in Love (and thus be saved from oblivion) is totally liberating, overwhelmingly life-affirming.

As rendered in the icon of Great Humility, the sacrifice of Jesus makes this supreme love possible. Though death claims him, his boundless love is stronger—he will rise on the third day and give life to those in the tombs.

And yet the love of Christ, as here portrayed in his demise, is not a thunderous, climactic love, but is hushed, obedient, faithful, non-struggling—the same quiet love Jesus radiates even as he de-scends into the tomb: *"Father, into your hands I commit my Spirit"* (Lk 23.46).

It is the love of trust and promise, a love that in silence denies itself, always giving the Father the glory. It is a love centred in submission and unconditional surrender to divine will. It is a patient love com-fortable in resigning all things to God, who knows (and loves us) more than we can possibly conceive. As Christ revealed, it is a love that is grounded in humility and repentence, and leads to salvation: "He who loses his life for my sake will find it" (Mk 8.35).[4]

In a world torn by hate and greed and overrun with hunger, disease, violence, natural disasters, and death, this humble, selfless love seems the most ideal (and expedient) way to live. *Agape* in Christ transcends the ravenous, inexorable ego and initiates a compassion-driven change: not "my will be done," but *Thy will be done.*[5]

In a crumbling universe where things often don't go our way and impatience and anger may surface at any time, it is prudent to follow Jesus' example and exercise extreme humility and love.

Inevitably, and especially as we age, we face the reality that we are not in control. Unpredictable hardships come into our lives. Physical and mental strength diminish. Like all things mortal, we perish. Our conscience therefore tells us to let go this fleeting world and stand before the Lord in awe and adoration, in a deep silence mirroring his own, listening to Him with all our being, that in Him we may find the pure calm of infinity.

The icon of Great Humility imparts that, like the crucified King of Glory, we are all waiting on God to raise us. And, like Jesus, we do not wait with trepidation, but obediently, confidently, just as we know that night turns into day, and spring follows winter. Even in death we continue to trust, for in all times and places we are close to him, and he with us, if we believe.

"Our lives are hid in Christ our God" (Col 3.3). In quiet awe, and with certain peace, we pray ourselves into his Mystery.

Dark Night

What if we can't pray? What if our hearts close, and we feel an absence of love?

On a grey September day, a listlessness bordering on emptiness had set into me. At first I tried to ignore this lingering malaise. It was, after all, the end of summer; the school year had commenced, and I had been assigned more than my usual share of classes. But as the days turned into weeks, my strange, persistent torpor intensified, and began to affect my spiritual life.

It became harder to pray. When I tried, my communication with God felt forced, born of obligation, not love. Simply going to church was prompted by a nagging sense of duty rather than desire. And when I made it to service, my mind often wandered instead of focusing on the holiness at hand—the Christ in our midst.

When after liturgy I remarked to an elderly parishioner (and long-time friend) that my faith life felt unsettled, she surprised me with her direct and emphatic reply.

"Professor, get out of your head and into your heart! Why is it so hard to believe in a loving God, and to trust him? *Stop doubting Jesus and get back to basics!*"

Though at that point I was not exactly "doubting Jesus," her words hit the mark. Secular scholarship, including the historical and archaeological study of the world religions, can indeed tend to undermine one's spiritual convictions, simply because so much of academic argument centres on demonstrative (and yet often inconclusive) evidence.

Faith, however, "hopes for what is unseen" (Heb 11.1) and is grounded in a dynamic *love* of the divine seeking a deeper *knowledge* of the divine. Small wonder that according to an in-depth survey conducted by Harvard University and George Mason University, the higher up in academia one goes, the less faith there is in God.[6]

One cannot discount how the constant stream of articles and books debunking the existence of a Supreme Deity may subtly (and cumulatively) affect believing academics, especially those teaching theology; their faith in a higher power is relentlessly challenged and may weaken over time.

Secular education's ever-growing emphasis on scientific and technological advancement can also make the very study of religion appear outdated and superfluous. As one college dean once heatedly asked me, "Compared to the sciences, what practical good has religion given the world?"

This naïve attitude and anti-religious sentiment, suggestive of Marxist ideology, may lead both faculty and students to regularly question their "antiquated" beliefs. Spiritual ideals and traditions—which have held societies (and psyches) together for millennia—may ultimately erode.

My autumn spiritual angst was probably also linked to various tragedies that my students had suffered throughout the semester, leading me to question where God was in the midst of their woes. One pupil had lost his mother to a sudden and unknown cause just at the beginning of the term. Another lost his mother to a fast-moving cancer, and then later his brother to a freak accident. Yet another student, who had begun living in a homeless shelter, dropped out of school after being infected with MRSA, a highly resistant and potentially dangerous bacterial infection.

Mid-semester, my own health was not the best. My mild asthma had been aggravated by a persistent chest cold and by a dense and lingering fog. As a result, I found myself rising from bed in the early morning hours until my discomfort subsided.

Somewhere around late October I began to wake at 3 AM, regardless of my respiratory condition. I couldn't go back to bed. Personal concerns relating to employment and financial security raced through my head like a shuffled deck of cards. The nation was just beginning to feel the effects of the coming recession. California in particular would soon be hit by state budget cuts that would severely hurt educators, resulting in job losses and the termination of classes.

These concerns were not entirely new. When they had surfaced before, I would take inventory of my life and reach the conclusion that no matter what, it was my faith in God that mattered most, and would guide me through my troubles.

But now, amid employment stress, I was experiencing a spiritual crisis; my relationship with Christ continued to feel strained. When I woke in the early morning, I did not sense him near. I often felt alone. And as my older, wiser church friend had foreseen a few months before, I began to deeply question the reality and existence of God.[7]

Where is God in a world where children are hit by stray bullets, by terminal diseases, and by drivers speeding through red lights? Every week, 200,000 infants die of malnutrition and disease. Millions of children are trafficked into forced labour, sexual servitude, and soldiering; their innocence is quickly and brutally lost. Twenty million of the world's poorest children are threatened by skyrocketing food prices and a "silent tsunami" of world hunger. As one student asked me years ago, "Is all the bliss of heaven worth one dead child?"

Especially at 3 AM, so much in the world seems to discredit the existence of a loving, personal Creator who intercedes for his creation. The holocausts of the twentieth century alone (in Germany, Soviet Russia, Cambodia, Turkey, and Tibet), to say nothing of the killing fields in Dafur, Rwanda, and Sudan, lend credence to the claim for a Godless universe.

Why didn't God intervene in the madness of Auschwitz or the murderous reign of the Khmer Rouge? Where was he when so many millions of Native Americans perished from a wide array of diseases brought to them by the influx of European explorers and settlers? What "heavenly father" could stand by and watch his children be annihilated since Genesis, and in the most agonizing and heinous of ways? How could all the horrific pain in the world be part of "God's plan"?

There were times in the early morning when nothing felt particularly holy. The universe came down to being a senseless meat grinder. A mindless entropy seemed to prevail, as marked by the world's steady stream of suffering, to say nothing of the inevitable dissolution of the cosmos. Chance alone appeared to be at the heart of all; everything indicated that the constant flux of fortune and misfortune operated randomly.

As winter approached, my spiritual dryness and inner aridity intensified, leading to an inner erosion of the soul. Nothing seemed to make lasting sense. Even my inborn ability to think and express myself fluidly (let alone creatively) felt uprooted. Though I tried to sleep off this psychic paralysis, I would inevitably wake to a grim and desperate meaninglessness that left me wholly desolate, dispossessed.

When I got up one morning in late December, an overwhelming wave of emptiness crashed through me. I felt cut off from God, reality, my very sense of self. Everything was deconstructing, breaking down to zero. My heart felt like it had fallen, shattered, and what remained of my disembodied consciousness was blown across burning sands. Whatever was left of my identity was being squeezed into a pinhole of light, a sky-blown ember fading fast.

Through my tears I looked out the window and saw dawn breaking by the coast. Desperate to drive anywhere, I headed for the marine sanctuary of Fort Funston.

It was a cold, blustery morning. The light streamed through the fast-moving clouds. I pulled into the empty parking lot and walked onto a wide deck overlooking the Pacific.

As I stared out to sea, buffeted by the pounding winter gusts, a hawk suddenly appeared overhead, its powerful wings outstretched. Motionless, the great bird rode the wind, and, like me, looked over the waters. Descending, it moved closer, about fifteen feet away, and hovered there in a keen and perfect silence.

Framed by the rising sun, the hawk's sudden appearance arrested my pain; its poised, majestic grace had abruptly cast me into a sacral state of wonder. The bird's balance and serenity—deftly maintained despite constant turbulence—sent incremental waves of peace through my soul, soothing and vivifying. Deep in my heart, I felt that the winged intercessor was showing me how my "night" might gradually be transformed into "light."

Simply by demonstrating how the stormy, adverse conditions of the physical world can be met with tranquillity and equilibrium, a hovering hawk—of all things in creation—had begun to lift me, ever so slowly, out of my inner hell.

I came to realize that no matter how violent the shudderings of a passing, fragile cosmos, human suffering can be met with a *transcendent love,* a love that rises above the pain, hate, and brutality of the world and ultimately abandons itself to the infinite *agape* that birthed the universe. Just as a bird trusts in the wind that bears it across the sky, so true lovers of God wholeheartedly embrace a higher love that carries its own through the darkness.

Such a "higher love" not only has the power to endure and heal, but to transform. Almighty love "bears all things, believes all things, hopes all things, endures all things" (1 Cor 13.7). This divine love rides out the storm of pride, faithlessness, inner doubt, anger, confusion, despair, even death, knowing that after a great darkness comes light. Love's ultimate aim is holy, all-renewing, exceeding any immediate pain: *the reconciliation of the universe in God.*

Traces of this transcendent love may still be found in creation. However defiled and wounded the world has become through collective sin, there remain vestiges of a firstborn Light, the explosion of love that was Genesis. These pure bright shards of divine agapaic energy, as manifested in the quiet grace of a hawk in mid-flight (or in an intercessory act of loving kindness), can give us the hope and strength to go on. They help to remind us of the world's holy and compassionate origins, how a supernatural power fashioned the universe in beauty, even entering into it, that we might be rescued from death, and return to the paradise that was Eden.

Like the sporadic sunrays now breaking through the overcast sky and glimmering on the water's surface, a tremulous smile broke across my face. All at once I knew that I was not alone, however dark the universe. An unmistakable *sympathia* (a deep and abiding inter-relationship) coursed throughout nature and ultimately pointed to its Maker, lest humanity forget its divine beginnings. The void was not empty; at the fundamental core of life, beyond all pain and suffering, all inner emptiness and sorrow, there was a merciful God who promised us *"life in abundance"* (Jn 10.10).

Abundant life is the only logical endpoint of a shared Mystery born of love. And because this Mystery intimately involves the entire cosmos (including the supernatural realm), great patience and trust is required before the present darkness becomes light, that the salvific works of Christ may be made manifest in all (Jn 9.3). As St. Paul said, "Here we can only see in a mirror dimly" (1 Cor 13.12). Here we wait for the living God in whom we shall one day be transfigured.

Rising, I spread my arms like wings and lifted my voice to Christ, thanking him for sending me one of his beloved creatures as a sign of hope, a restorative spirit-blessing meant to help me ride out my inner storm. With renewed faith, I quietly praised the Lord.

When the dark night comes, we do not resist it, however long and desperate its course, but like the sky-born hawk we spread our wings—that is, *open our hearts*—and ride whatever comes our way, for we dwell on a higher plane; we soar on the spirit-currents of love. We trust in the almighty God who ascended from the greatest darkness and gave life to those in the tombs, that with him, the dead might also rise, and wing their way back home.

> Prayer and love are learned in the hour
> when prayer has become impossible,
> and hearts have turned to stone.

Thomas Merton

> And they found the stone
> rolled away from the tomb.

Luke 24:2

Bird flies over Ocean Beach, San Francisco.

Christopher John Rozales, 2010

Night Becomes Light

In making greater sense of my "dark night" experience, I saw that my inner ordeal had not only tested my faith, but ultimately led to a *necessary deconstruction,* a refining rite of passage. At some point in the spiritual journey, believers endure this purgation, that they might renew their relationship with Christ. "The acceptable sacrifice," as Psalm 51.17 makes clear, "is a broken spirit, a broken and contrite heart."[8]

This "inner death" is essentially a dissolution of the ego. The distraught soul, beset with feelings of divine abandonment, wrestles with (and reflects on) the insufficiency of the temporal self. In this intense isolation, great doubts are experienced about heaven, earth, and the very essence of reality. Everything familiar dissolves; the inner pilgrim is stripped, like Adam cast out of Eden. A great despair ensues.

And yet this painful desolation is meant to serve as a means of purification. Purged of illusory needs and self-centred desires, the refined soul at last understands that all things depend on the love, mercy, and grace of God. As Søren Kirkegaard expressed in *The Sickness Unto Death,* "Despair to the full, so that the life of the spirit can break through; despair so that transformation can occur, that the eternal in the self may emerge .... Never forget that despair contains the seeds of salvation."[9]

Brokenness is the reality of life—sin has fragmented the cosmos. Thus in those desperate times when we feel the pain of the world and lament our alienation from the divine, we may come to sense the movement of something greater within. God begins to stir in the heart. The all-merciful love of Christ quickens and at long last breaks through, the sole power able to transfigure both a broken heart and a shattered universe.

Without Christ, the dark night has no meaning or definitive end. The Saviour takes on the pain of humanity and transforms it through conquering sin and death. Having suffered and died so that an alienated world might be reconciled to God, Christ is the sure means through which the "inner death" can lead to life and salvation. This is when human suffering is engrafted into Jesus' own salvific journey from darkness to light, and all pain and affliction becomes *sacramental*.

Moreover, when we suffer in Christ, our trials tie into the tribulation endured by the entire cosmos. The universe "groans" for his return, that all things may be liberated from the bonds of their transience. Even the very stones long to be renewed, transfigured: *"The whole creation groans and labours with birth pangs until now"* (Rom 8.21-22, Ps 96.11-13). In Jesus, an intimate, abiding solidarity may be felt with all of struggling creation.

Christ remains the irreducible centre, the unshakable foundation, the Rock of Faith on which life depends, in times of both darkness and light. Especially in an imperfect realm, Christ is the template of perfection, the model par excellence "before whom every knee should bow, in heaven, on earth, and under the earth" (2 Phil 2.9-10). As Pascal, the French physicist and philosopher, expressed, "Apart from Christ, we cannot know the meaning of our life or our death, of God, or of ourselves."[10]

Inevitably, the experience of the "dark night" leads to the recurring question *Why does suffering exist in the first place?*

Life is hard because sin (and the resultant Fall) have made this a temporary, perishing world.[11] We were created to inherit eternity, and yet we find ourselves caught up in a highly vulnerable, decaying dimension that strains for its liberation and rebirth. In such a precarious "limbo-realm" wherein fallen angels (Eph 6.10) and hostile forces rage, no holds are barred—tragedy can strike at any time. And because our position in this unstable existence continues to be perilous, God himself, in the person of Christ, urges us to "cast our anxieties" on him. The Redeemer cares for us; he *suffers with us* as the darkness of this passing age steadily transforms into light (1 Pet 5.7, Heb 4.15-16).[12]

All of creation is endeavouring to make it through the "cosmic dark night"—in essence, life itself. Suffering remains a universal phenomenon, an unavoidable mystery experienced through personal and communal trial. If the magnitude of the Fall (and the resultant sacrifice of the Son) are to be at all comprehended by humanity, then a deep experiential grasp of suffering would appear a necessary prerequisite to paradise. The "groaning of the universe" must enter the human heart, and shudder through it, before heaven opens.

> Beloved, do not be surprised at the fiery ordeal which comes upon you to prove you, as though something strange were happening to you … the same experience of suffering is required of all your brotherhood throughout the world … But rejoice in so far as you share Christ's sufferings, that you may also rejoice and be glad when his glory is revealed. (1 Pet 4.12, 5.9)[13]

This fervent disclosure indicates that human suffering will continue until Christ returns. Yet we cannot lose hope, because "to lose hope," according to the Eastern Orthodox *Philokalia,* "is more serious than to sin."[14] Rather than fall into despair, we must trust Christ, who counselled, "*Pray, and do not lose heart*" (Lk 18.1-8); "*I have conquered the world*" (Jn 16.33); "*I am with you always, even unto the end of the age*" (Mt 28.20).

St. Paul assures us that "no amount of suffering can separate our souls from the love of Christ" (Rom 8.38). Indeed, it is through the invincible *agape* of Jesus that we continue to endure our struggles, persevering nobly. All our pain will be eclipsed when the Saviour is ultimately revealed and his love is made wholly manifest. Then all prisoners, held captive by sin, decay, death, and the Adversary himself, "shall be brought forth from the dungeon, and set free" (Ps 102.20, Is 61.1).

For having been created in God's holy image, we bear the royal crest of the Trinity, the inner seal of love. We are the sons and daughters of a compassionate, all-merciful King.

In this King we have our inmost identity and hope. He carried the cross for all peoples everywhere. He gave his life for the ransom of many (Mt 20.28). Through the price of his own blood, he set humanity free.

Heaven and earth glorify him. Time and history point to him. All our strengths praise him; all our weaknesses are cries for him to "come soon" (Rev 22.20).

He is both Counsellor and God. He is the One who stirs human hearts and tests them, that they might grow purer, stronger, and open in authentic love.

And even if hearts should fail, he still keeps on loving creation, as only a loving God can do. He is the Alpha and the Omega, the First and the Last, "the Light that shines in the darkness, and whom the darkness has not overcome" (Jn 1.5).

Everything comes down to *waiting for God*. If embraced with patience and love, this "waiting" takes on a highly sacramental and creative dynamic. Greeting each day with an open heart, helping one's neighbour, crafting art, cultivating peace, planting trees, sending out prayers and joy—all these are means by which the waiting process may be fruitfully shared by pilgrims everywhere.

Indeed, as we mature in Christ, praying ourselves into his almighty love, we eventually see how the rhythm and spirit of our communal waiting helps to nurture and sustain creation.

We bless the world by waiting. Like stars emerging in the night sky, our faith-wrought blessings bring more light into the universe, helping everything find its way home.

> The whole world is waiting on God, praising him in the morning, keeping the faith through the night. Maybe every created thing is asking the same question—"*Why?*" I think we'll one day find out, all in his good time. But for now, let's not forget that it's love that keeps on holding everything together, even when things seem dark. Heaven still keeps on loving us in an abiding, always encouraging way. We just have to listen and be patient. We just have to keep on loving and hoping and praying and wait for his answer. Some day, everything will be heard right.
>
> Robert Lax[15]

Chapel

Seaside chapel near the port town of Skala, Patmos.

On a very warm Patmian night, Galatea, Vito and I had been discussing everything from Zen koans to Kandinsky. At half past eleven, we decided to take a leisurely walk through Skala, the main port town. We were navigating the narrow back streets, when Pantelis, an old friend of Robert Lax, happened to cross our path.

"Yassahs!" (Health be with you all!) he exclaimed. "Where are you going?"

"Phami peripato," replied Galatea, a Greek-American singer and dancer who visited Patmos often. "We're taking a stroll."

"Poli kalah!" (Very good!), he said heartily. Our conversation shifted from the benefits of exercise to the Aegean heat to the effects of tourism on the island. Then he leaned forward and in a quieter tone asked us if we would like to visit a charming little chapel in Skala, partly recessed, and half-hidden by a large pine tree. Having just come from there, he said that it would be an ideal place to find both peace and coolness, especially tonight.

Galatea's eyes lit up. "I think I know the chapel you're talking about. I've gone by it quite a lot of times, but never stepped inside."

Vito (my Italian friend) and I looked at each other and nodded.

"Sounds like a plan," I said. "Let's go!"

"Si, Andiamo!" Vito echoed.

Pantelis waved us on, saying, "You won't need a key. It's always open, like a lot of the chapels here are. *Kalinikta!"* (Goodnight!)

As we headed for our destination, I reflected on how many small, privately built chapels had been erected on Patmos. Most often they were commissioned by islanders who wished to thank a saint for his or her intercessions in effecting a miracle. The mountaintop village of Hora alone had over thirty such chapels, some dating back to the 1700s.

Amazingly, many of these holy sites continue to remain open to the public, despite a rise in icon thefts. Prayer remains a vital part of the islanders' everyday life; these tiny, whitewashed sanctuaries serve as simple and immediate places of retreat wherein anyone can light a candle and commune with God. A holy space consecrated for prayer is always available, at any hour of the day or night, for the passing pilgrim.

The number of tourists dwindled as we neared the chapel. It was situated beyond the harbour, well inland, on a less travelled sidestreet; next to it stood a bountiful pine tree, as Pantelis had said. To enter the recessed building, we descended a series of concrete steps, which gave us the feeling that we were going underground.

Perhaps it was wishful thinking, but we had already begun to feel a refreshing coolness as we popped open the old door latch and went inside. There was a cavernous feel to the place, a windowless structure large enough to hold ten people.

It was dark, and our voices echoed. The interior was lit only by an amber-coloured lantern and a few candles standing in a raised metal sandbox. Toward the front was a wooden iconostasis screen on which were portraits of Christ, Mary, and various saints; their images were adorned with wildflowers. Behind a thin embroidered veil, an altar was dimly visible, from which wafted a faint smell of incense.

There was a solemn, intense feel to the place, a profound quiet. The only audible sounds were our footsteps and the long, thin, sputtering candles. In their constant crackling, they seemed to be sending out prayers to the universe.

Our shadows darted about as we looked at the various icons. After a few minutes, Vito stepped to the rear of the chapel, where he sat on a bench and bent his head in prayer. Then Galatea, deeply moved by all that she had seen, began to sing (in Greek) an exquisite hymn from the liturgy of St. John Chrysostom: *Holy God, Holy Mighty, Holy Immortal, Have Mercy On Us.*

The walls reverberated with the sound. Her contralto voice—deep, dark, mournful, yet simultaneously blissful, even angelic—enhanced the mystery of the sanctuary. The haunting, ethereal notes, first descending and then ascending, took us to that sublime place that transcended time and space, leaving our spirits shuddering in an ecstasy that only the purest art could effect.

After the last long echo had receded and faded, Galatea repeated the ancient hymn, and asked me to participate in a lower register. So together we sang the *Ahgios O Theos* slowly, pausing to emphasize each line, every word, building to a crescendo, then dimming our voices until the music dissolved into the flickering radiance of candle flame.

Vito stood up and clapped his hands. *"Bravo, bravissimo!"* he said, cheering. "Again!"

Once more we sang the hymn. This time Vito opened the door, and within minutes a small group of people, mostly natives, peered in from above the entryway steps, their faces beaming. They, too, clapped after we had sung a few more rounds, some even throwing down flowers that grew around the chapel. Apparently, our midnight recital was a hit.

One islander, an old man with a dazed and almost troubled look on his face, came down the steps. "Please," he said. "Please, let me hear it again."

I motioned to Galatea, signifying that the stage was hers, then sat at the back of the chapel with Vito. As she sang, I saw the old man grow increasingly calm. He seemed lost in a rhapsodic sleep.

When the hymn concluded, he repeatedly said, *"Emorfo, tossoh emorfo"* (Beautiful, so beautiful). He chose his words haltingly, as if emerging from a dream; then he continued.

"I used to come here with my mother, to pray. She died early in life, so it's a very special place for me."

He paused for a moment to wipe away a tear. "Tonight I was deeply distressed, wondering where the years have gone. I was thinking about my mother, and then, when I was passing by, I heard the music. Everything came back—memories of her, of my friends, of everything. It was like I became young again, and everyone I ever knew was with me again, here in church."

Galatea embraced the old man. "I am happy we have made you happy," she said. And she, too, began to cry a little.

After lighting candles and saying a communal prayer, we went outside. It was almost 2 AM. The old man picked up some of the strewn flowers and headed toward an alley. Galatea returned to her cottage, and Vito to his hotel. Still charged with the beauty of the night's events, I took the longer route back to my guest house.

Clouds passed over a crescent moon. The streets were deserted. A warm Anatolian wind had picked up, coursing through the trees and swirling the road dust. The quiet, stark intensity of the early morning made me feel like I was the last man awake on Patmos.

Certainly all of us had been changed by what had transpired in the chapel. Through a wedding of spirit and art, something bright and very beautiful had been born, and had helped save a soul from darkness, giving it a hint of the impending transfiguration and unification of the cosmos. Dostoyevsky's famous quote, "*Beauty will save the world*," echoed in my mind.

This imminent salvation will not be accomplished by a temporal beauty, but by the heavenly Beauty that all earthly beauty participates in (and ultimately points to), which is ever in trinity with Goodness and Truth.

It was this very trifold Beauty that had touched Galatea and prompted her to sing; this same Beauty had, in turn, moved Vito, me, the Patmian audience, and especially the old islander, rescuing him from his despair; and it is this identical Beauty that calls us to hearken to its inner song, music playing since the world was made, that we might enter the chapel of the heart. Once within, we cannot help but also sing, and bring others out of the darkness.

Lumen Christi

While showing a video to my evening class, I noticed that one student's head, directly opposite me, was outlined with an intense glow. For a moment I was startled, but then discovered the source of the radiance. Behind the student rose a tier of windows; through them I could make out a newly installed security light shining in the distance, its steady beam pointed in our direction. Her upper body had blocked its rays, in turn giving her head a halo-like luminescence.

Though I tried to focus on the video, I kept glancing at the student framed by light. There was something intriguing, if not captivating, about her "aura," so enhanced in the dim room. Her white-gold radiance reminded me of the brightly haloed Christ and Apostles in Tintoretto's *Last Supper.*

Yet at the same time, the obscure darkness enveloping her face drew me in as well. It was somehow familiar, despite its austere severity. I had recently seen a similar darkness, even bordered by light, but where?

Then it came to me that a few days before, while running beneath a seaside cliff near Fort Funston, I had witnessed a magnificent sunrise. The face of the pre-dawn bluff was dark and ominous (like the student's visage), but as the sun rose, a stirring brightness began to radiate just above the dim summit (highly suggestive of the light "emanating" from the head of the pupil).

I recalled that the sun's rays slowly spilled down the mountain's face, onto the dunes, then out across the waves. The sky became a brilliant, deep blue. A gradual and intensifying warmth spread over the beach, coursing through me as well. Morning had broken—the daylight had eclipsed the darkness.

As I continued to look at my "haloed" student, I suddenly understood why the lamplight shimmering around her had so riveted me. I kept gazing at her "aura" because subconsciously I was waiting for her shadowy, indistinguishable features to gradually brighten and take shape in the light, much like the seaside cliff, illumined when touched by the dawn. Deep within the imagination of my soul, I expected her ring of radiance to wholly fulminate and extend its rays everywhere.

Later that night, while driving home, the image of the haloed student kept coming back to me. I sensed that the inner (or spiritual) meaning of what I had seen was near, coming to fruition, like the warmth building in my heart. And then I realized that halos, while representing individual sanctity, ultimately point to the glory of the Eighth Day, the *Unending Day of Light* when all things will at last be completely illuminated and reborn, entirely transfigured in God.[16]

Halos anticipate the hour when everything existing will become open and irradiant, rebaptized, supercharged, permeated and suffused with the glory of eternity.[17] All illumined beings will rise, converge in a kind of "high noon" in Christ, the Bright Lord of Creation. Together God and humanity shall fire a New Age, a hallowed, resplendent dimension of integral consciousness and transcendent being. As St. Augustine expressed in *City of God,* "There, in the kingdom, we shall find peace. We shall rest and see, see and love, love and praise."[18]

Our souls, whether we know it or not, long for that Day—we are hardwired for transfiguration. Deep within, our hearts sense that everything in this world is incomplete because there is no lasting joy save in God, in whom abundant life awaits. Our subliminal understanding of this concept explains why "dark into light" images (such as sunrises, candles making bright the night, and irradiant halos), both fascinate and intensely move us; they stir the deepest core of our being. We are reminded of the Eden to come, and we quicken to that imminent glory.

A powerful foretaste of this divine moment, when "all shall be changed in the twinkling of an eye" (1 Cor 15.51), may be experienced at the start of the Eastern Orthodox Resurrection Service.

Shortly before midnight, all the lights in the church, including candles, are extinguished, save for the vigil lamp on the altar. Everyone is in the darkness of the tomb. And yet it is not a darkness to be feared, only endured for a little while longer.

Christ has already gone down into the pit of hell and destroyed the Enemy. He stands at the Gates. God has detonated the void of death by filling it with light and life. The stone is about to roll away.

Instead of fear, there is awe, and joyful expectation. The faithful trust in "the Spirit moving over the face of the waters" (Gen 1.2), waters ready to part, that the sons and daughters of God might pass through the restless chasm of this age and enter the "Promised Land."

There is a flicker behind the altar. The priest has lit the Paschal candle, its wick ignited by the vigil light. The doors of the iconostasis are opened.

The pastor steps forward with the light of the resurrection raised high, chanting, *"Come, receive the light from the everlasting light, and glorify Christ who is risen from the dead!"*

Altar servers light their candles from the Paschal flame, then quickly move through the church to spread the holy fire, lighting the candles held by the congregation. As the radiance of the resurrection is disseminated, the church takes on the colour of a sunrise, of a halo extending its glory into the New World.

"Christos Anesti!" (Christ Is Risen!) cries the celebrant, his bright Paschal flame thrust to heaven.

"Alithos Anesti!" (Truly He Has Risen!) answers the congregation, their raised and radiant candles darting to and fro like a dancing sea of fire.

It is a New Genesis. Night has given way to Light. The Eighth Day dawns.

> Then I saw a new heaven, and a new earth; for the first heaven and the first earth had passed away, and the sea was no more. And I saw the holy city, the new Jerusalem, coming down out of heaven from God, having the glory of God, its radiance like a most rare jewel, like a jasper, clear as crystal ... There night shall be no more. And the servants of God will need no light of lamp or sun, for the Most High will be their light, and they shall reign for ever and ever. (Revelation 21, 22)

Christopher John Rozales, 2010

The "Royal Doors" of Holy Trinity Greek Orthodox Church, San Francisco. These magnificently wrought altar gates, fashioned in the form of peacocks (an early Christian symbol of resurrection), lead into the Holy of Holies.

Sand Dollars

It had been an unusually humid, muggy day, strange for early spring. My friend Jackie and I had arranged to take a late afternoon walk near Ocean Beach. When we reached a bluff that overlooked the coast, we were surprised to see fog hugging the shoreline below. A rare inversion layer had nestled itself along the sea cliffs, obscuring the beach; yet above the thick blanket of mist, where we were standing, there was sun and unlimited blue sky.

The low-lying fog was marvellously translucent; light flooded it, turning the vaporous clouds a faint purple-blue.

"That's where I want to go," said Jackie. "That's where the sand dollars are."

A bit of backstory: Jackie, a classical pianist and Benedictine oblate, was soon to leave for central East Africa on a faith trek.[19] She had met with me to find sand dollars, potential gifts for Camaldolese sisters in Karatu, Tanzania. Though I tried to impress upon her how rare it would be to find whole, unbroken sand dollars during this time of year (owing to the higher tides and pounding waves, which usually shattered everything except incoming stones), she insisted that we give it a go.

A steep stairway, made of logs fastened with steel cables, led down to the shore. It was an eerie descent. We had left the warm light and entered into a thick, wet mist that would momentarily part, then quickly close again. The sound of the breakers grew louder, though for the most part, we could not see them. We felt like we were entering a mysterious otherworld.

As we walked along the shoreline, I could tell that the coastal conditions were far too rough for finding much of anything, let alone intact sand dollars. It was high tide, and a strong westerly wind was driving the waves higher up the shore. The dense fog didn't help matters; a "wide angle scan" of the beach was impossible.

"Are you sure you want to go through with this?" I asked, trying to make myself heard above the wind.

She nodded vigorously, once more saying in an almost childlike way, "I want to go where the sand dollars are."

So we walked on, carefully searching the shore one step at a time— she nearer the water, and I, a few yards higher up.

We had been heading down the coast for about forty-five minutes and found nothing save shell shards, pieces of timber, stones, and bits of coloured glass. Remnants of sand dollars had washed ashore, but alas, no prize. When I asked her again about going back, once more stressing how the conditions weren't favourable for sand dollar success, she calmly replied, without a hint of irritation, "I think you should pray that we find sand dollars—good, whole sand dollars."

I broke into a wide grin.

"Why are you laughing?" she asked. "Isn't that a good prayer?'

"Of course it is," I said quickly, trying not to appear the spoilsport. "I mean, over the years, I've found some pretty neat stuff on the beach myself. But as far as your specific petition, well, I'm thinking that God and his angels might possibly, just possibly, have higher priorities."

Jackie shook her head. "Jesus said that whatever we ask of him, he'll do it, that the Son may be glorified in the Father."[20]

"Yes," I said, "but do you think he was thinking of people trying to find sand dollars when he said that?"

She laughed. "Jesus told us that whatever you ask in prayer, you will receive, if you have faith.[21] That's all I know."

Seeing that she was insistent, I began to silently pray the Jesus Prayer, saying it repeatedly within my heart, but with a different ending, to suit the needs of the hour: *"Jesus Christ, Son of God, Have Mercy Upon Us, Who Seek Sand Dollars ...."* I figured that even if we didn't find any sand dollars, the prayer would at least help to exonerate me from daring to think that God cared little about a woman's plea to find a marvel of his creation, especially since her intent was to gift it to others.

We continued on down the coast for ten minutes, then twenty. It was getting darker, and the wind had picked up. When we had walked for well over an hour in one direction, I was surprised to hear Jackie say, "OK, we've gone on long enough; we can go back now." An entire beach had netted zero, even with the added prayers.

The return was quiet, save for the rising wind and waves. Nothing was turning up except our footprints from the hour before. I was thankful, though, that the fog had begun to lift, allowing for less of a gloomy feeling, and, of course, greater visibility.

Then, like a sudden lightning flash, we both spotted a piece of drift-wood, half-coated in charcoal, a few yards away. On it, arranged in an almost cross-like pattern, were four smooth, round, perfectly proportioned and intact sand dollars, each bearing a very clear star-flower design on its clean white surface!

We looked at each other in total disbelief. It was like someone had placed the sand dollars on the wood to purposely set them off, that we might see them. And their arrangement even hearkened to Jesus! A little bit of heaven had rayed into our world, much like the sunlight breaking through the fog.

Over dinner at a nearby restaurant, most of our discussion focused on the "miracle find," on chancing upon the holy in the ordinary. Anybody listening to us would have thought we had found buried treasure, when all the while we were raving about discovering four simple sand dollars, a find that had cost us nothing, except the price-less value of faith.

A lot of our talk, in fact, centred on "keeping the faith" and the "pow-er of prayer." As Jackie had emphasized, all prayers, if said reverently, have a way of being answered, all in God's good time. Christ longs to have a personal relationship with each of us; our responsibility in making this happen is simply to remain open to his faithful, loving presence, and to return that love and faith as best we can.

Often when we read the Gospels, we forget that when Christ is speak-ing to various individuals or a large assembly, he is also speaking directly to us. All the narratives and wisdom lessons in the Bible are part of our own story, full of personal meaning and revelation, and are meant to be read in this fashion. Thus, when Jesus tells his disci-ples, *"Whatever things you ask for when you pray, believe that you will receive them, and you will have them"* (Mk 11.24), he is also speaking directly to us. And if such a saying may hold true for finding intact sand dollars, then how much more valuable might such a teaching be for those praying for their salvation, and that of the world?

After returning home that night, I happened to be looking through some old correspondence from Robert Lax. A handwritten poem of his, crafted in his simple, pure, minimalist style, caught my eye:

    an
    gels
    in
    hea
    ven
    lis
    ten.

Sand dollars. Ocean Beach, San Francisco.

Christopher John Rozales, 2010

Cutting Board

Sometimes we overlook things directly in our midst—even those that we handle most. A simple cutting board is an example. While my reappreciation of this utensil was valuable in itself, greater insights, having to do with the "poet of Patmos," came to me as I washed the surface of the board after dinner one night. So often items that we come to take for granted can, when rediscovered, infuse the memory and awaken perception; they may even serve as touchstones to a higher reality.

As I ran the sponge over the rich wood patterns and scrubbed at the cuts and fissures, it was not hard to see how every mark and slight discoloration could tell a story. Years of food preparation had been impressed into that smooth, solid piece of maple. There was a distinct earthy feel to its multigrained surface; it was perhaps the most rustic and natural article in the house.

Setting the wet wooden slab on its side to dry, I suddenly remembered that a small cutting board in my mentor's hermitage had also featured prominently. On occasion I'd walk into Lax's house and find him chopping carrots or some other vegetable on its well-used, indented surface (he was, for all intents and purposes, a vegetarian).

I, too, would pare foods on his cutting board, particularly fish to feed his outdoor cats. The heavy knife made a solid, definitive sound as it repeatedly struck the old wooden board.

Sometimes Lax stood by the kitchen door and, with a beaming smile, watched me cut the fish. He seemed to take a special delight in the sounds of things, most suitable for a poet-mystic who every so often would tell me, "There's lots of listening to do in the world."

"How best to listen?" I'd ask him.

"Cut off excess," he would answer. "Unclutter your life. The clearer you are, the freer you are."

"To do what?" I'd query.

"To get to the Source," he'd reply, still smiling.

The cutting board, then, had allegorical and metaphysical overtones. It not only hinted of Lax's grassroots lifestyle, but also typified his ascetic writing style. Stripped down and minimalist in form, his poems became increasingly reductionist, more refined, until they seemed to disappear into an apophatic nothingness that suggested the invisible presence of God.

The old poet said less so that the Creator could say more. He understood how language can only suggest; it cannot capture and contain. Words functioned as evocative channels for Lax, not endpoints. They best served as "portals of the Spirit," finely crafted blessings through which to glimpse the ineffable energy of God, a radiance that all too quickly fades, receding into Mystery.

When visiting Lax, sometimes I found him propped up in bed with what looked like a cutting board, but the thin grainy slab turned out to be a simple, flat piece of wood he could comfortably write on. And yet, the two were much the same. As he did when chopping vegetables, Lax was cutting down his verse to its barest minimum, concentrating on "organic simplicity" and "basic forms."

Perhaps what was most interesting about the hand-held flat board was the sage's use of it to draw circles. Whether on his bed or sometimes outdoors, by the water, Lax would position a page on the semi-stained, well-worn wooden board and, like a Zen master, would fashion an Enso-like circle in one brisk movement, an act he would repeat again and again.[22]

What was the meaning behind Lax's repetitive circles? When I asked him once, he smiled, then wordlessly drew another circle. This made me think of the Buddha, who, before an assembly, quietly held up a single flower, indicative of the brevity of life, and the consequent importance of being gathered in the *now moment* in which everything is contained.

Before drawing his circles, Lax might look around him, as if taking in all of creation, then make his single circular stroke. Perhaps he was suggesting that all things are essentially One. In order to best realize this foundational unity, it was important to participate in the "flow of love," as he would often say (hence the primary symbolism of his circles). For Lax, the popular phrase "Go with the flow" meant to "Go with God," whom the poet conceived of as an all-inclusive and everlasting love-flow. Love constituted the holy and interrelated round of life, a divine ring of *agape*.

Yet Lax's repetitive circles may have meant something more immediately personal, if not urgent: perhaps they hinted of the "full circle" he would make with his own life. Shortly before his passing in

September 2000, he travelled back to Olean, his hometown in New York, and died in the house where he was born. In doing so, Lax had literally made a circuitous passage from birth to death. His life of love had indeed become "a sphere encompassing beginnings and endings, beginning and end."[23] The poem cycle that was his life had traced out "a sphere of love in the void."[24]

Did the poet's fondness for drawing circles then suggest his ultimate return to God? Were they a final minimalist expression pointing to the purity of essentials, the "graced Nothingness," the "invisible Irreducible" (symbolized by the circle's empty interior) on which everything depends? Was he demonstrating how the radical divestment and emptying of the self (becoming "zero," or nothing) actually prepares one to receive the fullness of enlightenment in God? Did his repetitive swirls hint of how the meaning of life will never be fully realized until all of creation completes its circuitous return to the Creator?

Certainly all of the above are likely. But perhaps most powerfully, Lax was indicating how in the course of "riding the Flow," that is, in completing the full round of life in love (as illustrated by the circle's finished line of circumference), *another shape distinctly forms:* a mere "nothing" that had been there all along (represented by the circle's vacuous interior), a type of Cloud or Void given greater definition by the close of one's life, by the sealing of the circle, the return of ending with beginning.

It is this quiet, almost imperceptible "Presence" that Lax's poems, dreams, and wanderings consistently point to—the non-dual agapaic Power in which all opposites are reconciled and unified, and through which all of life incessantly swirls and passes into new form. It is this "unseen" and yet "seen" Mystery through which Lax is still spiralling, infinitely free and at play, as are we all. As he suggested to me in a poem he had enclosed in a letter,

> move freely, dance freely, sing freely;
> then I shall know, and you shall know too,
> that you are free.

Wired to Go Where?

One item regularly comes up at faculty meetings: how to manage the rising use of technology, such as laptops and smartphones, that students are bringing into the classroom. While some of these devices may assist student learning, aiding with their research and enabling pupils to take faster, better-ordered notes, all too often instructors have found that students are using high-tech tools to surf the Internet, blog, or email during class time.

Instructors also find it difficult to lecture while keyboards are incessantly clicking. There is little eye contact. Dialogue is forced. Even well-meaning students who Google the topic at hand (to better understand the material) often end up asking premature, complex questions that throw off the progressive rhythm of the lecture or discussion. Unless everyone is on the same site or webpage, class time cannot proceed uniformly.

Fitting comfortably into one's shirt pocket, a BlackBerry instantly connects the user with everything the world has to offer, be it information, communication, entertainment, travel arrangements, global positioning, banking—the list is endless. With so many options readily (and simultaneously) available, students using their high-tech devices for academic purposes may quickly find themselves sidetracked, clicking on intriguing sites that are unrelated to their work. And even if pupils can successfully multi-task, their attention is not collected and unified, but is diffuse and scattered.

For these reasons, students (even teachers, sadly) now find it increasingly difficult to immerse themselves in a lengthy article or book. Abridged versions of classic works are studied, rather than the works themselves. In-depth reading has been replaced with "skimming" because there is so much information on the Net that a good, long, focused read is nearly impossible. Over time, shallow reading habits make even the idea of deep reading irritating. In essence, our growing dependence on and addiction to technology may be short-changing education and rewiring the human mind.[25]

Since interaction with a computer does not require expertise in speaking or expository writing, it should not be surprising to learn that the rhetorical and composition skills of many students are in dire need of improvement. The Internet—which has become the prime "mentor" for many young people—teaches that facts acquired from a few Google searches, followed by some quick clicks on hyperlinks, neatly pasted together and edited, constitutes the essence of modern learning. Intellectual dialogue that gradually leads to a deeper, integrated understanding of things is, for all practical purposes, outdated, a product of "tech-less times." More than one student has asked me, "If I can get the info on the Net, do I have to come to class?"

One has only to visit the learning centres of colleges and universities (libraries, institutes, study halls) to find how pupils have answered that question for themselves. Ten years ago, these places would have been populated with students (and faculty) engaged in personal and communal research. Now, everything is online; much of education is conducted at home.

This social isolation may be morphing the personalities of Internet users. Alone and in front of a machine most of the day, many students are living in an increasingly self-centred and unreal (or virtual) world. Through the magic of e-books, iPhones, iPods, and iPads, everything can be accessed and actualized with the click of a mouse or a wave of a finger, and with little face-to-face counsel or peer interaction.

Quick, self-serving results are therefore expected in the online universe. "Stat" mode is imperative. If this immediacy is lacking—or, worse yet, if the Net is down—considerable impatience and frustration result.

The societal changes brought on by computer technology and the Internet extend well beyond higher education. One enters a coffee shop and all the tables are occupied by laptop users who have built imaginary walls around themselves. In restaurants, diners compare smartphone features or spend much of their time speaking with callers. When friends gather for a dinner party, the computer entertainment station takes centre stage. Both fascinated and mesmerized by the machine, *we are forgetting to be human.*

While my younger students appear to be happily "wired," eager to invest in the latest techno-gadgets (which may soon be obsolete), older pupils are realizing that a high-tech lifestyle has its limitations, even certain dangers. Inner tranquillity may be addled by online chatting, emailing, and texting, to say nothing of blogging, podcasting, and keeping up with Facebook/Twitter postings.

Many Net users, particularly college students, check their messages around the clock, anxiously hoping for something extraordinary to zap in. Razzle-dazzle advertising catalyzes impulse buying. Constant news reports, sensationalist in nature and updated every ten minutes, eventually leave readers numb to the world, desensitized.

Interestingly, a recent AP-Ipsos poll has found that the level of stress in fast-paced technological societies has been quickly accelerating, caused, in part, by addiction to technology itself.[26] For all the manifold benefits and personal conveniences of the Internet (and related techware), Web users the world over may be becoming increasingly isolated, self-centred, impatient, hurried, and jaded.[27]

But still the power and speed of technology is strong. Hooked to the Net, a Dell Alienware M15x laptop, brilliantly packaged and highly versatile, promises rewards well beyond success in school.

"It's all on the Internet," I recall a freshman saying to a classmate. "Know the Net, and you got it made—for life."

"Cold hard facts," agreed his friend. "Search and download."

For many young people, higher education (if not existence itself) is fast becoming a cyber-cerebral experience. The computer-aided mind is equipped to deftly process massive amounts of data. Scholarship especially centres on digesting gigabytes of information rapidly and regurgitating it on demand.[28]

Somewhere along the way, students (and, in some cases, teachers) forgot that education is about intellectual intercourse—that is, dialogue. In the tradition of Socrates, Confucius, and certainly Jesus, the essence of learning is about *direct human encounter*.

Facts remain "cold hard facts" until they are touched by flesh and blood: that is, pondered in the heart and brought into a circle of discussion. True learning (and teaching) is not about the acquisition and dispensation of data, but centres on *educing* ("bringing out") timeless truths indwelling in the human consciousness. Such an enterprise is not undertaken alone, on a keyboard, in the invisibility of cyberspace, but in the classroom, with fellow students, and in the presence of a supportive instructor who, through years of training and experience, can help guide those on the intellectual journey.

There are no shortcuts here. The trek from thesis to antithesis to synthesis takes time. In the deep realm of the mind, immediate downloads and colourful graphic displays are of little worth; far less valuable are instant answers. What matters are the questions—thinking, pondering, and, to quote the poet Rilke, *"living out the questions."*[29]

In an age when answers are everywhere, easily Googled within seconds, it is the questions that are most important. Only when the great questions of life are deeply discussed and explored do pupils gradually gain a sense of identity. Moreover, a developing sense of interrelationship with community (and cosmos) becomes progressively clearer. Students engaged in open, interactive dialogue come to develop their own unique perspective on things; in doing so, they are better able to make original and meaningful contributions to the world.

Few people know that Robert Lax had a computer in his hermitage, given to him by a friend. He used the Mac Classic in his last years to help organize his writing.

Lax also valued the Internet, comparing it to "a net catching fish." He felt that such an extensive information and messaging system is "knit up into the very framework of the cosmos."[30]

At the same time, however, Lax believed that the computer should be used conservatively. "Like anything else," he advised, "technology must be used wisely, in moderation. It's only when we slow down and relax that we can really understand anything. When we're calm, things sink comfortably in. Living, listening, learning, and loving become easier."[31]

It is this vital calm that technology, in excess, can erode. Too much time spent online, in communion with a machine, can obstruct both intellectual and spiritual development. Without deep peace and the soul-space that intense quiet brings, the inner journey is impossible. Even God spoke to his creation in a "still small voice" (1 Kings 19.12), allowing room for reflection. In holy silence, the mystery of a higher love unfolds.

Lax also understood that real learning involves physical presence. Though he had a telephone at home (usually covered with a blanket to muffle the rare ring), he encouraged me to visit him as often as possible rather than chat long distance. "Come here every time you can!" he would say. "Set a course now for the island!"

The sage knew that in-person sharing means everything. Dialogue "in the flesh" teaches much more than simply words can. This was especially true for Lax, who imparted wisdom through the slightest of sounds and gestures. When he spoke, he orchestrated his expressions according to the changes in the environment around him. One word, said in concert with a vibrant colour created by a sunset, could transcend ordinary speech.[32]

Ultimately, Lax valued the *holiness of presence*, which is impossible to communicate via the Internet. While well-chosen words alone may enlighten, their meaning is, in a sense, incomplete until their source is revealed, made present and manifest. God himself taught not through Scripture alone (as in the days of Moses), but somatically, taking on flesh in the person of the Christ. Therefore, unless we honour both mind and body as we live and learn, we will never enter into our deepest being, *the all-loving heart,* the spiritual-organic unity of what it means to be human. We will never be transfigured.

> The man of the atomic age makes no endeavor to produce a spiritual civilization that would match and govern technical civilization. While perfecting the machine to the utmost, we do nothing to shape the type of man who will put that machine under control and turn it to account. The higher we make our skyscrapers, the shallower we make their foundations. When the spirit is dead, technical progress becomes an instrument of ruin, not of life. Man makes machines he is no longer able to control. And so the machine kills man instead of serving him.[33]

IV. Kingdom of the Heart

For here we have no lasting city,
we seek the city which is to come;
A city which has foundations,
whose builder and maker is God.

Hebrews 11.10, 13.14

Approach to the Monastery of St. John the Theologian, Patmos.

S.T. Georgiou, 1999

Path of the Revelation

Halfway up the mountain leading to the Abbey of St. John is the Holy Cave (and Monastery) of the Apocalypse, where the Evangelist experienced his famous Revelation. An old cobblestone road that leads to the cave is the usual approach taken by pilgrims walking up from the port of Skala.

But as the steep road ascends, a dirt trail veers off from the main route. Hugging the hillside, it narrowly winds through a dense grove of pine and olive trees.

Eventually, the path widens and the ruins of a low-lying wall appear. The shady, secluded area, cooled by an offshore breeze, serves as a natural resting place, especially during the warm summer months. A beautiful view of the main harbour spreads out below.

A monk once told me that this was the "ancient path" leading to the cave, in use since the third or fourth century. Few tourists took this way up the mountain, he revealed. Far better for me, because sometimes I would walk the quiet trail, find a flat, comfortable stone, and pray or meditate.

From such a peaceful, wide-angle vantage point, it is not hard to sense a spiritual inflow-outflow coursing through Patmos. In the distance one can see ferries and cruise ships bringing in pilgrims eager to ascend to the cave and to the Monastery of St. John. After making "contact with the Holy," these travellers later descend and return to their ships; they spread word of their illumination, in turn attracting others.

This cyclic, sacrosanct flow remains constant throughout the year. Each dawn brings new pilgrims to St. John's isle. Here, on this remote sanctuary encircled by sea—a "centre ring" of love, power, and joy—voyagers from afar dance before the Lord, they praise God, then recede into the void of night, strengthened and reborn.

The natives also participate in this sacred round. In the early morning, when the abbey bells ring, they file into churches and chapels, pray a short while, then depart empowered, and attend to the day's work.

The carolling bells, their streaming notes carried by the wind and reverberating into space, peal throughout the day and into the night. By means of the bells the islanders keep track of time, whether they are caring for their goats, working the fields, mending their fishnets, or attending evening vespers. Every hour sings of God and the constancy of his love.

Whenever I looked out over the windy fields from the path of the Revelation, Christ's words came to mind: *"Consider the lilies, how they grow; they neither toil nor spin; yet I tell you, even Solomon in all his glory was not arrayed like one of these ..."* (Mt 6.28-29).

Here, along the "ancient path," everything seemed relaxed, gloriously simple. The Holy Spirit shone through creation precisely because of this simplicity. As C.S. Lewis said, "At these times, patches of Godlight radiate in the woods of our experience."[1]

One late afternoon, in midsummer, I walked up to St. John's cave to light candles for friends who had requested prayers. En route to the grotto, I stopped for a while at the familiar ruined wall along the path of the Revelation.

The green-gold leaves, fired by the falling sun, played against a blue-violet sky. The distant sea was also lightly coated with a purple iridescence. For a fleeting moment, everything on earth mirrored the tranquil beauty of heaven.

Birds sang in the nodding, whispering trees. Already the crickets were faintly chirping. Far off in the distance goat bells tinkled, and a farmer's occasional shouts echoed down the mountain. Somewhere in the back of my mind I kept on hearing St. John's last sermon on Patmos, repeated like a mantra and given when he was close to a hundred years old: *"Just love, just love, just love ...."*[2]

The scent of earth was strong. All day long the sunlight had worked its way deep into the soil, and now, as dusk approached, the fragrance of the land rose like an invisible mist, quickening my senses.

Wildflowers, olives and pine, birds, clouds, the pink-blue sky and lengthening shadows—in my deepening, reverberating bliss I felt an intimate contact with it all, as though all of nature had distilled into a cosmic elixir now coursing through my veins.

I shuddered in the exquisite stillness, the rapturous quiet. Long-forgotten memories, mostly of my first impressions of things (first poem, first prayer, first love), simultaneously rushed through my heart. Some kind of inner door was opening, beyond which infinite wonder and beauty dawned.

Everything felt incredibly new, as when I was a child. Wind on face, bird in flight, cool shade, light falling out of the sky—every event and sensation was an invitation to transcendence. Something Lax had once told me echoed in my soul like drops of falling water: *"Just to be is a blessing; just to live is holy."*

The dust of the road coated my sandals. This, too, felt holy. So did the scattered white-grey stones. Their hard, rough-hewn texture, abrasive to the touch, seemed pure, good, most necessary. The solidity of the rocks anchored my reverie, for I longed to kiss the trees, stretch myself out on the gravel-dirt road and embrace the scented earth, all of it, if I could.

Nature was my home; it was where I belonged. God had put me here to tend it. Adam's duties were mine. I wanted to name things, talk with every living creature, help them grow. This was my firstborn task, my only one, the one that ever really meant anything.

And I wanted to touch God. To take his hand and walk with him, like Adam. I wanted to feel his light, a radiance compassionate and wise, a bright warmth that would whisper to my soul,

> I have always been here,
> and you have always been my child,
> and I have always loved you.[3]

Everything around me, everything that I was experiencing pointed to the Lord, toward his infinite love, through whom life began and in whom all things continue to be sustained. The universe, down to its very atoms, and beyond, was *Soma Christou,* (Body of Christ):

> In him all things were created,
> things visible and invisible.
> All things have been created

> through him and for him.
> He himself is before all things,
> and in him all things hold together.
> He is the image of the invisible God.

(Col 1.15-17)

Creation was therefore God's love made tactile. On this theme, the religious thinker Simone Weil was moved to write:

> The beauty of the world is Christ's tender smile for us coming through matter. He is really present in the universal beauty. The love of this beauty proceeds from God dwelling in our souls and goes out to God present in the universe. It is like a sacrament ....[4]

All at once the thought came to me that nature had been created to prepare humanity for its Maker. Sacred in itself, creation is a kind of supernatural dress, and life is a "dress rehearsal" to meet the Creator and Life-Giver, in whom life (and love) abundantly await.

For while we thrill to sunsets, rainbows, and shooting stars, we still desire something more—we long to see and know the mysterious Source of that beauty, to lift nature's veil and gaze upon the divine core of beauty itself. As St. Augustine said, "Our hearts are restless until they rest in God."[5]

And yet we do not have to be restless, for God has come forth from his creation to meet us, and this through the Incarnation. God became human not so much to rescue us from sin, but that he might love us completely and divinize us in the ecstasy of his *agape*, in the infinite radiance of his all-creative being. For while a father may love his son from afar, how much greater is that joy when father and son embrace![6]

Heaven pulses and glows just beneath the "veil" of holy earth because God's glory yearns to shine in full. Christ, the "Light of the World," has indeed dawned, but when he comes again, our joy will be complete; the Son will have risen to an eternal noonday, and we shall be exceedingly glad in his radiance, wholly illumined by a love everlasting.[7]

Until then, let us wait for God "in the woods," along paths of light and in bright temples. Christ longs to meet us, to come through his creation and transfigure us, that even now we may breathe in the fresh clean air of the resurrection.

In the words of the poet Robinson Jeffers,

> It's time to let the leaves
> rain down from the skies,
> to let the rich life
> run through the roots again.[8]

S.T. Georgiou, 1999

Pathway leading to the Cave of the Revelation, Patmos.

Axis Mundi

When Robert Lax first came to Patmos, he often strolled along the path of the Revelation, eventually living close to the idyllic area for a few years. Sometimes he would continue on up the road to the Cave of the Apocalypse, where he lit candles for friends and fellow islanders.

"The cave has been a magnet for the Patmians since the days of St. John," Lax would tell me. "The site has permeated the whole psychology of the people here. It has made them loving, gentle, wise. I've found that they never say a word that doesn't emanate from a pure trust, a deep spiritual centre of which the cave is a part."[9]

I, too, found that the grotto (and surrounding abbey) exuded a powerful spiritual resonance. On first entering the simple, tree-lined grounds, I passed beneath a mosaic of St. John experiencing his Revelation—the same John, according to Eastern Orthodox tradition, who was the disciple of Jesus ("the beloved disciple" [Jn 20.2]), and later wrote one of the four Gospels.[10]

After moving through a long, descending walkway bordered by white stucco walls, I found myself in a roofed and windowed courtyard adorned with flowering plants. Forty steep and winding steps then led down to a large chapel. Turning to the right, I at last entered the famous cave, the most holy site of Patmos.[11]

According to early Church tradition, the small grotto gave shelter to the elderly St. John, who was banished to the remote isle by the Roman Emperor Domitian in 95 AD (Patmos then served as a penal colony). Here the elderly Apostle received a vision of the last days. The Evangelist, "caught up in the Spirit," was unable to record what he witnessed; instead, he dictated what he saw to Prochorus, his disciple and scribe, who is mentioned in Acts 6.5.[12]

The Cave of the Apocalypse, converted into a tiny chapel about 1000 AD, features a lamp-lit area near an iconostasis, believed to be where St. John slept (and later experienced his Revelation). Next to it is a flat extension of stone where Prochorus penned the vision.

Immediately above this area, the lip of the cave dramatically breaks into three sections. Patmian tradition has it that the rock was split asunder by the voice of the Trinitarian God who spoke to St. John with the force of an earthquake, saying, *"I am the Alpha and the Omega, the Beginning and the End"* (Rev 1.11).

It had taken a while for my eyes to adjust to the dim lighting of the cave. Long, thin beeswax candles illuminated much of the interior. Their darting shadows flickered on the massive, irregular grey walls.

I had taken a seat toward the rear of the cave, positioning myself on a flat portion of rock. Few pilgrims were present, which added to the intensity of the quiet. Though warm outside, it was cool in the grotto, and I meditated on what it might have been like to dwell here in the days of St. John.

Suddenly, a white-bearded monk rounded a corner. He looked very much like the saint himself!

"Nah zeesis!" he exclaimed when he saw me. "May you live!"

His face was full of compassion and deep warmth. He had empathetic, almost laughing eyes. I did not know it then, but I was standing before the "Keeper of the Cave," a soft-spoken elder who had watched over the grotto for over twenty years. His quiet, calming presence reminded me of a famous quote attributed to the Russian Orthodox hermit Seraphim of Sarov: "Acquire the Spirit of Peace, and thousands around you will be saved."[13]

After giving me a brief tour of the cave, he encouraged me to return whenever I should feel the need. He said that the *spylia* (cave) was the perfect place to pray and reflect on higher things, as exemplified by the thousands of pious travellers who journey to the grotto annually.

In visiting the holy site over the years, I have found that the cave is not only uplifting in itself, but also points to another cave, an inner cave that every Christian is called to enter—the *cave of the heart.*

Caves, in general, have long been thought of as sacred places. Many early people considered them to be axial points linking earth and sky, mystical junctions embedded into mountains that connected the terrestrial and celestial worlds. Caves were also seen as gateways that led to the underworld or to the next life, or both.

As such, caves were considered places of transformation, rebirth. Early religions thus made regular use of underground grottos in their initiation rituals. The darkness of the void-like and damp interior symbolized the womb, in which the initiate ritually prepared for new life; his egression into the light of day represented a fresh beginning.

Because of its deep-seated association with the Evangelist and Christ himself, the Cave of St. John may also be considered a place meant to foster rebirth, that is, the renewal of the soul. It is a Christocentric "axial point" wherein God and man, heaven and earth, the spiritual and physical keenly intersect. This "interlink," integrating spirit and matter, not only points to Jesus, the God-Man Incarnate, but also brings attention to our own spiritual-somatic makeup. Entrance into the Holy Apostle's cave (and meditation within) moves the pilgrim to look inside himself and find the inner axis point interconnecting body and soul.

If the cave represents a more *macrocosmic* intersection of heaven and earth, then what is the *microcosmic* core (or "inner cave") linking spirit and soma?

This mystic focal point is the human heart—the locus of intuition, insight, even the intellect, according to the Desert Fathers. Herein the dual power of the soul and body may be gathered into a single radiant point (and portal) brimming with infinite potential, an "access gate" through which to make contact with the Divine, so long as the heart remains open. Appropriately, this cardiocentric emphasis may be found in the following greeting read by pilgrims who enter the grotto of the Apocalypse:

> Your coming to this holy place is not a chance event in your life. God, who wishes all people to be saved and to come to a knowledge of the truth, who directs all things for humankind's spiritual benefit, has guided you here to listen deep within yourself, to the secret echo of the words that were spoken to St. John and to the Seven Churches of Asia Minor: "Behold!

> I stand at the door and knock! If any man hears my words and opens the door, I will come to him, and will eat with him, and he with me" (Rev 3.20) ....

> At this moment Christ stands at the door of your soul and knocks on it. *What will you do, searcher?* Will you open your heart to Christ or shall you keep it closed, condemning yourself to fatal isolation?[14]

Especially through his death on the cross, Christ somatically illustrates how the heart is the divine-human axial point, the psychic zone where man meets God. The cross's horizontal line represents what is *terrestrial* (earthly, mortal), whereas its vertical line delineates what is *celestial* (heavenly, eternal). At the place where the horizontal and vertical lines meet, the heart of Christ lines up.

The nucleic heart remains the *locus sancti* integrating body and soul. This mystic life-core spiritualizes the entire person through the almighty power of love. Through this "organ of illumination," humanity is urged to en-God itself in the Saviour.[15]

The heart is the "inner house," the spirit-chamber we are ever called to access, and therein wait on God. As Christ was born humbly, in a cave, so we, in drawing nearer to Jesus, are encouraged to quietly enter our "inner grotto." There, in the poverty of empty stillness (in actuality the bright promise of spiritual fullness), we patiently await rebirth in the Lord.

In loving trust and abandon we silently enter the darkness of our spiritual cave, knowing that in this "nocturnal communion" lives the hidden Christ, whose brilliance is too great for us to see in this present life. Placing our minds in our hearts, we wait in the night for his light to dawn.

Ultimately, there is an inward turning. "Hidden manna" is discovered—contact is made with the inner Christ. We at last realize that all that is required of us is to love God sincerely, devotedly, to respond, as much as we can, to the infinite *agape* he has given us.

Thomas Merton said that when this happens, everything becomes marvellously clear and flowing: "We are transformed into God, one Spirit with Him, so that everything we do, He is doing it, and it is all Love, and we ourselves are Love.[16]

Once this liberating energy is tapped, life is transfigured. There is only God consciously moving through all things, and all things moving through God. Everything becomes art. As Robert Lax said, "We are finally free to make, and rearrange with grace and skill, that which is being made in us."[17] We emerge from a long, patient darkness and enter an infinity of light, what Lax called the "Playground of the Lord."[18]

In *The Count of Monte Cristo*, Edmund Dantes discovers his earthly treasure in a physical cave, only to later realize that wealth supreme is found in the inner recesses of the heart.

In Christ, however, we find eternal riches from the very start. The God of Love is life and joy everlasting.

Galatea Psonis, 1995

The Cave of the Revelation wherein St. John witnessed the Apocalypse. "And I, John was on the island called Patmos on account of the word of God and the testimony of Jesus..." (Rev 1.9).

Fishermen

The fish has been a symbol of the Christian faith since the first century. According to the early Church, just as fish cannot live outside of water, so those who seek salvation cannot live outside the waters of baptism.

Numerous passages in the Gospels have to do with fish and fishing. Christ's Apostles were predominantly fishermen. Jesus preached to them, *"Be fishers of men"* (Mk 1.17).

Since Christianity was a religion persecuted by the Roman Empire until the fourth century, the early Christians recognized one another through the sign of the fish. Jesus was considered the "Great Fish," as symbolized by the famous acrostic ICTHYS, meaning Jesus-Christ-God-Son-Saviour. Those fishermen (searchers) who "caught" Christ would mystically consume everlasting life.

Christ could easily have surrounded himself with ascetics and distinguished men of faith. But instead he chose fishermen, rustic labourers who, as Thomas Merton said, "made themselves conspicuous only by their disregard for the moral gymnastics of the professionally holy."[19]

The disciples of Jesus worked closely with the rhythms of land and sea. Simple, unpretentious, they were the "salt of the earth."

When walking past fishermen along San Francisco's Ocean Beach, I was led to reflect on the grassroots holiness of Christ and his Apostles. This was especially the case when I happened upon anglers reading pocket editions of the Bible or praying with rosaries while they waited for the fish to bite.

Most of these faithful were from the Philippines and Guam. Nearly all were retired. As the years passed, I came to know a half-dozen of them.

Ben, Tomaso, Zoltan, Manuel, Carlos, Mario—they all exuded a basic goodness, a simple, refreshing honesty that is hard to find in a world where people keep to themselves, usually out of fear or self-centredness. Their faith and trust in the Creator reminded me of Lax and friends from Patmos, people like Demetrios, Pantelis, and various monks I had known.

Like my old acquaintances, the fishermen could teach valuable life lessons purely by example. Going about their assorted tasks with skill and grace, they radiated the merits of patience, endurance, and attentiveness. Their happily relaxed, easy natures demonstrated the importance of melding with a greater flow, with the wave rhythms of the sea, and, beyond that, God.

There was a peaceful, loving solidity about the anglers, a righteous joy that shone out of their deeply tanned and lined faces. When I'd approach them they would wave and shout, even from fifty yards away.

Holding a freshly caught perch, Mario might draw near, his free hand raised high.

"How goes it, bro?" he would ask, slapping my palm.

"All good!" I'd reply, returning the high-five greeting. "Saw a guy catch a bass a little while ago—hope you'll reel one in, too!"

Grinning broadly, he would flash a thumbs-up, adding a phrase the fishermen liked to say every now and then: *"It's not the fish—it's the fishing!"*

These simple words aptly summarized why the anglers were out at the coast, year after year. While the fish were good to catch and consume, it was immersion in the wilderness, by the beautiful, far-flung Pacific, that was most important. The fishermen had, in a sense, cast themselves into the bright and teeming depths of God—they had abandoned themselves to the infinite riches of his divine Providence.

Spending time along the shore was thus a tactile, wholesome way of experiencing an organic union with the Lord and honouring his glory. Direct contact with nature meant intimate communion with the Creator.

As I walked the beach and spoke with the anglers, I'd remember how Lax also enjoyed the company of fishermen, whom he called "the people of Christ."[20]

Throughout his travels in Greece, he routinely photographed them. In his journal he writes, "Taking pictures, so many, sometimes of one man, and never of merchants or doctors, but fishermen, fishermen, fishermen, fishermen, fishermen."[21]

Lax's black-and-white photos, taken decades ago, well portray the "people of Christ" immersed in their age-old occupation: baiting hooks, casting their lines out to sea, mending nets, repairing their boats. His photos capture a certain grace; they show fishermen flowing with the rhythm of life and the cosmos.

In spending time at Ocean Beach, I have felt a similar "spirit-flow" among the anglers there, particularly on a boulder-strewn shore a few miles down the coast, beyond the Fort Funston lookout point.

The most striking feature of this idyllic area looms high above—a long, rectangular church built near the edge of a towering peak. A steep semi-paved grade sharply winds down from the edifice along a flower-strewn bluff, ending at the breakers below.

Church atop a cliff, lower Ocean Beach, near Mussel Rock, Daly City.

I first noticed the church when it was being constructed. Looking up at it from the shoreline, I thought a sizeable ranger station was being fashioned. But about a year later, when I saw the large cross set into place on the roof, the building's purpose became clear, as did its spiritual place in the greater flow of things.

My understanding of this blessed flow all came together one late Saturday afternoon. I was walking along the coast and headed toward the boulder-strewn area. From a distance I could see about thirty people of various ages gathered in groups. Some were fishing. Most were sitting in the sand. A few tents had been set up, and a campfire was burning.

As I came closer, some of my fishermen friends waved. It turned out they had brought their families and friends with them.

Mothers were nursing babies or grilling perch. Children were building sandcastles. Laughing teenagers played Frisbee.

The older men, lined up along the shore, casually cast their lines into the sea or calmly reeled in, occasionally flicking their surf rods to avoid a snag. Some grey-haired women—grandmothers, it seemed— were digging for sand crabs and other bait. A few stripers, their scales gleaming in the sunlight, lay strung together, close to shore.

Everything seemed to be exactly where it should be. I felt like I had walked onto a movie set, that sooner or later a director would yell, "Cut and print! It's a take!"

But this was no set; it was life as it was meant to be lived, and more. It was life lived with united flow and direction, a coursing interactive harmony of God, family, nature, all radiant in love.

High above, near the cliffside church, I could see more fishermen and their wives and children descending down this *Monte Cristo* (Mountain of Christ) along the winding dirt road. Other families were going back up. The whole rhythm of descent and ascent reminded me of Jacob's famous dream, in which the Hebrew Patriarch saw angels descending and ascending from heaven to earth (Gen 28.13).

That seemed to be the great key to the whole movement of things, as I had witnessed them: outflow and inflow, emanation and return. Like life issuing from the Christ, so families descended from the distant church, its simple cross clearly visible against a serene blue sky. They came down to fish, eat, play, rejoice, and in all this praise the Lord.

And the Lord surely smiled, and saw that it was good. It was all like Eden, a eucharistic celebration, an unfolding afternoon of thanksgiving and joy, soon to be gathered up once more in God with the setting of the sun and the coming on of night. All things would return to the Christ from which they came, only to reissue again, at dawn.

Once more I turned to the fishermen. Casting out and reeling in, their movements were a microcosm of the seaside spirit-cycle I saw dancing before me.

Like cosmic conductors they let their surf rods fly. All of creation played, one organic orchestra making music with the singing, swirling angels, invisible, yet still visible.

With them, the anglers cast their lines far, "putting out into the deep," much like Jesus and his Apostles. In a figurative sense, their casting out and reeling in hearkened to the "great net" flung into the sea, the dragnet described in the Gospels (Mt 13.47). It was "cast into the depths to gather everything within," that all sons and daughters of the Fisher-King might be drawn unto heaven.

A well-known Greek Orthodox hymn, sung during the Divine Liturgy of St. John Chrysostom, intones:

> Blessed are you, O Christ our God,
> who rendered the Fishermen all-wise
> by sending the Holy Spirit down upon them.
> Into your nets all of creation is gathered.
> Glory to you O Christ, Heart of the Universe.[22]

Lost and Found

After completing a seven-mile run along Ocean Beach, I drove home to get ready for a late-afternoon class. My mother happened to be there. The first thing she asked me was, "Where is your cross?"

Immediately my hands went to my neck. Both cross and chain were missing.

I checked my tank top and windbreaker, hoping that if the chain had broken, the cross had snagged on my running gear.

There was nothing.

I retraced my steps to the car and looked inside.

Nothing.

The Byzantine-style gold cross, flared at the edges and similar to a Canterbury cross, had meant a great deal to me. But not in a superstitious, materialistic, or even sentimental way—much of my spiritual growth and personal faith history, for the past sixteen years, was deeply connected with it.

I had acquired the cross on Patmos, during my first trip there. It had been blessed in the Cave of the Apocalypse and in the Monastery of St. John. The cross had physically touched (and received the blessings of) many holy relics, both on Patmos and in other spiritual locales in Greece and throughout the Mediterranean, thus serving as a "secondary relic" in itself.[23] I had even dreamed about the cross shortly before Robert Lax died.

> Robert appeared to me in a memorable dream. He was about to move to a new home and was giving away his possessions. Eventually he turned to me and asked, "What do you want?" Rather boldly I replied, "Your house." He smiled and said, "You know you can't have that." Then I asked him, "What can I have?" And he bent down and kissed the small gold cross around my neck. In essence, Lax had demonstrated that the greatest gift was already within my possession, this being the Presence and Love of the Almighty—the *treasure within* which does not grow old or fail. It is this interior treasure which lies hidden in our souls, awaiting discovery.[24]

Memories of the cherished and holy keepsake kept running through my mind. It was hard to think I had lost something so connected with my faith. Without hesitation I called the department secretary to cancel class and then drove out to the beach, hoping that I'd find the cross where I had parked or somewhere by the water. All in all, finding the cross would be very much like locating a needle in a haystack.

A half-hour search of the lot yielded nothing. Then I combed the dunes leading to the shoreline. Luckily it was a weekday. Few people were on the beach, perhaps insuring that the cross lay on the sand exactly where it had fallen.

Making my way to the breakers, I continued down the coast, straight to Mussel Rock, the midway point of my earlier run. Sadly, I found nothing.

On the return, I desperately searched the surf itself, thinking that higher waves may have pulled the cross closer (if not into) the sea, but once more, nothing. Tired and empty-handed, I called it a day and drove home with a heavy heart, sorely distressed.

Though I well understood that the cross was a symbol of my faith (not Christ himself), I was upset by the loss for a long time afterward. More than once I searched my car and walked up and down the beach, hoping to find the treasured keepsake.

Friends who had lost their own crosses related how they had found them in the most unexpected of places. A local priest recommended that I pray to St. Phanourios, the Greek Orthodox saint of lost items. A few Catholic friends also lit candles for me in the Shrine of St. Jude at St. Dominic's Church in San Francisco.

Nearly a month had passed, and nothing had turned up. Rather than focus on a miraculous recovery of the cross, I instead began to ponder how its loss was meant to function as some kind of spiritual lesson. As I did so, my sadness gradually eased; moreover, it seemed that I had once more "found" the cross, that is, in an immaterial and transcendent way.

I had lost my cross during Christmas week, a time of gifts and sharing. With the "giving spirit" in mind, I reasoned that Christ had, for reasons unknown to me, dispossessed me of my precious cross, that another individual might receive spiritual benefit in discovering it.

After all, I, too, had once found a cross by the sea, and on the very beach that I had lost my cherished amulet. About five years before, I had been walking along this same shore during Holy Week, thinking about my father's death, when I saw something glisten in the surf.

Reaching into the sand, I fished out a small silver cross with a radiant centre.[25]

The unusual find buoyed my spirits and gave me comfort and inspirational strength. The cross must have been in the sand for years. It was worn away, save for some faint crosses carved on its face, and *Anno Domini* (In the year of our Lord) etched on its back, barely discernible, in Latin.

In a sense, the familiar phrase from Job 1.21, "The Lord giveth, and the Lord taketh away," had immediate personal meaning. God had given me another's cross from the sea, but now my own cross had been lost to the Pacific, meant to one day emerge from the mysterious depths and be found by a lucky (and needy) pilgrim.

A few months after losing my treasured keepsake, I happened to be jogging past the mountaintop church by the sea (described in the previous chapter). As I looked up the cliff I couldn't help but notice the edifice's tall, wide rooftop cross gleaming in the morning sunlight.

Suddenly it dawned on me that a massive cross had stood in the vicinity of every place I had recently frequented. This was clearly demonstrated in the seaside cross at the beach, the huge concrete cross near my campus (atop Mt. Davidson), and the striking neon cross on the heights of Patmos (its blue glow easily visible from Lax's hermitage at night).[26] A bold symbolism that glorified Jesus had remained consistent in my life, manifesting itself in those places that I had spent time in recreation, education, and contemplation.

As indicated by the three outstanding crosses, Christ was everywhere. Despite the fact that I had lost my personal cross, God had never really left me. *How could he?* The Lord was most especially in my heart, imprinted there through baptism, a holy seal that could never be lost or destroyed.

Indeed, as I spread wide my arms in prayer beneath the cross at the coast, my own outstretched body—head to the sky, arms open wide, feet together and rooted to the earth—was taking on the shape of a cross, and one that intersected at my heart, the integral crossroads of my being.

I felt a type of "somatic symbolism" setting in. My head represented my thoughts, my widespread arms depicted what I held and handled in life, and my legs delineated the path I was on. All four extensions of my "body-cross" led straight to my heart, like the four rivers in Genesis that ran to Eden.[27]

Again in happier spirits, I began to laugh by the water, not only because I had rediscovered my true and imperishable centre—the "cross of the heart"—but especially because I had just then found another cross, and on my very person. It had, in fact, been fastened to my wrist since I had last met with Lax in 1999.

The small silver cross once formed the centrepiece of a *komboskini,* an Eastern Orthodox prayer-rope that had eventually frayed and broken. On my last trip to Patmos, I had asked Lax to bless this cross. Later I set it into a prayer bracelet made of small blue beads and fastened it around my wrist with fishing tackle. It has never been removed.[28]

During the many weeks that I lamented the loss of my cherished gold cross, the wrist-cross had been with me all along. And yet my anxiety and despair had prevented me from taking notice of this all-consoling blessing. My stress-related "blindness" was akin to a man desperately searching for his gold (or, more importantly, his

God), when, throughout his journey, the "Great Pearl" was right by his side.

As Lax had revealed in my dream, our greatest gift, the presence and love of God, is ever within our possession. This interior treasure does not grow old or fail, but lies hidden in our souls, awaiting intimate discovery.

What is Truth?

> "For this I was born, and for this I have come into the world, to bear witness to the truth. Everyone who is of the truth hears my voice." Pilate said to him, "What is truth?" (Jn 18.37-38)

Pilate's famous question is also our own.

Every day we stand before the living truth of Christ, the Incarnation of Love through whom all things were made, who gave himself up for the life of the world and cleared a skyway to paradise, thus effecting our salvation.

Yet even after comprehending this, still we may come to ask, particularly when our faith is weak, *"What is truth?"*

I had been thinking of Jesus standing before Pilate, when a package came in the morning mail. It was a small icon, a gift from a friend who had recently visited the Holy Land. Depicted was the face of the famous "Sinai Jesus," the oldest known icon of *Christ Pantocrator,* Lord of the Universe. Painted in the late sixth century, the life-size original is from the Monastery of St. Catherine in Egypt.[29]

The face of Jesus is mysteriously captivating. Composed of two distinct asymmetrical halves, they come together to form a balanced, lifelike whole. The left side shows Christ as Lawgiver and Judge (thus his left hand holds the Gospels, the very truth of his Word). The right side of the Saviour depicts him as All-Merciful and Loving God (his right hand is consequently raised in blessing).

Could this have been the face that gazed upon Pilate when he asked, "What is truth?" Pilate knew next to nothing of Christ's teachings, and yet the quiet power of his unprecedented prisoner intensely moved him; he sought Jesus' release. The procurator's wife also "suffered much over him in a dream" (Mt 27.19).

Increasingly, I felt that the icon of the Sinai Jesus was meant to help me reflect on Pilate's famous question, which reverberates through history, straight into our own day.

"What is truth?" How great must have been the ensuing stillness as Pilate's words echoed through the praetorium. The same ominous (and yet empathetic) silence faces us when we find it difficult to sense the immediate presence of the Lord of Truth, whom all lesser truths point to.

Yet in the reverberating quiet, Christ is there, just as he was with Pilate. If we listen intently, praying ourselves into the seeming void, we begin to feel buoyed by his indwelling, all-loving presence that bears us through the dark, like a ship rolling through a midnight sea.

Though our vessel's inner timbers may buckle as the bow plunges into the deep (suggestive of the crucifixion), the next wave carries us skyward, and we have hope (indicative of the resurrection).

The eyes of the Sinai Jesus keenly show this necessary "spiritual tension," reflective of a universe en route to its ultimate union with Christ.

One orb, narrowed in scrutiny and arched like a wave about to break, sifts through our souls. Weighing our entire lives against Scripture and the living Fire that birthed the universe, the stern eye seems to darken, as if veiled by a cloud, and exhorts, *"I call heaven and earth to witness against you this day, that I have set before you life and death, the blessing and the curse; therefore, choose life, that you may live ..."* (Deut 30.19).

Since we are mere clay (wholly dependent on our Maker, like Adam), we humble ourselves before this intense, omniscient orb that ultimately asks, *"Who do you say that I am?"* (Mt 16.15).

The other eye, luminous as a sunrise, gazes out from eternity; its unconditional love straightaway comforts and reassures us. Guiding, all-renewing, its gentle, tender light radiates infinite blessings. Like dawn breaking over the sea, it whispers, *"I am the Way, the Truth, and the Life; I will always be with you, even unto the end of the age"* (Jn 14.6; Mt 28.20).

The arresting eyes of the Sinai Christ test the very core of our moral being. They penetrate the heart and quicken our inward movement to God. In their great silence and acute stillness, they quietly ask, *"Have you lived according to the truth? Have you testified to the truth of your life?"* (3 Jn 3-4).

The steady gaze of Jesus inspires reverence. Such fear of the Holy deeply moved Pilate's wife and shuddered through those who later gathered on Golgotha and in the Garden of the Resurrection, leaving them struck with wordless awe. According to Scripture, such ineffable silence will sound in heaven when the Lamb wordlessly opens the Seventh Seal (Rev 8.1).

Why will Christ be silent then? For the same reason Jesus said nothing before Pilate. God has no need to prove himself. *God Is.*

Truth Incarnate stood before the procurator, just as Truth will stand before us in that hour when earth and heaven shall be moved, and every living thing will tremble, both in fear and joy. *In fear,* because the all-consuming glory of God will irradiate the universe; *in joy,* because the fullness of the Truth will at last be made manifest.

What greater Truth could one conceive than a God of Love who in love created the cosmos, and in the image of *Agape* fashioned humanity? And even though humanity fell away, this loving God rescued his people from self-annihilation by becoming human, even enduring death by their hands, that every man and woman might become like God.

In this benevolent, compassionate Power all things were made good, having come from an All-Good Source. Heaven and earth, body and spirit, the invisible and visible, everything was created holy. An "organic spirituality" coursed through the newly born cosmos, perfecting itself in the God-Man whose almighty love delivered the world from dissolution and death.

A prime example of Christ's agapaic intent is recorded in the Gospel of John and concerns the woman caught in the act of adultery. When she was brought to Jesus, he did not demand that the law of Moses be executed to the letter—a moral code that would have sentenced her to death; instead, he preached compassion. Christ openly proclaimed the *law of love,* and in love forgave her, and gave her freedom, adding, "Go, and sin no more" (Jn 8.1-11). His writing in the sand at that moment is a sign of love's pre-eminence: all laws and commandments "set in stone" are as sand, unless they are balanced with the immediacy of love.

Jesus demonstrated that the highest truth is the "Now Moment" lived through the heart. Love is an eternal present and is made sacrosanct in its most perfect source, the Christ of Love himself. The journey toward the Incarnate God is thus a greater understanding of the divine *Agape* extant in all things, set into effect through Genesis and fully revealed in the birth and mission of the Saviour.

Late that afternoon I drove to San Francisco City College to teach an evening class. As I bounded up the many steps leading to the main entrance of campus, past the statue of St. Francis of Assisi shaped like a cross, its arms wide in blessing, I happened to look up and saw the school motto carved high atop the bronze doors. It seemed a perfect end to my day-long meditation on the nature of truth in Christ:

"The Truth Shall Make You Free"
(John 8.32)

City College of San Francisco, with statue of St. Francis of Assisi in foreground. Sculpted by Benjamin Bufano in 1968, the statue, aptly named "St. Francis of the Guns," was cast from two thousand melted-down firearms.

Trading Places

The colours in the late evening summer sky were slowly turning amber, then lilac. Lax and I had taken our regular 6 PM stroll along the waterfront, though this time it was a shorter excursion.

In his final years his strength had markedly decreased. At first he kept this to himself, but soon it became evident that the old poet was getting increasingly frail. Thinner, slower, moving more carefully with his walking stick, Captain Robo's life was setting like the sun, as every star inevitably must.

Halfway up the steep hill leading to his home, Lax appeared to be winded. It was the first time I ever saw him looking tired, fatigued. Head slightly bowed, he paused and took a few deep breaths, then turned to me and said, "You go on. I'll stay here and rest awhile," pointing to a whitewashed alley step. "Go on up and get the house ready. You know the routine."

"I'll stay with you," I insisted. "There's no rush."

Lax shook his head adamantly. "No, no, just go on up. I'll be OK. Here's the key. I'll see you there in a bit."

He waved me on, adding sternly, *"And don't tell anyone I couldn't make it up the hill tonight. I don't want word going around that I'm sick or something—I'm just a little tired."*

Though I swore to silence and obeyed his wishes, it felt odd walking up the narrow winding streets without him. It was strange leaving Lax there sitting by himself, resting in an alleyway. For the first time he and I weren't going up to the hermitage together. Our parting drove home how someday our walks and spirit-lessons would be but a memory.

As I passed broken doorways and cracked walls over which bougain-villea grew, I felt the intense emptiness that would sweep over me with his eventual death. Already I was imitating the cadence of our walks, half-thinking he was still alongside me, laughing or pointing out something interesting.

My fingers tightened around the key to Lax's house. His giving me the key took on a poignant symbolism. Though the poet had to stop for a while, he had given me the key to go on, much like the renewing example he had set with his words and life. They had kept me going at a time when I felt that I could not go on, fuelling me with spiritual and creative inspiration.

Stepping up to the porch, I opened the door to his little blue-and-white home that partially overlooked the bay of Patmos. In many ways, this was the house where I was born. The spiritual intensity of the dwelling was overwhelming, both back in 1993 (when I had first met Lax) and now. As recorded in *The Way of the Dreamcatcher*,

> Good and centered living had gone on here. It seemed the very air was charged with the harmonious life of the dweller. Rich tones permeated everywhere, much like those experienced at sunset. The activity within had left an afterglow.[30]

But now, and for the very first time, I was alone in the house of my teacher. There was a sanctity to the dwelling that made me think twice about what I was doing, even thinking. Though I knew I had to clean the kitchen, set the table for dinner, and cut fish for the cats, I was overtaken by the inner resonance of the place. Every chair, box, book, tile, and doorknob hinted of something more than what it was. Mere matter seemed to have been transfigured.

I put my bag down in the tiny kitchen and placed a few containers of yogurt and fish into the refrigerator. Silently, almost reverently, I then passed into the main room (which also served as Lax's study and sleeping quarters).

A dreamcatcher dangling from a large round Japanese lantern still swayed, set into motion when I had first opened the front door. I looked over the poems, photos, and art (mainly forwarded by friends) that he had carefully taped on his walls, then thumbed through a few books that lay on his bed. Next to them a writing pad lay open to a blank page, a pen beside it.

In the quiet of his hilltop abode, everything felt holy. Everything made perfect sense because all things seemed pure and open, like a garden after a rain, or the sun breaking through the clouds. The house had become a nadir point meant to stabilize the universe.

Stepping over to a table on which books and letters were piled high, I sat in a chair and took deep, meditative breaths. While centring myself in the pulsing peace of the room, I noticed some looseleaf papers off to the side, scattered beneath a desk lamp. They were one-line "spirit poems" written in his typical minimalist style, each sentence running down the page, each word broken into syllables, to give the reader pause for reflection. Yet even in standard sentence form, the words inspired meditation:

Every good deed will be noticed.

What you do to yourself you do to the world.

Infinite love brings infinite life into being.

What is exciting may not be fulfilling.

Angels are always with us.

Do not forget to love.

A hermit's work is never done.

Suddenly there was a knock on the door—it was Lax! And I had not even cleaned the kitchen!

Just as I sprang up to let him in, it occurred to me that one night, years before, it was I who had knocked on that same door, and Lax had allowed me entrance. This time, however, it was the other way around. In a sense, our roles had reversed.

"Who is it? Who's there?" I asked in a deep voice filled with concern, imitating how Lax had spoken to me when I had first knocked on his door in 1993.

"I dunno," Lax answered playfully, "but all I can tell you is I just keep on showin' up here" (this was what I usually said when visiting him).

"Well, son, make sure you show up as often as you can!" I replied (echoing what he, in turn, would tell me when I happened to drop in).

We laughed heartily, then went inside. Lax felt much better, but rather than focus on himself, he wondered why I had not yet fed the cats, now gathering on the porch.

"The cats are hungry," he growled, settling into his typically mirthful, unassuming nature. So together we cut up some fish and fed them, then proceeded to feed ourselves, dining on vegetable stew leftovers and tea.

As we ate, Robert asked me to read aloud the poems that I had found on the table. He nodded good-naturedly and smiled as I slowly and thoughtfully did so. His incredibly empathetic eyes were opened wide; somehow they brought into the room a higher, all-loving energy. Just reading the verse in this highly charged and luminous manner was enough; discussion seemed almost superfluous.

Shortly after I read the last selection, Lax said that he was going to look through a few books he had been studying. In the meantime, he suggested that I wash the dishes and take out the garbage to a trash bin a short distance away.

On my return, I found Lax in bed, the covers up to his chest, his head propped up with pillows. Only the table lamp, to his immediate left, was on.

"Pull up a chair," he said, his eyes tired, though still smiling. "I know it's only 9 PM, but I think I'm going to turn in early tonight."

"No problem," I said, placing a stool by his bed. "Get your rest. We'll talk tomorrow."

Lax laughed for a moment, then looked up at the old wooden ceiling beams and let out a long, contented sigh. Tired though he seemed, his dancing blue eyes twinkled; he appeared happy.

"God bless," he said, although for a moment I thought he had said, "Deep bliss."

"God bless," I returned, bending down to give him a hug.

Folding his arms on his chest, he regarded me with a warm smile, then gently closed his eyes, entering what seemed a calm and comfortable darkness, like a child finding its peace in the arms of its mother.

The lamplight spread over his lined, weathered face. Where its incandescence fell on his white beard it was very bright; its wide amber beam became increasingly diffuse as it spread over his bed, creating rippling shadows that highlighted the folds of his sleeves and blanket. He looked like he was being illumined by the dawn.

Even as my mentor became more relaxed, taking in deep breaths as he fell sleep, he appeared to be teaching. Lax travelled lightly, even in the realm of dreams. Even there, his heart remained awake.

Though frail now, the old sage's weakness made his words and presence grow that much stronger. The full intake of his breaths, going way down into the holy life-core of his spirit, emanated like ripples on a lake; they embraced the world with a wakeful serenity. Listening to their wave-rhythms, I once more heard my teacher saying,

> Live and breathe simply, openly. Relax, trust in God, go with the flow of love. Be forgiving, be compassionate. Pray and help others. Make an art of whatever it is you do. Bless all things, because everything comes from above. *Love, love, love* ....[31]

I stayed with him a little while longer, silently thanking him for everything he had given me. Almost without knowing it, my rate of breathing had melded with his, as if subconsciously I longed to travel with him in his sleep, through the night-world of dreams.

When I saw Lax turn slightly onto his side and settle into a deeper peace, I quietly switched off the table lamp, careful not to wake him. Somehow I felt that a circle of love had completed itself; and yet, in a mysterious, grace-filled way, it had blessedly begun.

On the way down the long, winding hill that led to the harbour, a poignant quote that I had read on his wall kept coming to mind. It encapsulated much of what had transpired that evening.

> The child is a person who has
> come from the Great Mystery,
> and I, who am an old man,
> am about to return to the Great Mystery.
> And so in reality, we are close to each other.

Black Elk

S.T. Georgiou, 1999

Shadows of Robert Lax (left) and the author.

A dam

Every year in October, faculty of the San Francisco Unified School District gather on the city's Presidio grounds for the annual BTS ("Back To School") night.

Located near the Golden Gate Bridge, the Presidio, a once-active military base, is now a bayside park and recreation centre famous for its tranquil forests, rolling hills, and scenic vistas.

In attending a recent BTS event hosted at the Presidio's Golden Gate Club, I saw that a sprawling cemetery bordered the premises—the San Francisco National Cemetery, composed of 30,000 war dead and veterans. The interred soldiers span the period from the Civil War to the recent conflicts in the Middle East.

Having arrived early, I began to take a walk along the many rows of gravestones, their identical grey slabs brilliant in the late afternoon light.

It was a very clear day. A slight nip was in the air, a sign of autumn's arrival. Framed by cypress trees and resting on a lush green slope, the idyllic (and yet solemn) setting quite naturally inspired reflection.

In all directions there were so many dead, some cut down in combat, others succumbing to disease or old age. The immaculate headstones spread over the hills like endless waves of granite.

Suddenly an overwhelming sadness came over me, accentuated by the lengthening shadows and the chirping of a lonely bird. Every marker hinted of a life lived, of wants, needs, hopes, dreams, joys, terrors, all suddenly (or slowly) reduced to dust.

For all my faith in an afterlife, in the resurrected Christ, a terrible finality rose up from the earth.

How to make sense of all the life that had become death? How to tie it all together? How to give it meaning?

Until now I had been walking behind the gravestones, rather than looking at their inscriptions. Something told me to stop at one.

My intuition had suggested that what I would read on its face would lift my spirits and show that death, however real, is not our ultimate end. Whatever I would see written on the stone would serve as a sign from above, indicating how our common "ending" is, in actuality, our common beginning.

I walked around the marker immediately before me, No. 1077. Carved in the granite was the name of an army private who had died in 1900: A.P. Adams.

Adams. Immediately I thought of Genesis, and the first human being created by God. Though the name on the headstone ended with an "s," the symbolism was close enough.

Seeing a name suggestive of "Adam" was intensely moving. It brought into play the cosmic whole of things, the entire gamut of where we came from and where we are going.

Born "of the earth" (as his name, in Hebrew, denotes), Adam is a microcosm of the universe, our common forefather, our primal link with all of humanity and creation.

However, as evident by the many graves around me, I could plainly see how Adam had actualized our mortality: the wages of sin, against God, was death.

Moreover, since life was created to be interrelational, the transgression of Adam (and Eve) had permeated and degraded the entire cosmos. Entropy was effected on all levels of existence, necessitating God's entry into time and space, that humanity might be saved and the cosmos be set on its path to collective transfiguration.

Thus while we are bound with Adam through sin and death, we also share with him the promise of a grace-born salvation, and this through Jesus, the Light and the Life: *"For as in Adam all die, so in Christ, all will be made alive"* (1 Cor 15.22).

While I stood by the grave of A.P. Adams and meditated on how everything in creation will be renewed in its divine Origin, the thought crossed my mind that already all of life was being remade, transfigured in the Christ (the New Adam). Ever since Jesus was born, the universe has been imperceptibly drawing nearer to the God who said, *"I shall gather all people to myself"* (Jn 12.32).

Since his baptism in the Jordan, Christ's nurturing energy has radiated throughout the world, quickening matter itself, preparing it for its ultimate transfiguration. The elements therefore "groan" for the

Second Coming (Rom 8.21). Creation longs for the rebirth of the universe in God's rejuvenating love.[32]

Surely, if all things were made "very good" (Gen 1.31), created through the love of God, then nothing can ever really die or remain dead forever. *Agape* calls all things back to life.

Jesus said to his disciples, "I am not the God of the dead, but of the living" (Mt 22.32). And the early Church proclaimed, "The faith of the Christians is the resurrection of the dead." Everything is therefore on track for renewal.

As seen throughout the Bible—especially in Ezekiel 37, where a dead army is raised, and certainly in the resurrection of Jesus—life after death is, in fact, a distinctly physical phenomenon. Spirit and flesh fuse to form a transfigured body. This demonstrates a profound organic spirituality where nothing in creation is lost, but is transformed into something greater (thus the tomb of Christ was empty). All things flowing from the Source of Life are holy, since the Source itself is supreme and almighty holiness.

Our God is therefore a *supernatural* God in whom we have a transcendent hope. While Christ is popularly likened to a gentle, loving Lamb, he is also the Lion of Judah, the *Mysterium Tremendum* who dwells in cloud and "formed everything out of nothing," as testified in Genesis.

Only a Deity of such power could shatter death and draw Adam and Eve (and all their innumerable descendants) out of the grave. Only a Lord of such forgiveness and love could rescue Israel and lead all nations and peoples to Mount Zion to enjoy life in the Spirit abundantly (Is 2.60).[33]

I had been standing by the grave of Private Adams thinking about these things when out of nowhere came a low rumbling, then a quaking, then suddenly a roar so loud I nearly hit the ground and covered my ears, expecting earth and sky to break open.

A millisecond later, I glimpsed the screaming source of the terrible, instantaneous fury—a jet fighter had shot past, almost skimming the earth. Wholly brilliant and blazing in the sunlight, its twin turbofan engines had shattered the quiet like thunder raining out of heaven.

Then I remembered that it was Fleet Week—the Blue Angels were in town. Naval cruisers and destroyers had gathered in the San Francisco Bay. Numerous air shows were scheduled.

But what a time for the F/A-18 Hornet to soar past—for a moment it felt like the graves were breaking open, supercharged with the glory of God! It was like a second Genesis, an explosion of light and fire, a fitting prelude to the Day of the Lord.

Indeed, the dramatic (and deafening) visitation by the Blue Angel fighter brought to mind the stirring Eastern Orthodox icon depicting the *Anastasis,* the Resurrection of the Christ in which he is shown raising Adam and Eve out of their opened graves, liberating creation from death and the power of the devil.

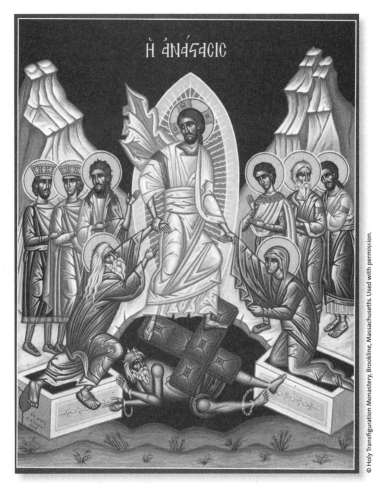

© Holy Transfiguration Monastery, Brookline, Massachusetts. Used with permission.

Icon of the Anastasis (Resurrection).

Jesus, surrounded by a mandorla bursting with light—the very Door of Paradise—stands at the centre, both arms outstretched. He tightly grasps the first couple's hands—Adam to his right, Eve to his left.

Exuding almighty strength and salvific energy, he straightaway lifts them out of their shattered sepulchres, raising the two awestruck beings into the eternal glory of the resurrection life.

The Saviour stands triumphant on the broken doors of hell. The chains and the locks that had once bound its inhabitants fall through a black chasm. Stripped and bound, Satan also plummets through the void, the dark angel who would have made humanity his everlasting prisoner.

Save for the devil, everything in the icon is moving upward, toward Christ; his creation is irrepressibly drawn to him. The Gates of Eternal Life are opening, the light of the New World is dawning, flooding through the cosmos and liberating all from the domain of death ….

However awesome and glorious this vision of Christ's coming kingdom, the many thousands of graves before me indicated that heaven still remains a destination to be hoped for, prayed for. Paradise is the great end (and eternal beginning) on which we have set our hearts. As written in the Nicene Creed, *"I await the Resurrection of the Dead and the Life of the Ages to come."* On this declaration rests the whole of the Christian faith.[34]

Once more, everything centres on waiting. Whether in life or death, everything is waiting for God, waiting for him to come again, "to free the prisoners" (Is 42.7), "to give light to those who sit in darkness and in the shadow of death" (Lk 1.79).

In his deeply reflective poem, "21 Pages," Robert Lax takes up the theme of waiting. While his voice hearkens to the fallen Adam, longing for the Lord, it also speaks for all who yearn to meet their God.

Waiting. I'm sitting in what we'll call nowhere,
looking into the dark, and waiting.
Like a prisoner waiting for a reprieve,
counting his days, not counting, not knowing
what to count or why to count it,
waiting for one thing, one moment, one event ...

I've wondered sometimes if you came, and I saw you,
and I knew you were there, if I'd continue to go on waiting ...
It could be like that, but I don't think it would, because if
you came, things would change. A thousand, maybe a
million things would change. My whole life would change.
I know that. I've known that since the beginning.[35]

The Ancient Beauty

In the beginning you formed me out of nothing,
honoring me with your divine image; but when
I disobeyed your commands, you returned me
to the earth from which I was taken. Restore me
to that likeness, that the ancient beauty may be
formed anew.

from the *Evlogitaria,*
Greek Orthodox Memorial Hymn

These words, sung at the end of the Divine Liturgy, commemorate
the dead. The entire congregation prays for the deceased and asks
that the soul(s) of the departed be granted safe and blessed passage
into eternal life.

Hearing this hymn at church one Sunday, I began to reflect on the
phrase "Restore me to that likeness, that the ancient beauty may be
formed anew."

What "ancient beauty"—first invested in Adam and Eve—will be
refashioned in the faithful when they inherit paradise? What will
our *resurrection bodies* (a transfigured composite of spirit and flesh)
look like?

As the choir sang the slow, moving hymn and the priest's golden
censer swung back and forth, emitting fragrant clouds of incense that

curled upward toward the light, I thought of how my own students, just a week before, had asked me similar questions during a session on early Christianity.

"What kind of shape," they wanted to know, "will people's transformed souls and bodies take on in heaven? What special attributes will the resurrected in Christ possess?"

Though certainly the answer remains veiled in mystery, definitive clues exist, as found in Scripture and in the lives of the saints.

According to Christian tradition, life in the hereafter is dependent on what the early Church fathers termed the "ancient likeness"—the *image of God* through which humanity was originally created (Gen 1.26). This all-empowering divine likeness, lost through the Fall, is renewed in believers through baptism: "Unless one is born of water and Spirit, he cannot enter the kingdom of heaven" (Jn 3.5).

Reborn in Christ, we are somatically being prepared, even now, for life in the New World. "Like formless and shapeless matter we go down into the water," writes Nicholas Cabasilas, the fourteenth-century Orthodox theologian, "to meet with the Form that is beautiful."[36]

The holy image of Christ is therefore planted in the "good soil of our hearts" like a seed (Mt 13.8), the fruits of which will be consummately realized in the age to come. For on the last day, in the hour when the Almighty moves over the face of the earth and gathers all of creation to him, the supernatural endowment that we have received through baptism (and carefully nurtured throughout our lives), shall quicken in our souls, and blossom.

Our inner eye—the eye of the heart—will open, and we will clearly see the Christ in us, the God coming to meet us, the very Lord who walked with Adam "in the cool of the garden" (Gen 3.8).

He will take our hand and lead us through the inward gate of the heart, to a throne where the Book of Life shall be opened (Rev 20.12).

There all our thoughts, words, and deeds will be revealed. And though our inner light and darkness shall be disclosed throughout heaven, there will be no need to fear; the Lord's compassion shall prevail. He will recognize that daily we endeavoured to live our lives according to a higher love, as best as we were able.

In his celebrated Paschal homily, the eminent fourth-century theologian St. John Chrysostom alluded to this manifold love of Christ, this triumph of *agape* in God. The much-loved sermon is still read in the Orthodox Church on Easter day:

> Let no one mourn their transgressions; forgiveness has risen from the grave. Let no one fear death; the Savior's death has set us free ... For the Master is gracious and receives the last even as the first. He gives rest to him that comes even at the eleventh hour, just as to him who has laboured from the first. He has mercy upon the last and cares for the first .... *Let all, then, enter the joy of our Lord!*[37]

On that day we shall indeed "be changed," suffused with the fullness and glory of the Christ (1 Cor 15.51; Phil 3.21). Endowed with "the image of the new man in heaven" (1 Cor 15.49), both our bodies and our spirits will be recast in the Creator's forge. Transfigured in love, the beloved of God shall take on a resplendent "resurrection body."

Like its prototype of flesh and blood, such a luminous body, irradiant and ineffable, will surely be centred in the heart, the inner sanctuary of love first made bright through baptism. Only through the heart can we understand the depth and vastness of God and draw near to the living Christ.[38]

With sighs "too deep for words" (Rom 8.26), the tripartite energies that had once fashioned Adam—truth, beauty, and goodness, all supercharged in love—will shudder out of the heart and spiritualize the entire soma, firing it like a newborn star.

The "ancient beauty" shall then at last be made complete—our true identity in God will become wholly manifest. We shall inherit the paradise meant for us since the beginning and join the many "partakers of glory" who shall "come from the east and the west to sit down with Abraham, Isaac, and Jacob in the kingdom of heaven" (Mt 8.11).

The resurrected body of Jesus gives us a fair idea of the higher qualities that our "glorified bodies" will possess. As evident by the solidity of his flesh (Lk 24.39), the scars of his crucifixion (Jn 20.27), and his eating of fish (Lk 24.41), the risen Jesus was distinctly human; yet as demonstrated by his ability to pass through matter (Jn 20.19), he transcended the mortal condition. In essence, his body was unlike mere "flesh," prone to decay. The risen Christ embodied the pre-Fall state of humanity—a somatic way of life not restricted by bio-physical laws. Christ's soma essentially displayed a natural-supernatural unity reflective of the harmonic balance between earth and heaven that will exist in paradise.

Saints throughout history have also demonstrated similar transcendent attributes, and while still in this life. Whether it be Antony of Egypt (fourth century), Catherine of Siena (fourteenth century), Padre Pio of Rome (twentieth century), or the late John Maximovitch, Archbishop of Shanghai and San Francisco, these holy people intermittently regained the pre-Fall blessedness of Adam and Eve. Through their intense compassion in Christ, saints were able to radiate a joyous, exquisite luminosity, levitate, in some cases even bilocate. Their fervent love allowed them to experience a creative and dynamic interrelationship with energy and matter.

Each of us, in our own special manner, shall bear a glorified body that will praise Christ through eternity and give heaven everlasting joy. I remember that three days after my father, a devout and patient man, had died, I saw him in a dream. Already he appeared to have taken on a form unlike his mortal body, and yet I still recognized him, and strongly felt that his transcendent soma approximated the glorified body that he would assume on the Last Day.

While he was tall and well-proportioned in life, now he was taller, more angular. He always had a full head of dark hair, even into his seventies, yet now his hair was even thicker, leonine, bound in a band set with diadems, and flowing down his back. His eyes, once blue-green, now were very blue, and shone like brilliant sapphires.

Around his luminous frame (amber-toned, it seemed), he wore a sleeveless mantle with hanging folds, the colour of red-ochre and gold. And then I saw that a pair of folded wings, almost diaphanous, ran down his back beneath his cloak, their sharp, tapered ends barely skimming the ground. They reminded me of the famous passage from Isaiah: *"Those who wait on God shall renew their strength; they shall mount up with wings like eagles"* (Is 40.31).

On waking, I realized that my father's transcendent body reflected a metaphysical union of heaven and earth. His translucent wings, sapphire eyes, and half-gold cloak were emblematic of the celestial realm, while his amber tones and the red-ochre folds of his mantle strongly suggested a terrestrial dimension.

In this somatic union it seemed to me that he was bodily taking on what Adam was meant to be in Eden: that is, a minister of creation, a cosmic caretaker ordained to bless and nurture heaven and earth, and to unite them into a holy and harmonious Unity.[39]

For in Adam, the realm above and the realm below were meant to meet and bring together all the energy of the universe, that something greater and previously unimaginable could, in time, be born—the ecstatic revelation of God to his creatures, and his direct communion with them.

While Adam and Eve briefly experienced this intimate friendship with their Maker, the cataclysmic Fall essentially broke their bond with him; ever since, humanity has yearned to find its God.

And yet through the Christ, *God has found us,* and this through the reclamation of our divine image, the holy seal, the "ancient beauty" of our baptism. The sacrament of Water and Spirit forms us anew and links us to Jesus, our source of life and power.

In dreaming of my father, I think what I saw was him becoming increasingly like Christ, a "New Adam," an anointed Spirit-Bearer of Truth whose baptismal energies were quickening in the world beyond, transforming and preparing him for paradise.

In all his rarefied beauty, he was taking on the image of the Everlasting, in whom he had been consecrated. Like all sons and daughters of God, he was assuming the supernatural abilities of what may be termed a *Worldbinder,* a sanctified steward of heaven and earth preparing the way for the coming of Christ, the Bright Lord of the Universe.

Priest of Creation

It was a magnificent spring day. Months had passed since I had visited the beach. A badly sprained ankle, coupled with a succession of late winter storms, had kept me away.

Sunlight poured out of a cloudless blue sky. I could see for miles up and down the coast, even out toward the Farallones. Since winter had just concluded, there was an invigorating chill in the air. All of nature pulsed with a tingling effervescence that swept through the core of my being.

In the distance, I could make out the ruins of a low-lying cliff; it had collapsed, undoubtedly due to the recent rains. A tunnel-like passage had formed, leading through the rock and out the other side. The dramatic portal aroused in me a deep sense of mystery and beauty. Eager to get a closer look, I doubled my pace.

As I approached the unusual archway, I soon realized that I had chanced upon what the Celts have described as a "thin place," a site infused with divine presence. Here, matter and spirit seemed to blend into one another. Time had slowed down; a certain holiness felt near.

Things suddenly seemed miraculously translucent. Looking through the dark, nearly cavernous passage I could see an iridescent sheen of blue reflecting off the shore, as if the sky had become the sand. Even the rocks jutting out of the surf took on an incredibly intense aquamarine lustre, the colour of infinite space. The azure light, rippling and spirit-charged, beckoned that I pass through the short tunnel, through this "stargate by the sea," and enter a wholly other dimension.

A remarkable clarity coursed through me as I did so. It seemed that for a moment I was everywhere at once, borne by the "supernatural blue" shimmering in all directions.

A distant land mass, poised like a faraway isle, felt as near to me as my own flesh—almost like a second skin. The salty wind and pounding waves sang in my veins. The curling crests roared free in my ecstatic soul. My open heart had nowhere to go because I was already there in God. For a millisecond I had become a cosmic, reflective vessel filled with the light of eternity.

In this grace-filled, blessed radiance I suddenly realized, more deeply than ever before, what Lax had meant when he would tell me, time and again, to "Go with the flow." The flow was love, and now, in my transcendent state, I was everywhere in it. Everything that had been created was sheer radiant love praising God. *"Holy, holy is the Lord of Hosts, for the whole earth is filled with his glory"* (Is 6.3; Rom 1.20).

Now I clearly saw how all of my journeys into the wilderness, whether on Ocean Beach or Patmos, were subliminal constructs designed to encounter Jesus, to return to the Christ through whom the cosmos was made (Jn 1.3). My regular forays into the wild had been unconscious attempts to enter "a place apart," away from worldly excess, artificiality, and pomp, and seed myself in his atavistic love, that I might grow according to his will.

I was trying to forget my egoistic sense of self, to lose it in wide-open spaces, that I might embrace a higher reality. Like the birds, trees, seas, and stars, I was longing to thank and praise God, to complete the "cosmic liturgy" offered him by the universe every moment of every day and night.

Now, more than ever, I understood my deeper mission in life, and the foremost duty of all people who love God: to be a *minister of creation,* a lay ministry into which every baptized Christian is called in order to help elevate, purify, sanctify, and bless everything in the cosmos (1 Pet 2.4-10, 3.21-22). The vocation of all Christians, lay or clergy, is to be a part of the holy priesthood of God in this world.[40]

Whether we know it or not, our souls yearn to complete what Adam and Eve had failed to accomplish. Through Christ the New Adam, this is made possible. Sealed with his almighty love, we are consecrated and equipped to play a powerful intercessory role in balancing earth and heaven and in maintaining harmony in the universe. As my dream indicated (wherein I saw my late father taking on the duties of a "Worldbinder"), baptism gifts us with the agapaic power to steward the earth and prepare creation for the coming of Jesus and the New Age in Christ.

There is something in the depths of our being that longs for wholeness and finality. The beauty of the cosmos catalyzes this yearning, but because nature is ephemeral, our spiritual hunger is ultimately satisfied in the God of the Heart, the all-loving Creator who calls us to cherish and nurture his creation. Via a kind word, a sharing of bread, a prayerful walk along the shore, or a Sunday service, this stewardship is intimately effected. All that matters is that we live, move, and have our being in the heart, our common temple.

This central sanctuary of spirit and soma is where Christ dwells outside of time and space. Existing like an "inner isle"—a domain distinct from a passing, self-obsessed world—the heart is the inviolable axis of communication between man and God, earth and heaven. In this thinnest of thin places, the Lord invisibly comes forth to meet us; as we pray all creation into him, he reciprocally prays his life-renewing love into the universe.

One loving prayer said in the heart gathers souls, as well as stars. In this integral spirit-shrine, the mystery of Christ and creation gently and exquisitely meld, like a light mist rolling through a valley, drifting to the sky. In the bright heart the ultimate meaning and purpose of life may be grasped. All things above and below are unified and at last transfigured in the merciful and compassionate God, "hidden as a treasure in our hearts," as St. Gregory of Sinai illumines.[41]

And yet this wealth is not to be kept secret and hoarded. Once the treasure of the Christ is found within oneself, his riches are meant to be joyfully shared and disseminated, that others may find their holy and life-giving centre. Having discovered God within us, we shine out of our souls like the dawn and bring his light to all who have lost their dream of home.

Love is therefore an inflow-outflow process; it imitates the very beating of our hearts and so sustains the cycles of life, on earth and in heaven. *Agape* is ultimately circulatory. Love always begins things anew.

Less than a week after my numinous experience by the sea, I went back to the mysterious azure portal, but only a dark, dense mound of earth was there. The "aperture of *agape*" had collapsed; the relentless wind and tides had done the rest.

While standing in the surf, reflecting on how for a moment I had entered a hidden dimension—a rarefied otherworld born of a fleeting union of matter and spirit—I saw a tattered piece of paper darting along the shore, driven by intermittent gusts. As it blew past, I quickly grabbed it. The very thin, near transparent page, half wet and flecked with sand, had been torn out of the Bible:

> Stand up and praise the Lord, who is from lasting to everlasting. Blessed be your glorious name, and may it be exalted above all blessing and praise. You alone are the Lord. You made the heavens, even the highest heavens, and all their starry host, the earth and all that is on it, the seas and all that is in them. You give life to everything, and the multitudes of heaven worship you. (Nehemiah 9.6)

In the Sanctuary of the King

Christopher John Rozales, 2010

Iconostasis (altar screen) shown with dome mosaic of the Christ Pantocrator. Robert Andrews, iconographer. Holy Trinity Greek Orthodox Church, San Francisco.

Toward the end of spring I received a call from Robert Andrews, a long-time friend and premier specialist in Byzantine-style mosaic iconography. The eighty-five-year-old Andrews, assisted by his son Timothy and a small team of Italian artisans, has designed and installed icons in Eastern Orthodox and Roman Catholic churches throughout the United States.[42]

For months, Andrews had been in San Francisco working on his greatest project—a 3,400-square-foot portrait of *Christ Pantocrator* (the Almighty Lord), to be set into the dome of Holy Trinity Greek Orthodox Church. The spectacular image—the largest mosaic face of Jesus in the Western hemisphere—was Andrew's long-awaited masterwork. In a half-century, he had created virtually all the icons within Holy Trinity.

"It's just about finished," Andrews said over the phone, in his usual soft-spoken manner. "If you're ready to climb up some scaffolding, I'd like you to see it."

The extraordinary mosaic was a project that had been decades in the making; now, after months of installation, it was nearly complete. Within the hour, I was there.

Swinging open the massive doors of the circular, neo-Byzantine style church, I saw that the pews within the dim nave had been removed to make room for eight storeys of scaffolding positioned just beneath the dome. The entire floor had become a construction zone filled with crates, cables, grout mixers. The only lights on were high above, illuminating the enclosed platform deck into which the zigzag scaffolding rose. Out of that distant workspace I could hear the installation team labouring. Their echoes reverberated through the cavernous interior of the concrete edifice, adding to the sense of mystery and expectation.

Rays of blue light, created by the stained glass encircling the church, filtered into the nave; the azure beams helped me to navigate my way to the centre of the building.

I looked up. Through the long maze of metal scaffolding I glimpsed two huge eyes, a nose, part of a mouth, all visible beyond a narrow rectangular crawlspace framed by a golden hue. The face of Jesus, which instantly reminded me of the Sinai Christ, beckoned.

Though Andrews had yet to meet me (he had momentarily left to pick up some supplies), I decided to go up the scaffolding alone. One hundred sharply inclined steps led to the dome. Quietly I ascended them, irresistibly drawn upward toward the light.

By about the third tier, as the floor receded beneath me, I began to realize that my going up was turning out to be both a physical and metaphysical experience, symbolic of my recent struggles and epiphanies in Christ. To borrow a phrase from St. John Climacus, I was climbing a "ladder of divine ascent."

Through the dark I was rising toward the light, to a kind of "rebirth" in Jesus. And strangely enough, as I was going up, I felt like I was *going in*, meditatively entering into the deeper recesses of my being. I was nearing the Christ both above and within, the Lord of Love who had been sealed in my heart since baptism, and through whom all things were born. In a sense, the transcendent (and yet intimate) God was gathering me up; within minutes I would be standing before his throne.

The climb was getting steeper, more arduous. It felt precarious to be moving along at such a dizzying height, surrounded by so much space. The golden icons of the saints, running up and down the walls of the edifice, glimmered intensely, as if they were encouraging me to go on. Suddenly the church felt like a mighty "prayer generator," a "spiritual accelerator" in which the life-enhancing love of the Holy Trinity (the very love-flow coursing through the Godhead) was being supercharged and beamed throughout the cosmos.

As I kept ascending, gazing on the life-size icons of the saints surrounding me, a familiar passage from Isaiah came to mind:

> It shall come to pass in the latter days
> that the mountain of the house of the Lord
> shall be established.
> Many peoples shall flow to it,
> and many nations shall come, and say,
> "Come, let us go up to the mountain of the Lord …"

(Is 2.2-3)

By the sixth tier, I felt like I had indeed been climbing a holy summit, an eight-storey mountain, a "Monte Cristo" of reinforced metal that led to Christ, "our High Priest in the heavens" (Heb 4.14), whom I could now see with increasing detail. His all-encompassing and exacting eyes, one gazing directly at me, the other deep in thought, instilled in me profound awe, if not reverence; they quickened my climb, and drew me higher.

Jesus' blue and brown-green robes, stunning and multihued, symbolized his dual nature, God and Man; they also represented heaven and earth, the two interdimensional realms that his salvific mission had sanctified and reconnected, creating for every believer a lightway to paradise.

The holy hands of Christ were enormous. One was raised in blessing; the other held a richly ornamented Bible. Already I could see that nine seraphim encircled Jesus; their many wings, replete with all-seeing, ever-watchful eyes, shielded their rose-hued bodies.

And then I saw the enormous gold halo surrounding the stern yet compassionate face of the Saviour. Composed of nearly half a million pieces of gilt mosaic glass, it shimmered like a sunlit sea.

Inside this brilliant nimbus flared a magnificent red-maroon cross, radiating from behind Christ's head. As of late, this most powerful sign of Jesus seemed to be everywhere in my life, readily indicating the Christ in all things, the treasured Mystery in whom the cosmos is converging.[43]

Just as I was about to hoist myself through the narrow crawlspace that led to the platform deck, a hand suddenly reached through the opening.

"Welcome to heaven!" cried Timothy, Andrews' son, with a big, wide smile. "I see you made it up here alone."

"Not without the prayers of the saints!" I grinned, grasping his hand and catching my breath. "Thanks for the lift!"

As we exchanged happy greetings, the thought came to me that whatever we were saying up in the dome, before Jesus, had a kind of literal-allegorical meaning. When I heard a worker say, "I'm going back down—I'll bring up Michael soon," he might have been speaking like an angel on a mission, charged to bring a soul before Christ. And when I saw the workers setting in the last of the mosaic tiles, their lean bodies brilliantly framed by the radiant spotlights, they, too, resembled angelic beings going about their appointed tasks in heaven.

Then my phone rang. It was Andrews.

"Sorry I was delayed," he said. "How is it up there?"

"It's paradise!" I replied. "The Pantocrater image is overwhelming! I don't think I'll be as close to Christ until the next life!"

Andrews laughed heartily. "Glad you like it. But remember, God's inside you, too. He's never too far away."

"You're absolutely right!" I affirmed. "That's what I've been learning lately—he's in my very heart."

Christ Pantocrator. Robert Andrews, iconographer. Inner dome, Holy Trinity Greek Orthodox Church, San Francisco.

After we arranged to meet for dinner that evening, I walked over to a part of the platform where there was less commotion and looked out over the church. The azure light continued to pour in through the surrounding stained glass windows; it reminded me of the blue iridescence I had witnessed by the sea, when I had chanced upon the mysterious portal there. Indeed, because of the pervasive blue light in the nave, the church interior suddenly felt like a sea, while the dome above appeared as if it were a sun (better yet, *the Son*), radiating his golden light over creation.

But even more than this, Christ in heaven seemed like an "isle apart," a blessed rock toward which the "Ark of the Church"—a travelling tabernacle in a passing world—was sailing. He shone like a hallowed sanctuary in the sky, the paradise all Christians have set their hearts on.

"Come to a place apart," urges Jesus, *"and rest a while"* (Mk 6.31). Only in his peace can we discover anything really lasting in ourselves, or in one another. For once we find his tranquillity in our hearts, then each of us, with time, may bring forth a new part of God into the universe, precious blessings to inspire our united journey toward Monte Cristo, the coming kingdom of love.

Robert Lax once revealed to me that despite our stellar advances, we continue to remain like children in the world. We are still maturing, and shall be, until Christ comes again. Through his saving grace and glory, he will ultimately transfigure us into the transcendent beings we were meant to be. On that resplendent day, the inner treasure will be ours for eternity.

Until then, let us keep on attending the "school of the heart," living each moment in God, that we might one day graduate to dimensions exquisite and vast, infinitely tranquil, supremely creative.

Agape knows no bounds. Love is forever.

> A new and kinder day is coming …
> There is only one way of preparing for the new age,
> by living it even now, in our hearts.[44]

E pilogue

While watching the summer sun dip into the sea at Fort Funston, I suddenly realized that almost seventeen years had passed since my first meeting with Lax. Following that serendipitous encounter, what had changed in my life? How were things now different?

Outwardly, much seemed the same. Despite my recently earned degrees in theology, teaching experience, and publication record, I remained a struggling part-timer, a "journeyman scholar" eking out a living from semester to semester. I was still single, living in the same modest quarters I had known as a graduate student. In the eyes of the world, my life had not particularly "advanced."

And yet inwardly, it very much had advanced. Through my mentor, I had learned how to relax more, to take delight in simple things, to let go of my "self," that I might become increasingly selfless, and so better flow with the Spirit. As Lax had counselled, the true treasures of life reveal themselves to those who live day by day, who trust in grace and give themselves up to the mystery of divine Providence: that is, the greater plan of God. Most of all, God's riches are discovered by those who exercise *agape*; love opens doors, on earth and in heaven.

Through meeting with Lax, and in my reminiscences of him, it has steadily become clear to me that this brief life is not about acquiring material wealth and gaining professional and social status, which are transitory goals. Good living centres on cultivating more love in the universe, an invaluable, eternal enterprise. Thus, my principal duty as a teacher consists not in landing tenure, but in helping students to discover ways of wisdom and compassion as expressed through the world faiths. My academic and spiritual journey has led me to function as an educator, a professor of religion, an "opener of inner doors," particularly for the young (and the young at heart).

By its very nature, my subject area is devoted to examining the inner life. All the major faiths point to human existence as being an inward passage, a quest of the heart, and this because everything in the world is finite and limited. Everything material wears out; there is no final good in a universe bound by entropy.

A born Christian, I have always believed this inner journey to be centred in Jesus. The life in Christ, deeply rooted in the love of God, yields priceless treasure. Yet in order to clearly perceive this, it is necessary to distance oneself from artificiality and excess. A "place apart" (as in a church or the wilderness) is required to cut through the illusions and distractions of our egoistic age, so steeped in mindless hedonism and greed. As Lax, a consummate minimalist, espoused, *less is more.*

Interestingly, the recent world economic crisis is now impelling us to live frugally, conservatively, to focus on the things in life that are most needful and worth pursuing.

We are learning how to reassess our values and priorities. We are gradually discovering the blessings of sharing versus hoarding, of helping others rather than giving in to self-centred obsessions.

In the process, many are waking to the spiritual life. In our "age of anxiety," searchers are finding that ultimate security rests in placing absolute faith in the Divine. The once-popular Christian motto "*God Alone*" is illuminating and inspiring a new audience.

This theocentric renaissance has much to do with an inborn, subliminal desire to renew life as it was in Eden. We desire the "fields of the Lord." The earth has become too complicated, noisy, polluted, wired. The blood of Adam and Eve quickens in our veins. Innately we know that our firstborn task is to steward creation and prepare it for its ultimate transfiguration in Christ. We long to make good the image of God within us.

My own desire to accomplish this task began on Patmos, itself a sea-ringed spiritual garden, a recreation of Eden. Here the gentle, wise, all-loving Lax, figuratively taking the place of the Lord in paradise, helped to create the conditions appropriate for salvation; he awakened in me the power of love.

For numerous summers I walked with him in the "cool of the garden" and learned vital spirit-lessons. Over the years, other writers and artists joined us in our excursions and talks. In the end, all of us went out from that Isle of *Agape* eager to spread the joy of love. With confidence and power we re-entered a world desperately in need of compassion. Lax himself had said for us to be as "lights in the world," that we might help guide all searchers home.[1]

It is this sacral rhythm of inward journeying and outward return that pervades the spiritual realm and the life in Christ. We enter our hearts and find our holy Treasure, then expand to share God's wealth with creation. And in freely giving of our spiritual bounty, we inevitably find traces of his everlasting glory in the universe, which, in turn, prompt us to search out once more the Divine in our inner depths, and this *ad infinitum.* As St. Gregory of Nyssa said, "The way of God is unending. We go from beginning to beginning by way of beginnings without end."[2]

Entranceway, Pacific School of Religion, Graduate Theological Union, Berkeley.

In an unstable, depersonalized world overrun by greed, cynicism, and human exploitation—a place where "innocent Adam" would almost certainly have been devoured—it may be hard to believe in the Mystery of God at work in the cosmos, steering life for the better. War, terrorism, economic chaos, and the global environmental crisis daily undermine our sense of personal (and communal) security, to say nothing of our faith in a caring, omnipresent Deity. Like the young Edmund Dantes, too often we find ourselves as hapless prisoners confined within a corrupt and fallen realm, victims of unseen mechanizations, both natural and perhaps supernatural.

And yet as Dantes himself eventually came to realize, we cannot lose hope. Someday our freedom—effected through our holy Liberator—will come. Our prayers will be answered and every good thing we have set our hearts on shall be realized; our faith will not have been in vain. As the Count of Monte Cristo expressed after his *metanoia*,

> Never forget that, until the day God deigns to reveal the future to man, the sum of all human wisdom is contained in these two words: *Wait and hope.*[3]

* * *

On a dim morning in late summer, a day of deep, thick fog, unusual for early September, I was out at Ocean Beach, running toward Pacifica. Eventually I had reached the area near Mussel Rock, above which loomed the recently constructed seaside church, its bright cross still visible in the mist.

Positioned right along my path, stretched out on a large boulder, was an oversized blue sweatshirt. Wet with drizzle, its sleeves were curiously flung wide in an *orans* (praying with arms extended) posture.

On each sleeve, four red Byzantine-style crosses were plainly visible; in the shirt's centre a much larger, sharply designed maroon-ochre cross radiated out of a smaller one. Exploding rays surrounded this central image, the symbol par excellence of the Christian faith.[4]

It was a powerful sight. The lengthy, oversized shirt looked something like a vestment. Its nine Eastern Orthodox-style crosses spoke for themselves, but its colours were also striking—they reminded me of the colours of the Christ mosaic at Holy Trinity, and especially brought to mind a unification of heaven (symbolized by the blue) and earth (represented by the maroon-ochre tones).

The unusual shirt seemed to me a kind of blessing, a validation of my intent to ever function as a Priest of Creation, a ministerial role all faithful Christians, who have been sealed with the image of Christ through baptism, are invested to perform, that it may be well on the earth until the King of Glory comes again.

Ultimately, the "spirit-shirt" made clear to me the great and holy Plan every Christian is a part of, a grand Design of Salvation in which each must play their blessed role, in times of light and darkness, until God's love transfigures all.

> For he has made known to us in all wisdom and insight the mystery of his will, according to his purpose, which he set forth in Christ, as a plan for the fullness of time, to unite all things in him, things in heaven, and things on earth. (Ephesians 1.9-10)

Rowboat, Sausalito Yacht Harbor, California.

Christopher John Rozales, 2010

Glory to God for calling me into life.
Glory to God who has revealed to me
   the beauty of the universe.
Glory to God who has opened to me
   heaven and earth
   like a book of eternal wisdom.
Glory to God for his eternity in a passing world.
Glory to God for his seen and unseen mercies.
Glory to God for every step of my journey,
   every moment of joy,
   every sigh of my heart.
Glory to God for all created things.
Glory to God from everlasting to everlasting.

(from the Eastern Orthodox *Hymn of Thanksgiving*)

The good dream of man
is to live happily
in a blessed city,
to live blessedly
in a happy city.
The good dream of man
is to live happily
in a blessed city,
to rise in the morning
and find himself
in a blessed city,
and to live in it
through the day,
and indeed through
all the days of his life.
The good dream of man
is the dream of a blessed city,
a city in heaven,
a city on earth.

Robert Lax, from *Writing Career*

Great is the Lord, and greatly to be praised
in the City of our God, in His holy mountain ...
Behold her citadels and towers, set your hearts
on her power that you may sing of her glory
to another generation. For He is God, our God,
forever and unto the ages of ages;
He will shepherd us unto the ages.

(Psalm 48.1-2, 12-14)

What no eye has seen,
what no ear has heard,
what no heart has ever conceived,
God has prepared for those who love Him.

(1 Corinthians 2.9)

NOTES

To the Reader

1 Thomas Merton, *The Seven Storey Mountain* (New York: Harcourt Brace, 1948) 181, 237.

2 Robert Lax, *Notes* (Zurich: Pendo Verlag, 1995), 8.

Prologue

1 In Christianity, the Greek word *agape* denotes the love of God for humanity and the whole of creation. *Agape* is an active, selfless love that is entirely volitional, intercessory, unconditional. The almighty energy of *agape* is rooted in the supreme and absolute love with which God embraces the world, and all things in it.

2 The "father-son" relationship between Abbé Faria and Edmund Dantes is poignantly rendered in the 2002 movie version of *The Count of Monte Cristo,* starring Jim Caviezel as Dantes (Caviezel is best known for his role as Jesus in Mel Gibson's *The Passion of the Christ*). The acclaimed Richard Harris is cast as Abbé Faria.

3 St. Paul refers to Christ as the "Second Adam," the incarnated "God-Man" who restores humanity to the state of grace lost through the disobedience of the first Adam: "For as by one man's disobedience many were made sinners, so also by one Man's obedience many will be made righteous" (Rom 5.19; see also 1 Cor 15.45-49). Subsequent Church Fathers would thus refer to Jesus as the "New Adam" who alone had the power to restore a universe corrupted through sin.

4 Alexandre Dumas, *The Count of Monte Cristo.* Lowell Blair, trans. (New York: Bantam Classic Edition, 1981), 66. Dantes' imprisonment, suffering, intense feelings of abandonment, and literal descent into death certainly suggest a "Christlike" comparison. Interestingly, when Dantes later transforms into the "Count of Monte Cristo," his self-designed heraldic emblem features what is essentially the summit of Calvary.

5 Edmund Dantes' escape from the depths of the sea (and the Chateau d'If) figuratively compares with Christ's victorious ascent from Hades (Eph 4.8-10; 1 Pet 3.19).

6 Dumas, *The Count of Monte Cristo*, 404. Not surprisingly, this change of heart opens the Count to new, life-affirming possibilities. He eventually unites Maximilien Morrel with Valentine de Villefort, the daughter of a bitter enemy. And he himself falls for Haydee, a Turkish slave girl whom he liberated, and with whom he will later sail off and depart the restless world.

7 Dumas, *The Count of Monte Cristo,* 178.

8 Dumas, *The Count of Monte Cristo*, 440–41.

9 From a conversation with Lax on Patmos in July 1997. See also Robert Lax, *Journal B* (Zurich: Pendo-Verlag, 1988), 46.

10 The early Church Fathers unanimously believed that meditating on the grandeur of the cosmos could impart spiritual edification. The "Book of Scripture" was reinforced with the "Book of Nature," an "organic text" through which theological and moral lessons could be gleaned. God was believed knowable by his works, and this knowledge helped the contemplative to praise the Creator. Bernard of Clairvaux, the twelfth-century French saint, wrote, "You will find something more in woods than in books; trees and stones will teach you that which you can never learn from masters" (Epistle 106).

11 Isaiah 2.2-3 is one of many examples of mountain-centred symbolism occurring throughout the Bible. More popular examples include Moses' trek up Mt. Sinai and the transfiguration of Jesus on Mt. Tabor. The image of the "holy summit" recurs in Christian symbolism, as evidenced in such spiritual classics as St. Teresa of Avila's *Interior Castle* and Thomas Merton's *The Seven Storey Mountain.* The perennial image of a summit relates to the arduous climb of faith to God and the bountiful return from his Presence (the illuminated seeker returns to the world to help others make the ascent). Mountains are also linked with sacred activity because of their close proximity with the sky, functioning as "nadir points" connecting earth and heaven. The peaks of mountains tend to be covered in cloud; according to Christian theology, this expresses how the divine is incomprehensible, beyond anything the human mind can grasp. Thus, mortal knowing must ever rest in the "mystery of unknowing"; it is God alone (in the person of Christ) who must come forth from the cloud with illumination and salvation. All things "wait on God." (Tomas Spidlik, *The Spirituality of the Christian East, Vol. 2: Prayer.* Anthony Gythiel, trans. [Cistercian Publications, 2005], 206–09).

I. Gates of Entry

1 At 925 feet (282 metres), Mt. Davidson, situated near the geographical centre of the city, is the highest natural point in San Francisco. The concrete cross at the summit is 103 feet (31 metres) high and was built in 1934. Sunrise services are held at the cross every Easter.

2 For more on the author's mentorship with Robert Lax, see S.T. Georgiou, *The Way of the Dreamcatcher: Spirit-Lessons with Robert Lax, Poet, Peacemaker, Sage* (Ottawa: Novalis, 2002), 32–46 (hereafter, this source will be referred to as *Dreamcatcher*). On Lax as a hermit, sage, and mystic, see also *The Merton Seasonal,* Spring 2001 (Vol. 26, No. 1); the entire issue is devoted to Lax. A contemplative chapter on Lax appears in Murray Bodo, *Mystics: Ten Who Show Us the Ways of God* (Cincinnati, OH: St. Anthony Messenger Press, 2007). Additional works of interest include Peter France, *Hermits: Insights of Solitude* (New York: St. Martin's Press, 1996); David Miller and Nicholas Zurbrugg, eds., *The ABC's of Robert Lax* (Exeter: Stride, 1999); and James Harford, *Merton and Friends: A Joint Biography of Thomas Merton, Robert Lax, and Edward Rice* (New York: Continuum, 2006). A touching essay commenting on Lax's loving, mentoring qualities, written by one

of the poet's close friends, Moschos Lagouvardos, appears in the *Merton Seasonal,* Fall 2004 (Vol. 29, No.3), 25–32.

3   Merton, *The Seven Storey Mountain*, 181, 237.

4   *The Merton Seasonal,* Spring 2001 (Vol. 26, No. 1), 25–26. See also Br. Patrick Hart, O.C.S.O., *Patmos Journal: In Search of Thomas Merton with Robert Lax* (New York: Ring Tarigh, 1996).

5   Catherine Doherty, *Not Without Parables: Stories of Yesterday, Today, and Eternity* (Notre Dame, IN: Ave Maria Press, 1977), 76–79.

6   Jack Kerouac, *The Selected Letters: 1957–1969,* Ann Charters, ed. (New York: Penguin Books, 1999), 321.

7   Harford, *Merton and Friends,* 104. The Italian poet Francesco Conz, associated with the Surrealist and Fluxus art movements in Europe, said of Lax, "He was the last of the mystics to close a former epoch" (Miller and Zurbrugg, *The ABC's of Robert Lax*, 218).

8   Lax's only screenplay to be made into a film was *The Siren of Atlantis* (co-written with Rowland Leigh), starring Maria Montez.

9   The author's doctoral dissertation, *Sea and Sky: Robert Lax and the Spiritual Dimensions of Minimalism* (Graduate Theological Union, Berkeley, 2005), examines how the poet's life and thought sequentially shaped his minimalist creative philosophy and spiritual beliefs. Lax's "less is more" lifestyle and peacemaking concerns are also studied in light of the theme of minimalism.

10   Thomas Merton, "Circular Letter to Friends," September 1968. From *The Asian Journal of Thomas Merton* (New York: New Directions, 1973), xxix.

11   "A Song For Our Lady" is also known by the title "A Song For Notre Dame de la Garde, Marseilles." Lax travelled to the port city of Marseilles numerous times in the 1950s, while acting as a roving reporter for the celebrated national Catholic magazine *Jubilee: A Magazine of the Church and Her People,* published between 1950 and 1967.

12   Excerpt from "A Song For Our Lady" by Robert Lax, *Jubilee: A Magazine of the Church and Her People* (March 1957), 44.

13   *Jubilee* (March, 1957), 1–2.

14   While in Marseilles, Lax sought to establish a hospice for the poor (something like the Catholic Friendship House he used to volunteer at in Harlem, while working under Catherine de Hueck Doherty), but the project never came to fruition. Lax eventually travelled to Greece and settled into his hermitage on Patmos. He believed that he had been "divinely directed" to travel there through a sign he saw in his Marseilles hotel room: above his bed was an icon of St. John writing the Revelation. The icon was regularly highlighted by the setting sun (Georgiou, *Dreamcatcher,* 79–80).

15 In Marseilles, Lax received a "theopoetic vision" of the world transfigured, touched by the light of God: "The sun stood on one hand above the town but straight above the town, its light fell upon the street and every ray was like a string, each living ray was like a string of music. Each object then leapt from the street and spoke; each object said its name, proclaimed its name in glory ..." ("Port City: The Marseilles Diaries," in *Love Had a Compass,* James J. Uebbing, ed. [New York: Grove, 1996], 192–94).

16 Robert Lax, "Port City: The Marseilles Diaries," from *Love Had a Compass: Robert Lax: Journals and Poetry,* J.J. Eubbing, ed. (New York: Grove, 1996), xiii, 138, 159.

17 "In Christ are hid all the treasures of wisdom and knowledge" (Col 2.2). See also Is 33.5-6; Mt 6.21, 13.44, 19.21; Mk 10.21; Lk 12.33, 12.34, 17.21, 18.22; 2 Cor 4.7.

18 For more on Gianvito (Vito) Lo Greco, see "Desert Secret" in Georgiou, *Mystic Street,* 257–62.

19 Excerpted portion of a letter from Vito Lo Greco, January 2007. Used with permission.

20 All the great faiths indicate that an interior journey is necessary in experiencing the bliss of transcendence. This communal inward trek should especially be kept in mind when engaged in interfaith dialogue—since all inner roads lead to the Heart, the ideal attitude toward other faiths should be grounded in the spirit of loving exchange wherein humility, integrity, patience, discernment, and a deep sense of mystery prevail. While *The Isle of Monte Cristo* is written from a Christian perspective, how Christ works outside of Christianity is treated as an apophatic mystery in this book, and, as such, points to the freedom of God, who in his work of providence and redemption transcends all limitations. As the Eastern Orthodox theologian and author Fr. John Garvey makes abundantly clear, "Each of us is capable of understanding only the most fragmentary and dim aspects of the Truth we hope to encounter fully .... We cannot know what God wills for those who are not Christians. We do know that God has created all out of love and that God is merciful, and the fullness of the joy God wishes for all of us is beyond our imagining" (Garvey, *Seeds of the Word* [New York: St. Vladimir's Seminary Press, 2005], 125–26). It is also vital to remember that the earliest Christian apologists taught that Christ the Word (the Logos of God) is accessible in "seed form" in both non-Christian and pre-Christian faiths and philosophies. While Christian traditions may claim to teach the "fullness of the truth," they cannot claim a monopoly on truth (Garvey, *Seeds of the Word,* 7–13). Thus it is the "mystery of God"—and our experience with it—that must remain pre-eminent in both interfaith dialogue and everyday living.

21 "Jerusalem," in *Robert Lax: 33 Poems,* Thomas Kellien, ed. (New York: New Directions, 1988), 51–52.

22 Paul Chryssavgis, *Light Through Darkness: The Orthodox Tradition* (Maryknoll, NY: Orbis, 2004), 111.

23 Robert Lax, *Psalm* (Zurich: Pendo-Verlag, 1991), 22–26. Works by Lax that demonstrate the belief that this life is a "training ground" for spiritual discovery include *21 Pages, Psalms, Dialogues,* and *Notes,* all published by Pendo-Verlag, Zurich.

24 C.S. Lewis, *The Problem of Pain* (New York: HarperCollins, 2001), 57.

25 St. Augustine, *The Confessions,* R.S. Pine-Coffin, trans. (London: Penguin Classics, 1986), 21.

26 See Georgiou, *Mystic Street,* 229.

27 *Beowulf,* D. Wright, trans. (London: Penguin Classics, 1986), 68.

28 From a conversation with Lax on Patmos, October 21, 1999.

29 Lax, *Notes,* 90.

30 Georgiou, *Dreamcatcher,* 204.

31 Lax, *21 Pages* (Zurich: Pendo-Verlag, 1984), 12.

32 The interior of an Eastern Orthodox church may be said to replicate the interior of the mystic heart, most significantly during Divine Liturgy. Early Church Fathers often refer to the heart as an "inner kingdom." This kingdom is invoked at the beginning of every service ("Blessed is the Kingdom of the Father, and of the Son, and of the Holy Spirit, both *now* and forever, and unto the ages of ages.") The treasure of the Christ is available immediately. God is in our midst. God's kingdom is at hand, a holy realm visually and tactilely demonstrated by icons, incense, and ethereal hymns. This material richness reminds the worshipper that the "kingdom to come" may be readily glimpsed, and this through the Resurrection. God's saving, renewing grace is already transforming this fleeting world into paradise.

33 Though "all the elements will one day melt with fire" to form "a new heaven and a new earth" (2 Pet 3.10-13), the new creation will be born out of the old, fallen world through its transfiguration in Christ. Since creation is the product of an eternally good God who transcends any imperfection brought on by Adam, nothing will be ultimately lost, but rather changed, perfected, according to divine mercy and unconditional love (and humanity's response to that love). This supernatural rebirth will transform both the *macrocosmos* (the entire universe) and the *microcosmos* (the human person), because both are intrinsically related—Adam was fashioned from the earth. That God shall use both matter and spirit to create a new world demonstrates a profound organic spirituality, distinct from other religions, which profess a purely spiritual afterlife.

34 "God is love" (1 Jn 4.8); "We love because he first loved us" (1 Jn 4.19).

35 On baptism conferring inner illumination: "The true light *that enlightens every man* was coming into the world …." (Jn 1.9). St. Gregory of Sinai (thirteenth century) describes baptism as a treasure buried within us, a gift we have received

from Christ that must be brought to light (*The Art of Prayer*, Timothy Ware, ed. [London: Faber, 1966, 114]).

36 This "inward and upward" double movement, in which the contemplative enters his heart and rises above his temporal condition, is common among Christian mystics. On entering the heart via prayer, the contemplative feels the concentration of love so profoundly that he "ascends," oftentimes in a spiral fashion, as if winding up a mountain. The image of divine ascent appears in pre-Christian mysticism (Plato's *Symposium*) and is also evident in the Torah (Jacob's ladder of ascending-descending angels, Moses climbing Mt. Sinai) and in the Gospels (the Sermon on the Mount, the Transfiguration of Jesus on Mt. Tabor, and his Ascent on Mt. Olivet).

37 For Christians, this perpetual "inward-outward" flow sustaining creation is based on the supernatural model of "divine contemplation, emanation, and return": in essence, God in heaven creates, incarnates himself in his creation, and then returns to his blessed domain. In similar fashion, the contemplative Christian recreates himself through inward prayer (prays himself into God), emanates with blessings, and then returns to his salvific Source. Interestingly, all the great faith leaders— Moses, Jesus, Muhammad, Buddha, Lao Tsu, the Hindu Rishis—withdrew from the noisy, materialistic world, that they might enter into themselves and commune with a higher reality. All the mystics (Kabbalists, Hesychasts, Sufis, etc.) have departed the illusory trappings of society in quest of a quiet inner refuge where they might discover their true selves and cultivate their connection with an infinite Source, after which they return into the world to illuminate others.

38 For more on this topic, see Tobin Hart, *The Secret Spiritual World of Children* (Philadelphia: Quaker Books, 2006).

39 Lax, *21 Pages*, 6, 16.

40 Thomas Merton, *The Inner Experience: Notes on Contemplation* (New York: HarperCollins, 2003, 128–29).

41 On the struggles of this passing world, the Elder Amphilochius Makris, a modern holy man of Patmos, said "Where there is no struggle, there is not victory; where there is not victory, there is no crown." (Paul Nikitaras, *Elder Amphilochius Makris: A Contemporary Personality of Patmos, 1889–1970* (Patmos: Monastery of St. John Publications, 1990), 111.

42 See Georgiou, *Dreamcatcher*, 211.

43 Especially in the past decade, science is discovering that there may be a "hidden world" beyond our perception where particles and forces are helping to stabilize the cosmos and ensure its continuity on every level of existence. "Seen and unseen worlds" interact beyond our imagining, dimensions in which we constantly (though imperceptibly) participate, perhaps suggestive of a transcendent cosmic directive. See Ian Sample, *Massive: The Hunt for the God Particle* (London: Virgin Books, 2010).

44 *The Upanishads*, Juan Mascaro, trans. (London: Penguin Books, 1965), 120.

45 *Pensées*, A.J. Krailsheimer, trans. (Middlesex: Penguin Books, 1966), 154, 216.

46 For more on Lax's concept of "going with the flow" (the flow of God's love), see Georgiou, *Dreamcatcher*, 75–76. Interestingly, the word "God" relates with flow. "God" is derived from the Germanic *Gudam*, which in turn stems from the Indo-European root *gheu*, meaning to "pour blessings," as in libations. So when we hearken to God and feel God's presence, we are literally "going with the divine Flow."

47 Simone Weil, *Gravity and Grace* (Lincoln, NE: Bison Books Reprint, 1997), 132. Weil's *metaxu*, or "intermediary" concept (that every separation may also serve as a link) is borrowed from Plato's *Symposium*.

48 Weil, *Gravity and Grace*, 132.

49 *Modern Greek Poetry*, Friar Kimon, trans. (Athens: Efstathiades Group, 1982), 224.

50 With the Incarnation of Christ (made evident during his momentous baptism in the River Jordan, in which the Trinity revealed itself [Mt 3.13-17]), a "new creation" began. The salvific energies of his holy baptism radiated throughout the cosmos, resanctifying it, preparing creation for its ultimate transfiguration on the last day. Likewise, the Incarnation bridged the abyss between God and humanity, heaven and earth, because Christ is the long-awaited and heralded *Theanthropos*, simultaneously both God and Man.

51 "God became man so that man could become like God" is from Athanasius' *On the Incarnation*. The famous quote reveals the intimate connection the Creator shares with his creation. God so loved the world that he entered into it and took on human form. In this way, humanity could receive his Spirit, and by an infinite series of ascendant degrees, be made divine. God's plan to enter the world is seen in Leviticus 26.12 ("I will walk among you, and will be your God, and you shall be my people") and 2 Corinthians 6.16 ("I will live and move among you").

52 Christian tradition relates that these dark forces were originally angels, but fell from heaven as a result of a "supernatural schism" led by Satan, whom Jesus describes as the "Father of lies, a murderer from the beginning in whom there is no truth" (Jn 8.47). All evil is traced to this fallen angel, who still endeavours to disaffect humanity from God. Though Christ, having risen from the dead, is victorious over Satan and his minions, the demons still have power in the world until Jesus comes again in glory. Until then, the Christian soldier fights with the "sword of the Spirit," and is equipped with the "armour of light" (Eph 6.13-17), mystically received at baptism.

53 John 20.19 reveals that Jesus "walked through walls," appearing to his disciples in an enclosed room. Related to this supernatural ability is the phenomenon of *bilocation*, wherein saints are able to be at two distinct places at the same time. In bilocating, the holy can project their forms through matter unimpeded. A recent

example of a popular bilocating saint is Padre Pio (1887–1968), who briefly served as Robert Lax's confessor.

54 That the soul of the dead is thought to "wander" for a period of time (usually around forty days) before entering the next life remains a popular belief in both Western and Eastern religions. In Christianity, this concept is based on the resurrected Jesus remaining on earth until the fortieth day, when he ascended into heaven. Contrary to popular opinion, ghosts and spirits are not unfamiliar entities in Judeo-Christian tradition (1 Sam 28.8-15; Mk 6.49). The Nicene Creed also states, "I believe in all things, both visible and invisible [seen and unseen]."

55 In the Eastern Orthodox liturgy, immediately prior to the recitation of the Nicene Creed and the preparation of the Eucharist, the priest loudly exclaims, *"The doors! The doors! In wisdom let us be attentive!"* These words not only herald the preparation and dispensation of Holy Communion (the heart of the Christian mysteries), but also remind us that life is an inner passage that ultimately leads to the compassionate Lord of Creation.

II. Spirit Currents

1 Heinrich Zimmer, *Myths and Symbols in Indian Art and Civilization*, Joseph Campbell, ed. Bollingen Series VI. (Princeton, NJ: Princeton University Press, 1946), 221.

2 Georgiou, *Mystic Street,* 183–84.

3 Jean Pierre de Caussade, *The Abandonment to Divine Providence*, John Beevers, trans. (New York: Doubleday Publishing Group, 1993).

4 A few of Lax's early works, such as *Circus of the Sun* and *Mogador's Book,* especially emphasize the creative repetition of life. For more on Lax and divine flow, see Georgiou, *Dreamcatcher*, 75–77.

5 Robert Lax, *A Thing That Is: New Poems of Robert Lax*, Paul Spaeth, ed. (New York: Overlook Press, 1997), 42.

6 Robert Lax, *New Poems* (New York: Journeyman Books, 1962), 5.

7 See Georgiou, *Mystic Street,* 107–112, 199–202.

8 Chrysostom, *On the Incomprehensibility of God*, Sermon 5.

9 An "arrow prayer" is a quick intercessory prayer said in a moment of need. Oftentimes such prayers are the most honest and straightforward supplications because dire necessity propels them. The arrow prayer follows the teaching of Jesus: "And in praying do not heap up empty phrases as the Gentiles do; for they think that they will be heard for their many words" (Mt 6.7).

10 The prayer "Deliver us, O Lord, from all affliction, wrath, danger, and distress" is from *The Divine Liturgy of St. John Chrysostom* (fifth century), the dominant liturgy in the Eastern Orthodox Church. The Greek word for liturgy denotes "a work for the people."

11 Georgiou, *Dreamcatcher,* 237.

12 Robert Lax, *Journal A* (Zurich: Pendo Verlag, 1986), 84.

13 Robert Lax, *Mogador's Book* (Zurich: Pendo Verlag, 1992), 62.

14 Robert Lax, *Dialogues* (Zurich: Pendo Verlag, 1994), 120.

15 Lax, *Notes*, 90.

16 For more on the crisis in higher education, two classics in this genre are Alan Bloom, *The Closing of the American Mind* (New York: Simon & Schuster, 1987) and Page Smith, *Killing the Spirit: Higher Education In America* (New York: Penguin, 1991). Though written two decades ago, the sentiments expressed are timeless.

17 *San Francisco Chronicle*, May 22, 2009. The July 2009 issue of *Pediatrics* magazine reveals that in a study based on a survey of 20,000 college students, fifteen percent of students felt that they were going to die young.

18 Georgiou, *Dreamcatcher*, 241, 243. In a similar manner, St. Augustine said, "Love it is that asks, love that seeks, love that knocks, love that reveals, love, finally, that assures the permanence of what is revealed. Take away love ... and the proofs will no longer hold" (Eugene Portalie, *A Guide to the Thought of St. Augustine* [Westport: Greenwood, 1975], 107–08).

19 As Carl Jung, Mircea Eliade, and Joseph Campbell have made evident in their scholarship, nearly all the shamanic traditions and world faiths have beliefs centring on heroes and/or powers that enter into human existence, die, and are reborn. Oftentimes these heroes/gods act as sacrifices to ensure crop growth, the continuity of the seasons, and so on. A sacrificial and saving power runs deep in the human psyche. In a sense, Jesus came not to subvert pre-Christian traditions, but to *perfect* them. See *Psychology and Religion: West and East* (Jung), *The Sacred and the Profane* (Eliade), and *The Hero with a Thousand Faces* (Campbell).

20 Versions of the Jesus Prayer include "*Jesus Christ, Son of God, have mercy upon me*" and "*Lord Jesus Christ, Son of God, have mercy upon me, a sinner.*" For more on the Jesus Prayer (which is essentially derived from Lk 18.13), see Archimandrite Lev Gillet, *The Jesus Prayer* (New York: St. Vladimir's Seminary Press, 1987) and *The Art of Prayer,* Timothy Ware, ed. (New York: Faber and Faber, 1966).

21 Georgiou, *Dreamcatcher*, 222.

22 A "holy fool" is someone who enlightens people under the guise of foolishness and eccentric, if not bizarre, behaviour. Holy fools prefer to appear mad so as not to draw attention to themselves; they would rather give all the glory to the Divine. The holy fool is popular in Eastern Orthodoxy, Zen Buddhism, Taoism and Sufism.

23 Intermittently, I prayed for Nick's safety during these months. I had already known one transient killed in his cell by a psychotic inmate. See Georgiou, *Mystic Street*, 47–52.

24 *Mother Maria Skobtsova: Essential Writings,* Helene Klepinin-Arjakovsky, ed. (Maryknoll, NY: Orbis, 2003). Mother Maria Skobtsova (1891–1945), also known as "Saint Mary of Paris," is often compared to Dorothy Day, who founded the Catholic Worker Movement. Mother Maria emphasized love of one's neighbour, even in the harshest of conditions. During World War II, she sheltered Jews and helped many to escape. Eventually, the Nazis discovered her operation. She perished in the gas chambers of Ravensbrük prison.

25 To view the "Crossbow Jesus" online, go to www.famsf.org/legion. Search the Imagebase using "Pendant" as the key search word. Go to page 13—the medallion is listed as no. 121.

26 Gregory of Nyssa, *Homilies on the Song of Songs,* 4.

27 The pendant was worn by a member of a German sharpshooter's guild. Such medallions were common among bowmen throughout the Renaissance, and usually integrated images of St. Sebastian (third century), the patron saint of archers in Western Christendom. Sebastian, a soldier ordered by the Emperor Diocletian to be shot to death with arrows for his secret faith in Christ, survived this ordeal; later, after publicly declaring his religion, he suffered martyrdom. As the life-giving "Arrow of God," Jesus—who pierces death and sin and opens up a "skyway to heaven"—complements and completes the pendant.

28 *Greek Orthodox Holy Week and Easter Services*, George Papadeas, ed. (New York: Archdiocesan Press, 1973), 384, 454.

29 See Georgiou, *Mystic Street*, 217–23.

30 John Neihardt, *Black Elk Speaks: Being the Life Story of a Holy Man of the Oglala Sioux* (Lincoln, NE: University of Nebraska Press, 1972), 32.

III. Riding the Waves

1 The two fingers of Jesus also relate to his dual natures: Christ is both fully divine and fully human. Additionally, his two-toned robes (blue/crimson-brown) represent how heaven and earth are contained in him.

2 All three angels bear attributes of each member of the Trinity. The mansion (or temple-kingdom) relates to the *Father*; the Oak of Mamre (symbolic of the Tree of Life and the Cross) associates with the *Son*; the mountain and cave suggest the *Holy Spirit*, who may be likened to both a mysterious void (hence the cave) and to the ineffable mist swirling atop a mountain, the sacred axis point where heaven and earth allegorically meet.

3 C.S. Lewis writes, "The whole dance, drama, or pattern of the Three-Personed Life [the Holy Trinity] is to be played out in each one of us" (*The Weight of Glory* [San Francisco: HarperOne, 2001], 153.

4 On the rewards of humility, Robert Lax said, "The 'humus' in the word 'humility' means earth. When we touch the earth, we can't help to grow, all in God's good time ...." (Georgiou, *Dreamcatcher*, 188).

5   "True mystics are those who know that they transform the universe by accept-
     ing the will of the Father" (Tomas Spidlik, *The Spirituality of the Christian East,
     Volume 2: Prayer*, Anthony Gythiel, trans. [Cistercian Publications, 2008], 269).
     All saints understand that the highest wisdom is to cut off selfish desires and "go
     with the divine flow." Every true believer lives out what John the Baptist said to
     Jesus: "He must increase, I must decrease" (Jn 3.30).

6   See *Biblical Archaeology Review*, March/April 2007 (Vol. 33, No. 2), "Losing Faith:
     How Scholarship Affects Scholars," 50–57.

7   This "separation" from God is commonly referred to in Christianity as the "dark
     night of the soul," a phase in a person's spiritual life marked by intense feelings
     of loneliness, doubt, depression, and diabolical despair. Though the individual
     practises a devout life, he or she may gradually (or suddenly) find it difficult to
     pray, leading to feelings that God has abandoned him or her. The expression was
     originally coined by the Spanish poet and mystic St. John of the Cross, who used
     it as a title for a poem and treatise describing his arduous journey toward union
     with God. Many Christian mystics have experienced lengthy "dark nights," some
     lasting decades, as in the case of Mother Teresa of Calcutta (see *Come Be My
     Light: The Private Writings of the Saint of Calcutta* [New York: Doubleday, 2007]).
     Robert Lax, in his poem-book *Psalm*, describes his own inner passage from divine
     light to darkness and then to divine light again. Though the "dark night" may be
     excruciatingly painful, in the long run it is seen as both a means of purgation and
     a test of faith. While the "tested" believer is stripped of the divine joy he once felt,
     he inwardly becomes more virtuous because he quietly and reverently waits on
     God. The "dark night" is also based on the life of Christ, who in agony prayed to
     the Father in the Garden of Gethsemani and on the cross uttered the ultimate cry
     of desolation: *"My God, my God, why have you forsaken me?"* (Mk 15.34).

8   St. Paul said that he "died daily" to himself, that he might experience Christ all the
     more (1 Cor 15.31). What is significant in the Christian "dark night experience" is
     that the *self* (the egoistic "I") is crucified with Jesus (emptied of its illusions). Once
     this refining process is complete, the purified self is renewed in the resurrected
     Christ. Hence St. Paul exclaims, "It is no longer I who live, but Christ who lives in
     me" (Gal 2.20, 5.24).

9   Søren Kierkegaard, *The Sickness unto Death: A Christian Psychological Exposition
     for Upbuilding and Awakening* (Princeton, NJ: Princeton University Press, 1983).
     The dark night impels the penitent individual to realize that he/she must let go of
     everything (sin, ego, self-centred desires, illusory pleasures), save God. Coming to
     terms with this "unconditional surrender" is difficult and painful, much like the
     aging process, which in itself teaches that all things decay and perish, except that
     which is rooted in the Spirit. In many ways, the illumined soul remains in "hell"
     until it makes Christ the conscious centre of its existence, and this through love.
     Recognizing its inward Light, a soul is made free.

10 *Pensées*, 148. Jesus himself said to his disciples, "Apart from me you can do nothing" (Jn 15.5). Thus St. Paul states, "I can do anything through Christ who strengthens me" (Phil 4.13). This complete trust in the Lord has its roots throughout the Old Testament.

11 That the earth and cosmos are perishing is a belief common to many of the major world religions. Certainly the popular phrase "Ashes to ashes, dust to dust" (based on Gen 3.19) speaks of creation's transience. The Hebrew and Christian scriptures affirm that one day, "the elements shall dissolve in fire and the earth will be consumed" (Is 34.4; 2 Pet 3.12). St. Paul consequently exclaims, "Here we have no lasting city; we seek the city which is to come" (Heb 13.14). Repeatedly, the Judeo-Christian God promises a new and everlasting creation: "the tribulations of the former age shall be no more" (Is 65.17, 66.22; Rev 21.5). Islam also declares that "life in this world is nothing but a brief passage" (Koran 40.39). And the Eastern religions (Hinduism, Buddhism, and also Taoism, to an extent) even go so far as to stress that since everything present is in flux (and consequently impermanent and decaying), the cosmos is utterly empty of true existence; essentially, all is already void. The only reality we may discern is our awareness of the moment at hand.

12 That Christ empathetically suffers with a suffering world (and is enduring our tribulations with us) is alluded to in Luke 21.18: "For I will not drink of the fruit of the vine until the Kingdom of God shall come." In essence, Jesus will at last drink of the "new cup" when his faithful shall be gathered around him in the New Age.

13 The fact that spirit-centred suffering remains a *universal phenomenon* should never be forgotten, especially in the midnight hour (or "Dark Night"), when one's intense pain may easily become wholly self-centred. Thus it is during the early morning (2 to 3 AM) that many monks in both the East and West rise to pray for a world too wounded and/or weak to pray for itself. The Sixth Prayer in the Eastern Orthodox "Office of Orthos" states: "Lord, remember them who cry out to you in the night; hear them, and show them mercy ..." (from the *Liturgicos*, Northridge, CA: Narthex Press, 1993, 31). Whether in tribulation or joy, no one stands alone.

14 The Discourses of St. John of Karpathos, from the *Philokalia*, Vol. 1, G.E.H. Palmer, Philip Sherrard, and Kallistos Ware, eds. (London: Faber and Faber, 318). Christ's statement, "When the Son of Man comes, will he find faith on earth?" (Lk 18.8) illustrates how harsh and void of love the end times may be.

15 Georgiou, *Dreamcatcher*, 229–32. The theme of "waiting for God" resurfaces in Lax's writing, as especially exemplified in his lengthy and introspective poem, *21 Pages*.

16 The "Eighth Day" corresponds to the image of timelessness in the world to come, and points to the "New Creation." (As Genesis 1–2 indicates, the original creation lasted seven days.) The Eighth Day was consecrated by the resurrection of Christ;

therefore, all Christians are already living in the "Eighth Day," and, as such, have already tasted life everlasting. The Eighth Day will fully dawn and come into glory with the Second Coming of Christ. Since the beginning of Christianity, the number eight has symbolized the resurrection; hence, numerous baptisteries are octagonal in shape (Jean Danielou, *The Bible and the Liturgy* [Notre Dame, IN: University of Notre Dame Press, 2002]).

17 Existing in both Western and Eastern religious iconography, halos define the holy and enlightened. The nimbus is a natural, visible outcome of *theosis*, the "Godward journey." The saint who intensely loves comes to take on the "all-loving Christ energy" that sustains the universe; the holy individual irrepressibly and joyously exudes it, and this for eternity, as demonstrated by the circular halo, which has no beginning or end (like God). For more on this topic, see Vladimir Lossky, *The Mystical Theology of the Eastern Church* (Crestwood, NY: St. Vladimir's Seminary Press, 1957, reprinted 1997).

18 St. Augustine, *City of God*, Book 22, Chapter 30.

19 For more on Jackie Chew, see the "30 Good Minutes" website found at http://www.csec.org. Click on "Short Videos" and search for Jacqueline Chew.

20 John 14.13

21 Matthew 21.22

22 The *Enso* is a Zen Buddhist creation. In its circumference, the circle represents the physical totality of the universe, while its vacuous interior imparts ultimate voidness—the luminous emptiness (or domain of potential) in which all things are. The circle, executed with a single fluid movement, symbolizes absolute and true enlightenment. When a Zen adept's mind is clear, the drawn Enso is strong and well balanced.

23 Robert Lax, "Circus of the Sun," in *33 Poems*, 10. For more on Robert Lax's last days, see Jack Kelly, "Robert Lax: Coming Home," *The Merton Seasonal*, Spring 2001 (Vol. 26, No. 1), 3–6.

24 Lax, "Circus of the Sun," 10.

25 For more on the hazards of the Internet and technology overuse/addiction, see Jonathan Zittrain, *The Future of the Internet—And How to Stop It* (New Haven, CT: Yale University Press, 2009); Lee Siegel, *Against the Machine* (New York: Random House, 2008); John Freeman, *Logging Off: The Tyranny of Email* (New York: Scribner, 2009); Clifford Stoll, *Silicon Snake Oil: Second Thoughts on the Information Highway* (New York: Anchor Books, 1996); Nicholas Carr, *The Shallows: What the Internet Is Doing to Our Brains* (New York: W.W. Norton, 2010).

26 AP-Ipsos Poll, November 2006.

27 Benny Evangelista, "High Tech Taking Toll on Attention and Relations," *San Francisco Chronicle*, November 15, 2009. To quote Dorothy Day, "God meant

things to be much easier than what we have made of them" (Day, *Meditations* [New York: Newman Press, 1970]).

28 Benny Evangelista, "Americans Gorging on Mounds of Data," *San Francisco Chronicle,* December 9, 2009.

29 Rainer Maria Rilke, *Letters to a Young Poet,* M.D. Herter Norton, trans. (New York: W.W. Norton, 1993). Original edition 1929.

30 Georgiou, *Dreamcatcher,* 147.

31 Georgiou, *Dreamcatcher,* 144, 146.

32 See Georgiou, *Dreamcatcher,* 258.

33 A.N. Tsirintanes, *Knowing Where We Are Going* (London: Cassell & Co., 1973), 84. This quote by Tsirintanes compares to a famous "prophecy" of the early desert father St. Antony the Great: "A time is coming when people will go mad, and when they see someone who is not mad, they will attack that person, shouting, 'You are mad! You are not like us!'" (Enzo Bianchi, *Words for the Inner Life* [Ottawa: Novalis, 2002], 7).

IV. Kingdom of the Heart

1   C.S. Lewis, *Letters to Malcolm* (New York: Harvest, 2002), chapter 17.

2   D.G. Davaris, *Patmos: The Sacred Island* (Athens, 1989), 52. According to the monks of the Monastery of St. John, the Evangelist's last sermon may have also consisted of the simple phrase "Just love one another." See also Georgiou, *Dreamcatcher,* 82–83.

3   Robert Lax, *Journal E: The Hollywood Journal* (Zurich: Pendo-Verlag, 1996), 68.

4   Simone Weil, *Waiting for God* (New York: G.P. Putnam's Sons, 1951), 104.

5   St. Augustine, *Confessions,* Book 1.

6   While the original transgression of Adam and Eve necessitated the coming of Christ to repair the break between Creator and creation (a wrong no mortal could right because of its cosmic and integrative magnitude), numerous theologians in Western and Eastern Christianity rejected the view that the Incarnation happened solely because of the shared sin of the first couple. Most notable among these theologians was Blessed John Duns Scotus, the medieval Franciscan philosopher. Scotus believed that the Incarnation principally transpired through the "fullness of divine love." In essence, God had *always intended* to become human, to love humanity intimately, as a Father, and to take rightful possession of His kingdom.

7   All of nature is, in a sense, "jelling" for something infinitely greater than itself to issue from its sacral core. Many spiritual writers speak of creation as an interconnected "matrix." The Latin root of this word denotes womb.

8   From Robinson Jeffers, "Return," in *The Wild God of the World: A Robinson Jeffers Anthology* (Palo Alto, CA: Stanford University Press, 2003), 151.

9   Georgiou, *Dreamcatcher,* 81.

10 Whether or not "St. John the Disciple-Evangelist" and "John of Patmos, the Seer of the Revelation" are one and the same has remained a subject of debate among theologians. Eastern Orthodox tradition has, for the most part, asserted that John the Evangelist is indeed the author of Revelation. Numerous early Church Fathers (Justin Martyr, Hermas, Papias, Ireneaus, Tertullian, Clement of Alexandria, Athanasius, Cyril of Alexandria, and Gregory of Nyssa) believed that John the Evangelist and John the Seer were the same individual. Since the fourth century, critics have argued that the writing style of the Revelation is far different from that of the Fourth Gospel. However, it should be noted that the elderly John, around ninety years of age at the time of the Revelation, was "caught up in the Spirit." In such an altered and mystical state, John's language and form of expression would have certainly parted from the norm, accounting for irregularities in the document. Interestingly, Church tradition maintains that John did not "write" his Revelation; it was physically recorded by his disciple Prochorus (R.A. Culpepper, *John, the Son of Zebedee: The Life of a Legend (Including a Study of the Acts of John)* [Columbia, SC: University of South Carolina Press, 1994]).

11 The buildings and grounds of the Monastery and Cave of the Apocalypse were erected in successive stages, beginning in 1000 AD and extending into the nineteenth century. Perhaps as early as the third century, pilgrims began visiting Patmos to pray within the hallowed cave of St. John. Some of the earliest monastic settlements on Patmos are found at the Rock of Kallikatsou, formerly known as "Petra."

12 Little is known about the mentor-disciple relationship of St. John and Prochorus. Eventually, an oral tradition emerged that resulted in the apocryphal *Acts of John,* a late fourth-century or early fifth-century work spuriously attributed to Prochorus.

13 Seraphim of Sarov (1756–1833) remains one of Russia's most beloved saints. He taught that the primary aim of life is to acquire the Holy Spirit through *theosis* (deification, becoming like God through divine, superabundant grace). In doing so, one comes to increasingly radiate love. A great lover of animals and nature, Seraphim of Sarov may be likened to St. Francis of Assisi.

14 Courtesy Archimandrite Efthimiou Koutsanellos, Superior Emeritus, Holy Cave and Monastery of the Apocalypse. Portions of this document have been edited.

15 In most Eastern Orthodox icons depicting the crucifixion, Christ's heart is positioned at (or very near) the intersection of the cross, illustrating the pre-eminence of the heart in the spiritual path.

16 Letter to Robert Lax, from *When Prophecy Still Had a Voice: The Letters of Thomas Merton and Robert Lax,* A.W. Biddle, ed. (Lexington, KY: University of Kentucky Press, 2001), 102.

17 Lax, *Journal B*, 54.

18 Lax, *Mogador's Book*, 68.

19 Thomas Merton, *New Seeds of Contemplation* (New York: New Directions, 1961), 250. In choosing fishermen (instead of scholars) to be his disciples, Christ revealed that salvation does not depend on degrees and accolades but centres on cultivating an honest, loving heart.

20 Francesco Conz, "Impressions of Robert Lax," in *The ABC's of Robert Lax*, 217–18.

21 Robert Lax, *Journal C* (Zurich: Pendo-Verlag, 1990); *Journal B*, 28.

22 *Apolytikion, 4th Plagal Tone.* Our existence may be seen as a rhythmic oscillation of love, the prime expanding-contracting pulse of life. The universe as a whole may operate according to this outflow-inflow principle, beginning with the Big Bang, functioning much like a universal heartbeat.

23 "Primary relics" are the body parts of saints (usually bones), whereas "secondary relics" are objects that have come into direct contact with primary relics, thus conveying the holy energy, sacredness, and blessings of the saint. A scriptural example of this faith practice may be found in Acts 19.11. Interestingly, this transference of healing/empowering/protective energy from "primary relics" is found in many religions and tribal societies throughout the world. For more on relics, see Georgiou, *Mystic Street*, 243–46.

24 Georgiou, *Dreamcatcher*, 275–76. Robert Lax died in his sleep on September 26, 2000, on the Feast Day of St. John the Divine, the patron saint of Patmos and author of the Fourth Gospel and the Revelation.

25 See Georgiou, *Mystic Street*, 110–11.

26 For more on the blue neon cross at Patmos, located across the Bay of Skala and atop a mountain in Koumana, see Georgiou, *Dreamcatcher*, 82.

27 This somatic cross has remained a consistent personal symbol. See Georgiou, *Mystic Street*, 87–91.

28 See Georgiou, *Dreamcatcher*, 255.

29 The Monastery of St. Catherine in Egypt was built in the sixth century. It is the oldest continually inhabited Christian monastery in the world. Nestled in a valley between Mt. Sinai (where Moses received the Decalogue) and Mt. St. Catherine (named after the fourth-century martyr), the monastery houses the most extensive collection of Byzantine icons in existence. The monastery is also famous for the *Codex Sinaicticus*, which contains the oldest complete copy of the New Testament (dated 350 CE). For more information about the monastery and its extensive treasures, including the "Sinai Jesus," see http://orthodoxwiki.org/St._Catherine's_Monastery_(Sinai).

30 Georgiou, *Dreamcatcher*, 38–39.

31 Lax's last book, *The Peacemaker's Handbook*, contains many of these sentiments. See *The Peacemaker's Handbook* (Zurich: Pendo-Verlag, 2001).

32 According to the Psalms, even matter is imbued with a kind of "creator consciousness" receptive to the divine Presence. Thus, when Christ comes again, "The trees
of the wood shall sing, the seas shall roar, the fields will exult, the floods shall clap
their hands and the hills will sing for joy …" (Ps 96, 98). On the deeper mysteries
of Jesus' baptism and its association with creation, see K. McDonnell, *The Baptism
of Jesus in the Jordan: The Trinitarian and Cosmic Order of Salvation* (New York:
Michael Glazier Books, 1996).

33 Here the question may be raised, "Will all the dead, even the most heinous and
justly condemned, be 'made free' when Christ comes again? Will there be salvation for all?" Numerous early theologians (Origen, St. Gregory of Nyssa, St. Isaac
of Nineveh) have suggested this possibility, arguing that in perfect love, all things
are forgiven and liberated and so find their proper and blessed place in renewed
creation, "that God may be all in all" (1 Cor 15.28). A common point also made
is that it would not make sense to have infinite punishment (hell for eternity) to
chastise those who have committed only a finite number of sins. Hence St. Paul's
declaration, "God has imprisoned all in disobedience, that he may be merciful to
all" (1 Cor 11.32). Ultimately, the nature of the *apocatastasis* (hope in all things
reconciled) remains a mystery "to be revealed." Once I asked Robert Lax what
he thought about the *apocatastasis,* and he replied by drawing a circle. Inside the
circle he wrote, "There's nobody left in the Beat-Up Room but---." He then placed
"me" outside of the circle, adding, "And I give him a pretty rough time." In other
words, while all may be saved, we must live as obedient to Christ as possible.

34 The Nicene Creed was formulated in 325 in the town of Nicaea by the First
Ecumenical Council. This declaration of faith contains the foundational beliefs of
early Christianity. The Creed was instrumented in order to unify the early Church,
which had been had been persecuted for 300 years by the Roman government.
During this time, the religion was practised underground, in secret throughout
the Mediteranean world. The Creed was therefore needed to effect clarity and
cohesion in the early Christian Church.

35 Excerpt from Lax, *21 Pages,* 20, 28, 80.

36 Nicholas Cabasilas, *The Life in Christ,* Carmino De Catanzaro, trans. (New York:
St. Vladimir's Seminary Press, 1974), 79.

37 Based on *Greek Orthodox Holy Week and Easter Services,* compiled by George
Papadeas (New York: Greek Orthodox Archdiocese, 1973), 481–82. Portions of
this passage have been slightly edited.

38 The heart represents the holy core of our being, the "inner shrine" made in the
image of God in which the union between the divine and human is consummated.
Since the seal of baptism is impressed on the heart forever, this "inner sanctum"
can never be destroyed.

39　There is an old theme in the Christian tradition (going back to Judaism) that reveals how humans were created actually superior to the angels. This idea is based on the ancient belief that humans are a *microcosmos* (a smaller universe in which elements of heaven and earth, the two realms created in Genesis 1.1, are contained). In us, spirit and matter, heaven and earth therefore *co-join*. Moreover, how we live affects both the world above and the world below. Ultimately, we have the graced potential to be ministers (overlords) of all creation, while angels are limited to performing specific tasks; they cannot nurture, elevate, and unify the universe. According to Christian tradition, Lucifer (Satan) became jealous of Adam and Eve's greater cosmic role, and so fell from grace. As stated in Isaiah 14.12, "How you have fallen, O Daystar, son of Dawn! How you are cut down to the ground, you who laid the nations low! You said in your heart, 'I will ascend to heaven; above the stars of God I will set my throne on high ....'"

40　Those ordained to the priesthood of the clergy offer back to heaven an organic "microcosm" of creation—wine and bread, supernaturally changed into the God-Man Jesus, the "New Adam" and High Priest linking heaven and earth. Water and oil are also natural elements used in the sacraments. Christianity is thus a very "green" religion. See Meletios Webber, *Bread, Water, Wine, and Oil: An Orthodox Christian Experience of God* (Ben Lomond, CA: Conciliar Press, 2007) and Ian Bradley, *God Is Green: Christianity and the Environment* (London: Darton, Longman, and Todd), 1990.

41　*The Art of Prayer*, Timothy Ware, ed. (London: Faber and Faber, 1966), 114–15.

42　For more on Robert J. Andrews, see http://www.helleniccomserve.com/robertandrews.html. To view the Jesus mosaic, search for "Holy Trinity Jesus Christ Mosaic CBS" on YouTube.

43　St. Maximos the Confessor (580–662), wrote of the divine Mystery, "Christ is the great hidden Mystery, the blessed goal, the ultimate purpose for which everything was created. Christ is the point toward which Providence is tending, the Power in whom creatures accomplish their return to God" (Olivier Clement, *The Roots of Christian Mysticism* [New York: New City Press, 1995], 39). "All things were created through him and for him" (Col 1.16).

44　Robert Ellsberg, *All Saints: Daily Reflections on Saints, Prophets, and Witnesses for Our Time* (New York: Crossroad Publishing, 2007), 521. Ellsberg refers to Etty Hillesum (1914–1943) as the "Mystic of the Holocaust." Though this young and highly gifted Jewish woman perished in Auschwitz, she dedicated her last years to "bear witness to the inviolable power of love and to reconcile her keen sensitivity to human suffering with her appreciation for the beauty and meaning of existence" (Ellsberg, *All Saints*, 521). For more on Etty Hillesum, see *The Letters and Diaries of Etty Hillesum* (Ottawa: Novalis, 2002).

Epilogue

1   Georgiou, *Dreamcatcher*, 267.

2   *From Glory to Glory: Texts from Gregory of Nyssa's Mystical Writings*, Herbert Musurillo, trans. and ed. (New York: Crestwood, 2001), 68–69.

3   Dumas, *The Count of Monte Cristo*, 441. All things wait on God, that divine love, mercy, and justice be ultimately realized, both individually and collectively. Thus the Christian's anticipation of "Judgment Day," the cosmic and climactic event that will call into account the whole of creation, that all things may be transfigured in God, and therein find the shared bliss of eternity.

4   While the cross clearly represents death (as in the Crucifixion), it also heralds life (the Resurrection). It is the supercosmic axial point where all paths lead, and where the terrestrial and celestial dimensions intersect, the point of ecstatic reconciliation from which new life is born. In this sense the cross takes the believer beyond the dichotomy of life and death. Presumed emptiness leads to fullness because death was annhilated *in the body of Christ*, leaving God (and life in God) alone to reign—the sacral promise of the world to come. For the Christian, then, death becomes not an ending, but a necessary passage leading to a new beginning. For more on the inner meaning of the cross, see Georgiou, *Mystic Street*, 87–91.

Praise for S.T. Georgiou's
Mystic Street: Meditations on a Spiritual Path

Available in Canada from Novalis (www.novalis.ca) and in the United States from Twenty-Third Publications www.twentythirdpublications.com; 1-877-944-5844

"Mystic Street describes Georgiou's contemplative journey while studying for his doctorate at the Graduate Theological Union in Berkeley. The integrated wisdom of both the Roman Catholic and Eastern Orthodox traditions rises strikingly to the surface. A helpful guide to anyone on the spiritual quest."

—*Michael Shackleton, The Southern Cross, South Africa's National Catholic Weekly*

"A spiritual tour de force."

—*David Miller, SF Gate, San Francisco Chronicle Online Edition*

"A beautifully presented work; a gift of great value."

—*Paul Fromont, Refresh: A Journal of Contemplative Spirituality, New Zealand*

"A charming collection of images and reflections. Often touching, sometimes deeply moving, each chapter is a meditation that is, in its own way, fresh, arresting, and wise."

—*Living Spirituality Network, London*

"A natural follow-up to *The Way of the Dreamcatcher.* Wonderfully insightful and spirit-filled."

—*Tom Gilbert, Living the Solution, Albuquerque, New Mexico*

"Georgiou speaks as a theologian in many chapters as he points out the operations of divine *agape.* Recommended for all."

—*Fr. Charles Cummings, O.C.S.O., The Cistercian Quarterly*

"A beautiful spiritual tapestry. The reader will be transfigured by the insights of Georgiou, who draws from the richness of Eastern Orthodoxy."

—*His Eminence Metropolitan Nikitas, Director of the Patriarch Athenagoras Orthodox Institute, Berkeley*

"Building on his mentoring with Robert Lax, Georgiou shares his journey with God and makes us aware that the way is ever forward."

—*Sr. Bede Luetkemeyer, O.S.B., Spirit and Life*

Praise for S.T. Georgiou's

The Way of the Dreamcatcher: Spirit Lessons with Robert Lax—Poet, Peacemaker, Sage

Available from Templegate Publishers (1-800-367-4844; www.templegate.com)

"Joyful tranquillity flows through this book. Here Lax emerges as a Gandalf-like figure who has found refuge on a quiet island off the shore of Middle Earth."

—Jim Forest, Founder and Director, Orthodox Peace Fellowship

"Georgiou has provided us with a very full and connected portrait of Lax as no one has before."

—Paul Spaeth, Director, Lax Archives, St. Bonaventure University

"This book of conversations presents Lax as a hermit full of wisdom who is much aware of the immanence of God in all of creation."

—Brent Aldrich, The Englewood Review of Books

"This book will be cherished for its radiance of spirit."

—James Grey, O.S.B., The Prairie Messenger

"This book enables Lax to continue sharing his wisdom with readers, poets, priests, and artists who strive to bring good to the world."

—Nimble Spirit: The Literary Spirituality Review

"A book of visions … The symbols that Georgiou and Lax share will bear fruition for eternity."

—D.K. Phillips, editor of Thomas Merton: Monk and Poet

"Through his luminous interplay with Robert Lax, Georgiou has painted a loving portrait of a remarkable human being. A doorway to a man who deserves much attention has been opened."

—Peter Maravelis, City Lights Books, San Francisco

"The subject of this book is the most difficult and most necessary thing in the world—*intentional love*, the love that transcends all desire for pleasure or personal gain. The capacity for such love is what we human beings are here for."

—Jacob Needleman, author of What Is God?